The Reb and the Rebel

Jewish Narratives in South Africa 1892–1913

The Reb and the Rebel

Jewish Narratives in South Africa 1892–1913

Edited by
Carmel Schrire
and Gwynne Schrire

UCT PRESS

KAPLAN CENTRE
JEWISH STUDIES & RESEARCH, UNIVERSITY OF CAPE TOWN

The Reb and the Rebel: Jewish narratives in South Africa 1892-1913

First published 2016 by UCT Press
an imprint of Juta and Company (Pty) Ltd
First Floor
Sunclare Building
21 Dreyer Street
Claremont
7708
South Africa

PO Box 14373, Lansdowne, 7779, Cape Town, South Africa

www.uctpress.co.za

www.rebandrebel.com

ISBN 978-0-79922-493-1

Editor and proofreader: Sandy Shepherd
Typesetter: Scan Shop
Indexer: Carmel Schrire
Cover designer: Pippa Skotnes and Celeste Beckerling
Printed in South Africa by Scan Shop

Typeset in Whitney AND 10pt on 12pt

This book has been independently peer-reviewed by academics who are experts in the field.

DEDICATIONS

To the descendants of Yehuda Leib Schrire, in recognition of his decision to leave Lithuania for South Africa, and that we may know a little more about him.

Whoever saves a life, it is considered as if he saved an entire world.

Babylonian *Talmud Sanhedrin* 4:8 (37a)

and

To the memory of my beloved sister Tamar Schrire Smith (1939-1997) who, like her great-grandfather, loved both Cape Town and Israel (CS).

CONTENTS

ACKNOWLEDGEMENTS

Interest in publishing the Schrire manuscripts was sparked when Millie Pimstone, of the Isaac and Jessie Kaplan Centre for Jewish Studies and Research at the University of Cape Town, was doing preliminary research for an exhibition at the South African Jewish Museum — *The Jews of District 6: Another Time, Another Place* — and discovered part of a memoir by Harry Schrire in the archives of the District Six Museum. The Centre then offered to publish the full memoir dealing with his childhood in District Six in the early years of the twentieth century. They subsequently learned that Harry's father, Yehuda Leib Schrire, had written a long autobiographical poem in Hebrew dealing *inter alia* with his life in District Six, and agreed to translate and publish that as well. This is turn led to the revelation that a Hebrew diary (1891-93) detailing Yehuda Leib Schrire's journey to South Africa, his sojourn in Johannesburg and his settlement in Cape Town, was also available.

The owners of the manuscripts, Arthur, Vivienne, Gwynne and Carmel Schrire, express their gratitude to Professor Milton Shain, Director of the Isaac and Jessie Kaplan Centre for Jewish Studies and Research, University of Cape Town, for his support in translating and publishing what we consider to be a unique contribution to Judaica and Africana.

Publication would not have been possible without the translation of Yehuda Leib Schrire's difficult pre-Ben Yehuda Hebrew by Devis Iosifzon, Jacob Gitlin Library, Cape Town; Michal Solomon, Westchester, NY; and Professor Andrew Plaks, East Asian Studies Department, Hebrew University, Israel. The high-end rendition of this book by Scan Shop is due in part to the timely advice of Professor Pippa Skotnes, who insisted that her beautiful cover design be matched by an elegant production. This generated an effort to cover the costs over and beyond the generous subvention from the Kaplan Centre. Heartfelt thanks are due for donations by various members of the Schrire clan, some of whom insisted on anonymity but others of whom include Gail and Michael Flesch; Daniel, Melinda, Dylan and Mia Flesch; Sharon and David Godfrey; Isabel and Barry Gottheiner; Stephen, Dina, Jack, Adam, and Sam Lucas; Brian Schrire; Jonathan and Gail Schrire; Margot Schrire; Mervyn Smith; Debbie Ginsberg; Paul Amit; Raphael and Abigail Smith; and in memory of Tamar and Rinah Smith. Finally, Nina Steiger and Andrew and Zachary Muir; Reuben, Hilary, Theo and Phoebe Steiger; and Vivienne Stein.

We would also like to thank other members of the extended Schrire family for their assistance, advice and editing, including Gail Flesch; Sharon and David Godfrey; Daniel Pfeffer; Roy Robins; Dani Schrire; Jonathan Schrire; Samuel Schrire; Shoshanna Shapiro; Mervyn Smith; Raphael Schrire Smith; Leslie Sohn; Reuben Schrire Steiger; Nina Steiger; and Vivienne Stein. We are grateful to Rabbi Dr Lionel Mirvish for calculating the *gematria*, and to Rabbis Desmond Maizels, Reuben Suiza and S. A. Zaiden for their help. Other assistance was provided by Janine Blumberg of the Kaplan Centre at the University of Cape Town, by Ute Ben Yosef and Dr Veronica Belling. We also thank Peter Hall, head of the James Hall Museum of Transport, Johannesburg, and the staff at the Jacob Gitlin Library and Western Cape Archives and Records Service, in Cape Town. We are grateful to Adam Mendelsohn, Director of the Kaplan Centre and Associate Professor of Historical Studies at the University of Cape Town, for his careful reading of Chapter 1. We owe a special debt of gratitude to Dr Janet Monge, at the University Museum, University of Pennsylvania, for using forensic protocols to identify and date a number of our photographs. Carmel Schrire thanks the Department of Anthropology and the Center for Human Evolutionary Studies at Rutgers University, for their support.

Genealogist Paul Cheifitz provided generous advice and skillful navigation of sources in the Cape repositories. Likewise, we thank Professor Pippa Skotnes, Michaelis School of Fine Art, University of Cape Town, who designed the original cover with her customary panache.

LIST OF ILLUSTRATIONS

PREFACE

The origin and development of the South African Jewish community is one small part of a vast and varied literature on the formation of nineteenth-century diasporic communities, worldwide. Records include primary sources such as ships' passenger lists, transit placements, immigration papers, memoirs, reminiscences and letters home and abroad — all of which are often integrated into a rich and learned academic framework.

Personal accounts of the diasporic experience are far from rare. Embedded in this panoply are the occasional voices of the immigrants themselves. Where South Africa is concerned, some boom with pride about the height of Table Mountain and the wealth of the gold fields, others weep for a taste of pickled cabbage or the cantorial cadences in their *shul* back home. Some tell of new kids born to Cape sunshine, others long for the bracing snow of a Baltic winter. More formal publications reveal the spread of institutions in places like Cape Town, Oudtshoorn and Johannesburg, itemising such details as the business deals and marriages that bound them into communities.

However, for all these personal moments, lengthy, unedited, unbowdlerised memoirs that purport to tell how it actually was are few and far between. Such are the manuscripts of two members of the Schrire family published here. None was ever intended for wide distribution nor for the discipline of an editor. The *Tolada*, however, was written to remind the children of Yehuda Leib Schrire of his struggles, so that they might better understand his picaresque life. Harry Schrire's memoir was deliberately written as he spoke, and he forbade the transcriber to change the original in any way whatsoever.

The voices of these two men differ: one is a foreign immigrant, and the other, a Cape-born native of South Africa. Threads of his European Talmudic learning are braided tightly into the travels of Yehuda Leib, while Harry's words are studded with turn-of-the-century Cape Yiddish such as once echoed through the alleys and parlours of District Six. You might catch an indignant yowl as Yehuda Leib recalls his former colleagues, and sense his wife patting his arm as he stamps his stick. You might hear the rattle of tea cups as Harry's wife Lily interrupts his recollections of the old gang commandeering the corner of Harrington and Commercial Streets almost a century ago. These manuscripts are the stuff of which history is made, and their publication represents a labour of love by its editors, translators and donors, in the hope that the manuscript will earn them a place in the archives of South African Jewish studies.

Carmel Schrire
Princeton, New Jersey, 2016

1. THE SOUTH AFRICAN CONTEXT OF THE SCHRIRE MANUSCRIPTS

Gwynne Schrire and Carmel Schrire

This book contains three previously unpublished autobiographical works: a diary, a poem and a memoir. The first two were written by Yehuda Leib Schrire (1851–1912), and the third, by his son, Harry Nathan (1895–1980). These texts mainly cover the period of 1892–1913, and are set in a number of countries, including Lithuania, Germany, Holland, England and South Africa. Few of the early immigrants to South Africa were writers, let alone poets, and the social history here embellishes and enlivens the picture of South African Jewish communities at the turn of the twentieth century. This chapter focuses on their contribution to South African Judaica and Jewish Diaspora studies.[1]

The genesis of the present book is worth summarising. The main archive of Yehuda Leib Schrire was housed in the extensive scholarly library of his grandson, Theodore (Toddy), in Cape Town.[2] It included an abbreviated copy of Harry Schrire's memoir donated by Gwynne Schrire's mother, Mary, some years earlier. Carmel discovered this hoard when her mother, Sylvia, suggested that she go and find "your great-grandfather's histories in the big cupboard". Carmel commissioned a rough translation of the autobiographical poem for use together with the Harry Schrire memoir in her book *Digging through Darkness*.[3] The full Harry Schrire memoir remained in the possession of Gwynne Schrire who quoted from it in articles on early Jewish life in Cape Town.[4] Carmel and Gwynne did not discuss these matters directly until a fortuitous meeting in 2007, when Carmel met Professor Galit Hasan-Rokem of the Hebrew University at a conference at Rutgers University. She mentioned that she was supervising the doctoral research of a certain Dani Schrire, son of Gwynne's brother, Samuel. At his request, Carmel sent Dani a number of photocopied manuscripts together with a catalogue of the manuscripts and ephemera of Yehuda Leib (Appendix II, this volume), which he, in turn, showed to Gwynne.

Coincidentally, the Isaac and Jessie Kaplan Centre for Jewish Studies and Research at the University of Cape Town was mounting an exhibition on the life of Jews in District Six and located one of Gwynne's articles in the District Six Museum.[5] When the Director of the Centre, Professor Milton Shain, learned of Harry's memoir, he offered to publish it together with the poem. Gwynne contacted Carmel who agreed to pool their resources. Devis Iosifzon, Director of the Jacob Gitlin Library, was contracted to translate and annotate the epic poem, which was written in pre-Ben Yehuda Hebrew.[6] Recognising the importance of this work, Carmel sent Gwynne the 1892-3 Hebrew diary that was later translated by Michal Solomon in Cape Town. Thus, through the fortuitous collaboration of several of the descendants of the writers and the enthusiastic support of the Kaplan Centre and its Director, these three original and previously unpublished works are now being made available to a wider readership.

The Reb: Yehuda Leib Schrire (1851–1912)

Reb Yehuda Leib Schrire, author of the Diary and the epic poem *Tolada,* is the central figure in this book. He was born in 1851 in Oshmanya (Ašmiany), in the Vilna district of the northwestern Krai, the Russian administrative district that incorporated Lithuania and Belarus. Vilna was a buffer region between Russian and Polish cultures which held little appeal for its closely-knit and deeply religious orthodox *Litvak* Jews (Fig. 1). Although Lithuanian Jewry was one of the least acculturated of Eastern European Jewish communities, this centre of religious scholarship faced intellectual challenges from within. The *Haskalah*, Bundism and Zionism began to present new forms of identity and models of belonging. These movements offered exciting alternatives — socialism, Jewish nationalism, modern ideas — as well as access to a broader world through new styles of Hebrew and Yiddish literature. The young Yehuda Leib Schrire epitomised these rising trends. He was a cantor, who had also trained as a *shochet*, a *bodek* and a confectioner (Fig. 2).

Fig. 1: The travels of Yehuda Leib Schrire, first in and around his home (A) in Neustadt Sugind (now Žemaičių Naumiestis), and his birthplace, Oshmanya (now Ašmiany), and then on his journey to Africa via Insterborg near Koeningsberg (now Kaliningrad), Berlin, Hamburg and Vlissingen (now Flushing), where he boarded the *Dunbar Castle* for the Cape. Amended from Google Maps/ GeoBAsis -- DE/BKG. (2009). [Northern Europe]. [Political Map]. Retrieved from: https://maps.google.com/maps/ms?ie=UTF8&oe=UTF8&msa=0&msid=212310978236458572729.0004cf07a34a6967d67f3

A deeply orthodox man, he was also interested in the *Haskalah*, was a Zionist, and was a creative writer in Hebrew and Yiddish, publishing a novel and articles in Hebrew in Eastern Europe. One such article, *O' lam Ha' fuch* ("Upside-down world") was published in the Koeningsberg weekly *Kol la' Am* on 15 and 22 June 1877.[8] He contributed to the journal *Kobez al Jad*, and published his Hebrew novel a mere 25 years after the first Hebrew novel appeared in 1852.[9]

In Cape Town, he contributed articles to *Haor, Der Yiedisher Herold, Der Afrikaner Telegraph, Yiedishe-Volkszeitung, Der Afrikaner Israelit, Haohev* and *Kinneret.* [10] Many of these were short-lived journals, published by his friend from Lithuania, Nechemiah Dov Hoffmann, a journalist and publisher who described him as:

> *... a devout man who was respected and loved by all. He was a scholar and an accomplished writer who was able to bridge the gap between the young and the old generations. He was orthodox yet tolerant of the spirit of his times. He was an outstanding Hebrew and Yiddish writer ....*[11]

Advertising one of his newspapers, *Kinneret*, which was devoted to "... wisdom and science, literature, criticism and the Jewish question in South Africa ...", Hoffmann boasted that "the best Hebrew writers participated in it—the late Judah Leib Sherira ... and many more enlightened people in Africa."[12] On a more practical level, Yehuda Leib played and taught the violin, composed cantorial music, mastered calligraphy and constructed mechanical toys. He fashioned sugar confectionery, once building a model of his synagogue for a visiting governor. He was a folk artist who painted and fashioned fretwork views of Zion and Jerusalem, notably a memorial tablet, some of which were proudly exhibited in the personal library of his grandson, Toddy Schrire. Such was his skill that he

Fig 2: Yehuda Leib Schrire and his wife Gela, probably taken in Vilna before he left for South Africa.

was commissioned to carve a traditional Lithuanian ark for the Oudtshoorn synagogue.[13]

Yehuda Leib left Neustadt Sugind (Žemaičių Naumiestis) on the Russian- Prussian border, where he had served as the cantor, and arrived in South Africa in 1892 (Figs 3, 4). He had received a job offer with passage money to Johannesburg through his brother-in-law, Mr Globus. He departed "... with excitement and confidence and without fear ... [to] minister to English Jews ...."[14] His anticipation was fervid: Johannesburg had gold mines and a magnificent synagogue where he would work as a *chazan, shochet, bodek, mohel* and preacher.[15]

The venture appeared to have been doomed from the start. Johannesburg had two competing congregations. The Park Synagogue had been established by a former chairman of the first synagogue in Johannesburg, the President Street Synagogue (opened in 1889) following a disagreement with the rabbi. The chairman and his supporters left and established their own synagogue—the Park Synagogue—for which they imported Schrire (Fig.2). The difference between them was lampooned in the London *Jewish Chronicle*, saying that the members of the first were proud to call themselves Jewish, the second thought Jewish, and the third acted Jewish.[16] Yehuda Leib Schrire, a proud Jew who certainly acted Jewish, was hired to serve the Park Synagogue where people only *thought* Jewish! He found himself thrust into communal disunity. The President Street Synagogue committee took their dispute with the Park congregation to the newspaper complaining that the new

Fig 3: The route travelled by Yehuda Leib Schrire, 1892-1893, from Lithuania to Vlissingen, Holland, where he boarded the *Dunbar Castle* for Cape Town via Las Palmas. He then went from Cape Town north by rail and wagon to Johannesburg and back. Adapted from www.Theodora.com.

Fig. 4: "British Interests in Southern Africa and Boer Wars c. 1880-1920" showing places mentioned in the Schrire manuscripts. Adapted from A.C. Cave and B. Trinder (eds), *Pergamon General Historical Atlas* (Oxford: Pergamon Press Ltd, 1970), p. 60

synagogue was absolutely not required in Johannesburg and that it therefore fulfilled no purpose.[17]

In an 1893 article, Meyer Dovid Hersch remarked that while the rabbi at the President Street Synagogue preached only in English, the Park Synagogue minister sometimes preached in Yiddish and that "... the new congregation has built itself a veritable palace ...".[18] The Park Synagogue congregation of acculturated Anglo-German Jews was supported by mining magnates whose wealth derived from the fabulous gold mines of Johannesburg. Their place of worship was a monument to the enterprise and energy of the Johannesburg Hebrew Congregation (Fig. 5).[19] Designed in Italian Renaissance style, it seated 800 worshippers. It was embellished with magnificent entrances, richly decorated pillars and moulded wreaths and had a blue and gold dome dotted with golden stars. The Synagogue was opened by the Transvaal President Paul Kruger on 15 September 1892 (Fig. 6). From the start Schrire disliked the congregation he had come to serve and refused to attend the opening banquet, saying:

> *I knew in my heart that it was not for a man like me to mix with presidents and ministers and among the English who speak English and Dutch. I would just look a mockery in their eyes. Furthermore ... they were going to have an abomination of a soup and a non-kosher wine ... That is why I came to the dedication of the synagogue but I did not go to the banquet ...*[20]

Schrire's criticism of the Jewish structures in Johannesburg was echoed in three roughly contemporary works, by Morris Abrahams, Meyer Dovid Hersch (edited by Joshua I. Levy) and Leibl Feldman, all of which have been recently recovered and published.[21] Abrahams, an English Jew, wrote in English; Feldman in Yiddish and Hersch (also known as M. Ben Yishai), in Yiddish and, for the same ideological reason, in a Hebrew similar to that used by Schrire. Rappaport described it as "... the picturesque Hebrew of the *Haskalah* period ...". [22] Schrire's Diary is actually the earliest of all, but unlike the others was intended as a souvenir for his family only. The accounts by Abrahams (writing before 1899) and by Hersch (in 1895)[23] were factual journalistic reports addressed to people in Europe interested in immigrating to Johannesburg. Feldman arrived in Johannesburg only in 1910 and did not publish the first version of his book *Yidn in Johannesburg* until 1950, as an anti-establishment history for Yiddish immigrants.

Schrire arrived in Johannesburg six years after the discovery of gold in 1886, by which time speculators had poured in, making the town even larger than the port city of Cape Town, founded almost 250 years earlier. He was horrified at the state of religious observance by the Jews on the goldfields, a dismay shared by all the writers mentioned above. Schrire, a cantor, *shochet* and *bodek*, pulled no punches in delivering his harsh, sarcastic and uncensored opinions. Like Hersch, he preferred the services of the Orthodox *beth ha-midrash* to those of the English-oriented Witwatersrand Hebrew Congregation's President Street Synagogue and the new Johannesburg Hebrew Congregation's Park Synagogue, which had

Fig. 5: Composite view of three Johannesburg synagogues: President Street (1888), Park (1892) and Doornfontein (1905). Only the first two existed when Yehuda Leib Schrire came to work at the Park Synagogue in 1892, and only the Doornfontein Synagogue remains standing today. See Oscar I. Norwich, *A Johannesburg Album. Historical Postcards* (Cape Town and Johannesburg: AD Donker Pty Ltd, 1986), p. 87, no. 186. (Courtesy Rabbi S.A. Zaiden, London UK)

brought him out of Europe. His friend Nechemiah Dov Hoffmann reported: "... [t]he religious state of Jews in South Africa is very bad. I am filled with shame to have to report publicly that our brethren have forgotten ... their people, their religion and language."[24] Meyer Dovid Hersch complained: "In the whirl of making money, who gave a thought to matters spiritual? In the realm of Jewish faith the spectacle was very very sad. There was complete neglect ...".[25] Likewise, Feldman reported that the new immigrants, many of whom were religious Jews, regarded the President Street Synagogue as a Jewish church, and could not understand how the leaders of a *shul* could possibly work on the Sabbath.[26]

The arrival of immigrants from the more traditional Jewish communities in Eastern Europe in the early 1890s created serious tension with the Anglo-German pioneers, leading to dissension in the synagogues.[27] Yehuda Leib grumbled that "they quarrelled strongly with strife and complaints" at the congregation's meetings.[28] He complained that the congregation did not observe the commandments. They did not eat kosher food, they spoke English rather than Yiddish, their women were immodest and men shaved with a razor. Indeed, the group photograph of the dignitaries at the opening of the Park Synagogue features very few bearded men other than the minister, Rev. Wolfers, and President Kruger (Fig. 6).[29]

Fig. 6: Consecration ceremony of the Park Synagogue, Johannesburg, 1892, showing President Paul Kruger of the Transvaal Republic (seated centre front), but apparently not Yehuda Leib Schrire, who attended the dedication but refused to attend the banquet. See Gustav Saron, *The Jews of South Africa. An Illustrated History to 1953 With an Epilogue to 1975*, edited by Naomi Musiker, (Johannesburg: Scarecrow Books in association with the South African Jewish Board of Deputies, 2001), p. 25. (Courtesy David Saks, South African Jewish Board of Deputies)

Yehuda Leib's particular problems began as soon as he arrived. In Hersch's words: "The congregation engaged a new minister but their first choice was not a very happy one ...".[30] The *shul* committee demanded that he update his appearance by shaving his beard and sidelocks, and by altering his old-fashioned clothes. Schrire had already anticipated this by shortening his knee-length coat himself, but their insistence on hiring a tailor to amend his efforts rankled even more. He smouldered with resentment.[31] As a result of this and many other perceived insults to his orthodoxy, he served the Park Synagogue on the High Holy Days only, and for the rest of the time he worshipped with other East European Jews at the Orthodox *beth ha-midrash* whose services were "conducted exactly as in the old country."[32] A reconstructed timeline of his stay there shows that his job lasted only eight weeks, after which he tried to find work as a baker or a businessman, and did the odd religious duty at a *bris* or a wedding. But for the most part, he sat around at his brother-in-law's house, unemployed.

The differences in outlook between the more traditional East European Jews and the acculturated Anglo-German Jews emerge clearly in a comparison between Schrire's critical article "Israel and its Baggage" and the account of Morris Abrahams.[33] Both discuss the synagogues and religious organisations in Johannesburg, and deplore the lack of attention paid to educating children, but there their agreement ends. Schrire criticised the customs of the English Jews and Abrahams those of the Russian Jews. Abrahams called his synagogue, the Park Synagogue, "the moderate progressive" Johannesburg Hebrew Congregation, whereas Schrire described it as catering to "ignorant English types".[34] Abrahams described the Russian Jews as:

> *The first group of malcontents ... and this was their grievance ... They wished to spend the greater part of* Shabbos *in* Shool, *repeating* Tehillin *and gossiping. No mode of harmoniously working together was devised and they seceded from the Congregation.*[35]

They were:

> *... sticklers, extremists when in any way what they consider their "rights" to make the Synagogue a place of rendezvous ... they persisted in gregariously flocking to certain districts, and forming a local Ghetto ... They swarmed like bees in a hive around this centre [the* beth ha-midrash*] ... which was open from early morning till late at night.*[36]

Schrire was shocked that the Park Synagogue was not open for daily prayers, unlike the *beth ha-midrash*, which also had a *Mishnah* study circle which he joined.[37] He complained that the cemetery was for rich Jews only, while Abrahams, for many years the *Chevrah kadisha* secretary who ran the cemetery, claimed that no distinction was made between the rich and the poor.[38] Schrire grumbled that the burial society paid poor people to stay with the sick and dying and only turned up for the funeral. Abrahams countered, saying that the *Chevrah kadisha* were all volunteers and performed their duties punctiliously, never shirking their duties in this hot country,[39] and Hersch confirmed that the leaders of the burial society had "well-thought-out regulations". [40] Schrire objected that poor relief was hemmed in with onerous regulations, was limited to once a week, and required sponsors to stand security. Abrahams praised the "charity" night meetings, which ensured that only the deserving poor received relief and commended it for lending money while expecting borrowers to find securities for the refund of the money.[41] He praised the society while reminding members to pay their fees.[42]

Whatever the truth of these matters, Schrire, like many other disillusioned immigrants, decided to return home, and to this end, he approached the local religious leadership for money for his ticket back. Jewish welfare organisations were inundated with requests for passage money to Europe, and they granted partial payment for the ticket but expected the immigrants to raise the balance.[43] It is salutary to realise that between 1897 and 1903 the Cape Town Jewish Philanthropic Association had 160 requests for assistance to return to Europe.[44] When Schrire reached Cape Town with every intention of heading back to Oshmanya, he was offered a very attractive position as *shochet* to a newly developing congregation that had been founded in opposition to the English one. He accepted the offer and named the congregation in a marginal annotation as *Agudat Achim,*[45] noting with justified optimism in his diary that "The society would be built and the community established around me."[46]

This was more than mere self-promotion. Schrire had arrived at a most opportune moment. Friction already existed between the established Anglo-German Jews and the newly arrived East European immigrants. It was more than a matter of beards and Yiddish. The only synagogue, the Cape Town Hebrew Congregation, or "Gardens *Shul*", as it was commonly known, was established in 1841 and followed the customs of the British chief rabbi who provided candidates for colonial synagogues but did not choose their ministers. Chief rabbis existed in Eastern Europe but in a different form from those in Britain. They spoke and preached in English and lacked the in-depth scholarship associated with those from Eastern Europe where chief rabbis did not exist. Not surprisingly, the new arrivals did not approve of the congregation or its rabbi, and these feelings were reciprocated. In fact, on first being introduced to their rabbi, Rev. Ornstein, Schrire instantly dismissed him out of hand:

> *I saw that he did not have the spirit of the* Torah *about him and he did not live Judaism. The English ways were his ways ... They would eat non-kosher vermin and were not impressed by the holiness of the* Shabbat.[47]

The Gardens *Shul* rabbi, Rev. Bender, who succeeded Rev. Ornstein, reciprocated the criticism in equal measure. He was reported as giving:

> *... a diatribe against all Jews generally and Russian Jews in particular ... Why can't they wash? Is water so expensive? Why can't they wear a clean suit? Must their* arba kanfoth *hang a mile out of their shirts? Even the* Talmud *does not say so.*[48]

It was the provision of kosher meat for Cape Town Jewry that Rabbi Israel Abrahams described as a "*casus belli*".[49] Anglo-German Jews already looked down on what they regarded as the primitive, ignorant, Yiddish-speaking "foreigners" like Reb Schrire, with their unfashionable dress and beard. In turn, the "greeners" (*grienes*) looked down on the ignorant, English-speaking old-timers who aped the English with their clean-shaven appearance and dress. The new immigrants mistrusted the practices of the Gardens *Shul* and the kosher meat provided by its *shochet*, which could be purchased only by *shul* members. Some East European Jews banded together to break the monopoly. They formed a society called *Agudat Achim* (Association of Brothers) and declared their independence and lack of respect for its *kashrut* by employing their own *shochet* to provide their own kosher meat without having to pay membership fees to the *Englishe Shul*. The *Agudah* had lost its *shochet* just before Schrire arrived, and by employing him, they got a "twofer", a *shochet* who was also a cantor and could lead their services. The end result was the formation of a rival congregation that broke the 60-year dominance of the Cape Town Hebrew Congregation.

Schrire signed a three-year contract[50] and on the strength of this new job was able to bring out his wife Gela, sons Max (aged 14) and Samuel (aged 5), and little Annie (aged 3).[51] They arrived in 1894, on a Saturday, and walked all the way from the harbour to the town (Fig. 7). The following year, his youngest son Harry was born. His plans blossomed: he established a *shtiebel* and invited people to his house to pray; he rented a hall and bought a larger house to accommodate his flock; he established a study group and planned a school for children.

Fig. 7: Harbour, Cape Town, c.1890.

All in all, "... our life became like that in a European town."[52] A sense of cohesion, camaraderie and community grew around him as the East European Jews bought their meat from his butchery and prayed in his *minyan*. Their numbers grew, and the following year, in August 1895, they held a meeting at the Masonic Hall on St. John's Street (up the road from the Cape Town Hebrew Congregation) to establish a new congregation to be called *Agudat Achim*. They drew up a constitution and elected a committee, one of whose members was the Rev. A. F. Ornstein, embittered because his own contract had not been renewed at the Gardens *Shul*.[53] In September 1900, after a mass meeting in the Masonic Hall, they formed their own Roeland Street Synagogue.[54]

Schrire's implication that the Roeland Street *Shul* and its *Talmud Torah* emanated from his flock is confirmed by Hoffmann[55] and by Rabbi Abrahams of the Cape Town Hebrew Congregation.[56] Harry Schrire's memoir attests to their involvement in the Roeland Street Synagogue, where Yehuda Leib's eldest son, Max, served on the committee.[57] His study group became the Roeland Street *Shul's Chevrah Gemara*, where he read the *blat*. Hoffmann confirmed that Reb Y. L. Schrire was one of the founder members:

> *A group of old-time students of the Talmud, worthy citizens, meet every evening in Roeland Street Shul to study* blat gemara. *About 12 years ago the group met once a week, later they met twice a week. The group has grown to 50 members.*[58]

Harry Schrire remembered a *Siyyum Ha-Torah* held amid a joyous celebration. Yehuda Leib also built a *mikvah*, initially in his own house, and later elsewhere, that was "marble floored and painted vermilion".[59] But if his religious life was flourishing, Schrire's business was not. He discovered that the butcher who employed him (Bayers Etkampf)[60] had gone bankrupt and fled. In a panic he rushed to the organisers (? ...tzky and Berman)[61] who convened an urgent meeting, where it was decided that, in addition to working in the abattoir, Schrire would run the butchery and retain some of the profit. His wife, a better businessperson than he, helped in the shop, and they expanded into other items of trade. They prospered and started investing in houses.[62] Houses of poor quality were being built rapidly to cater to the new immigrants, and loans and mortgage bonds were easily obtainable. For example, the Wicht brothers, "moneylenders turned slum landlords", were speculative builders who built 460 houses, many in District Six around Harrington Street.[63] A quarter of J. A. H. Wicht's estate came from promissory notes, bonds, mortgages and debentures. After their parents' deaths, the Wicht children started selling the properties in the 1890s.[64]

In time, the Schrires went on to own numbers 37, 39, 41 and 41B Constitution Street, 78 and 80 Boom Street (now Commercial Street), 96, 98, 100 Harrington Street, and 1 and 3 Bryant Street, all of which they rented out for a total monthly income of £50 (an amount whose purchasing power might be around £5000 today) (Fig. 8). An obvious question is how did these newly arrived immigrants accumulate sufficient capital to purchase so many houses? The answer is that at that time mortgages were easily available: Yehuda Leib and Gela Schrire took out joint mortgages to buy properties in 1896 and 1897 and thereafter Gela Schrire took out mortgages in her own name in 1898 and 1900 and again in 1904.[65] The Schrires seemed to have moved around a great deal. In February 1898, when Reb Schrire became naturalised, he was described as a butcher living at 56 Boom Street with bonded property in Cape Town.[66] The 1899 *Juta's Cape Town and Suburban Directory* listed a Scheire L, Butcher, 38 Harrington Street and a Scheira, Mrs, Boarding

Fig. 8: Commercial Street, Cape Town c.1930, showing a grand house (c.1790s) flanked by more modest ones similar to the Schrire house at number 80, where Yehuda Leib died in 1912. See Hans Fransen, *A Cape Camera. The architectural beauty of the old Cape. Photographs from the Arthur Elliott collection in the Cape Archives* (Johannesburg: AD Donker and Jonathan Ball Publishers, 1993), p.38. (Courtesy Western Cape Archives and Records Service, E1926)

House, Leicester House, 56 Boom street. This must have been their house on the corner of Harrington and Boom streets, which had about a dozen rooms. Gela would go down to the docks to bring back immigrants to stay with them. On 17 June 1907, property owner Louis Schrire ("Leib") testified to a police officer that a Mr Press, who was applying for a naturalisation certificate, had been living with him at 80 Commercial Street from January 1902 to March 1905, returning to the "Commercial Hotel" in 1907.[67] Schrire's death certificate in 1912 gave his residence as 180 [sic] Commercial Street.[68] Apart from 80 Boom/Commercial Street, these addresses do not coincide with those later provided to the Insolvency Court, where Gela Schrire stated that "she came from Europe in April 1893"[69] and joined her husband who was a minister of religion of the Hebrew Church of Cape Town. From him she received £360 with which she bought the property on Commercial Street for £1,060, raising a bond of £700. After this time she started a business as a general dealer and in 1898 had made a profit of £130 out of this venture.[70]

Whatever his domicile, Reb Yehuda Leib Schrire pursued his religious duties and continued his efforts to increase religious observance. He acted as an unofficial *beth din* to judge cases of Jews, who, experienced as they were in Russian justice, had a healthy distrust of state structures. He often judged cases with the Lithuanian Rabbi Mirvish who came out in 1908 to minister to the more orthodox Eastern European Jews in their newly established *beth ha-midrash he-chadash.* Mirvish was a great Talmudic scholar and the first rabbi with *smichah* to arrive at the Cape Colony.[71]

Hoffmann complained in 1891 that the "children grow wild in the absence of any schools to give them Jewish education so that when they grow up they will be completely ignorant of their people and their faith."[72] Yehuda Leib shared this concern, especially after his youngest son, Harry, was born at the Cape in 1895. In spite of considerable opposition, he turned his attention to founding a *Talmud Torah.*[73] He installed two paid teachers, Shulman and Morrison, and made monthly rounds to collect contributions.[74] Despite some uncertainty about exactly when this *Talmud Torah* was established, it was probably the first one of its kind in Cape Town.[75] Myer Katz tracked down the 1915 Annual General Meeting's 19th report of the *Talmud Torah Ivris b'Ivris* whose date suggests that the school had been in existence since 1896 or 1897.[76] Likewise, in 1947 an article in *The South African Jewish Chronicle* stated that the *Talmud Torah* had been established in an old house.[77] Certainly two purpose-built classrooms formed part of the Roeland Street Synagogue, which was opened in 1902.[78] The school was situated in Palm Villa on Roeland Street with a staff of three and J. Geffen as headmaster.

Harry attended this school, which operated in three *cheder* rooms at the back of the synagogue. As it was outside the influence of the Cape Town Hebrew Congregation, Louis Herrman regarded this *Talmud Torah* as being "in the orthodox mode" and therefore heralding the beginning of "fractionation" caused by setting up independent organisations within the community. Herrman adds that this *Talmud Torah* was opened in 1899, and that it was given impetus by the children of the war refugees from the Transvaal.[79] Rabbi Abrahams agreed that the school was established in 1899, on Brown Street off Caledon Street, because the new immigrants were dissatisfied with the "Sunday School"-type of education being offered by the Gardens Synagogue and wanted greater emphasis placed on what Reb Schrire called *Talmud, Tefillah* and *Torah*. He added that it was only established because the influx of "foreigners from the Transvaal as a result of the outbreak of the South African War made it imperative that Jewish education be provided to their children in a satisfactory way. The *Talmud Torah* enrolled about 100 pupils, most of whom returned home when the war ended."[80]

These discrepancies in the foundation date of the *Talmud Torah* may be due to Herrman and Abrahams seeking to elevate the success of their Cape Town Hebrew Congregation school by downplaying the pedagogical motives that led to the formation of the *Talmud Torah* and attributing its establishment to the needs of war refugees. Whatever the reasons, prior to the present publication of his epic poem, *Tolada*, the only record of Schrire's contribution to Jewish education in Cape Town was a 1947 article noting that "among those who during this period gave yeoman service to [the *Ivris b'Ivris* school] which set up its headquarters in Palm Villa in Roeland Street, must be remembered the name(s) of ... Mr L. Schrire."[81] His poem, which was not intended for publication or self-aggrandisement, restores his central role in establishing Jewish education at the Cape. As such, it places him at the forefront of the Hebrew Revival movement, which formed part of an emergent Jewish nationalism aimed at establishing a homeland in the Holy Land where Hebrew would become a living language.

Harry Schrire wrote warmly of Morrison, the *shammes*, a learned man, whose daughter, Dr Deborah Sagorsky, would become the first woman to chair the Western Province Zionist Council. Harry's father's Hebrew was so good that when he sent letters excusing Harry from attendance, they were used as a grammar exercise in his classes. Harry complained that when he went on holiday with family friends, M. J. Cohen the *shochet*, known as the "Krakenover Cohen", who was a great admirer of his father, forced him to write home in Hebrew to his father (corrected by Mr Cohen), in Yiddish to his mother, and in English to the rest of the family.[82]

Harry was expected to conform to his family's religious standards, and when his parents went out, the housemaid was instructed to check that he had prayed. On his mother's return, the maid would often report, "*Nee. Master Harry het nie gedaven nie.*"[83] Harry called himself the black sheep of the family, because his *yichus* was less than those of his siblings, who having been born in Lithuania, were listed as the children of a reverend, whereas he, being native to Cape Town, was listed as the son of a mere butcher. Part of the problem was that he grew up in a different culture from his parents and siblings and was therefore a product not of the *shtetl* but of the streets and lanes of District Six. He was the *laat lammetjie*,[84] born in Cape Town in 1895, and therefore a South African, not an East European. Harry rejected his parents' old-fashioned ways and rebelled against their orthodoxy, saying that he had had an overdose of religion. As an adult he refused to go to synagogue except to please his wife, and was very sceptical about all religions. His son Arthur saw this as a reaction to the high standards of the old man. For all his resistance, Harry obtained a thorough grounding in Hebrew, and was so well-versed in the *Torah* that he was able to teach his grandsons their *bar mitzvah* portions.[85]

Yehuda Leib, like other members of the Roeland Street Synagogue, was a Zionist, and theirs was the first congregation to become affiliated with the South African Zionist Federation. It bought *shekalim* for all its members, thereby making every congregant automatically a member of the World Zionist Organisation.[86] Schrire also founded the first Zionist society in Cape Town — the *Bnei Zion* — at the time of the First World Zionist Congress on 27 November 1897.[87] He gave an impassioned speech in the Masonic Hall on St John's Street on Jewish suffering and hopes for national regeneration, and a committee was elected with him as chairman. But seven months later, *Hamelitz* reported that "the heat of their ardour [had] been quenched for the moment," and it disbanded,[88] or, as Rabbi Abrahams scoffed, was "almost still-born, within a few months of the initial meeting it was to all intents and purposes defunct."[89] The society may have been short-lived but Schrire's public ardour was not. He was one of the speakers in September 1903 at the opening of the *Zeire Zion* Association's Zionist Hall and Library on the corner of Canterbury and Caledon Streets. *The South African Jewish Chronicle* reported that there were about 250 ladies and gentlemen present, and that "many other speeches followed [after the key note speaker] both in Hebrew and in the Jargon, amongst the most eloquent and most important being those of Schrire and Genusov."[90]

Fig. 9: Max Schrire at work as a Boer War photographer, De Aar, c. 1901-02. (C. Schrire coll.)

When the South African or Anglo-Boer War (1899-1902) began, over 25,000 refugees who had been expelled or fled, arrived in Cape Town from the hinterland. Thousands of troops were stationed in the city either permanently or *en route* to the front. Business boomed and property was at a premium. Along with troops and supplies drawn from many parts of the British Empire came horses, fodder, rats, fleas and their attendant zoonotic diseases. The bubonic plague that began in China in 1894 reached India in 1896 and finally arrived in Cape Town in 1901. Accepted wisdom attributed it to unsanitary human living conditions, and in 1898 the Bombay Plague Research Committee defined the plague as a "disease which is essentially associated with insanitary conditions in human habitations, the chief of which are accumulation of filth, overcrowding and absence of light and ventilation."[91] Professor W. J. Simpson, the local authority, concurred, calling Cape Town with its heterogeneous population a magnet for the plague.[92] An idea of its toll may be seen in the figures for March 1901, when deaths peaked with 81 people hospitalised. By May there were about 33 deaths a week.[93] Jewish plague victims were buried in the Cape Town Hebrew Congregation's 7th Avenue Cemetery in Maitland. When his wife Gela fell ill, Yehuda Leib plummeted into despair. He mistrusted the local doctors and feared that accusations of unsanitary conditions might lose them their butcher shop.[94] Given that their rental income provided enough money to live on, he decided to take the family back to Europe.[95] His efforts to hide Gela's illness by bribing the quarantine officials, tipping the ship's staff, and making her mask and glove herself before disembarking, combine to reveal a willingness to compromise his normally strong ethical stance for his family's personal needs.[96]

The family settled happily in Frankfurt-am-Main, where his elderly parents came to visit. His older son, Max, stayed behind in Cape Town, working as a photographer on the war front at places like De Aar (Fig. 9),[97] and later using his savings to go into partnership with a friend, Israel Mauerberger. However, all was not well with Yehuda Leib's investments. After the war, refugees from the north returned to their homes on the Witwatersrand and the property market at the Cape collapsed. There was a recession, no rent was coming in, and their properties became dilapidated. Max wrote to his father begging him to return immediately.[98] The family headed back to Cape Town, leaving Samuel behind to complete his studies. They stopped over in London long enough to meet Joseph Mauerberger, the father of Max's business partner. Joseph's daughter, Rebecca, was an educated woman. She spoke Hebrew, had corresponded with Herzl and Nordau, and later that year she would attend the Sixth Zionist Congress in Basel.[99] She would also become Max Schrire's bride (Fig. 10).[100]

Fig. 10: The Mauerberger family of Whitechapel meet the Cape Town Schrires in London, c.1908-09. Standing L. to R. Morris Mauerberger, Rochel Mauerberger, Bertha Mauerberger Goodman, Joseph Theodore Mauerberger, Israel Mauerberger. Seated L. to R. Max Schrire with Theodore (Toddy) and Rebecca Mauerberger Schrire with David. (C. Schrire coll.)

The family boarded the *Avondale Castle* at Southampton on 25 April 1903 and headed home.[101] There they found that the full employment of the war years was over and there were signs that the country was passing into a depression exacerbated by the worst drought in 40 years.[102] Writing that year in the *Hatzefirah* (a weekly Hebrew newspaper published in Warsaw by Haim Zelig Slonimsky), Meyer Dovid Hersch warned that "... the situation of many of the immigrants who have come here is dire: they are unable to make a living and there is no end to their financial distress ...".[103] Depression struck in 1904. Prices plummeted and many lost their fortunes ...[104] Max Sonnenberg, who later established Woolworth's, wrote:

> *Things went from bad to worse. Properties and houses in Cape Town dropped in value by 50% and more, after all the refugees had returned to the Transvaal, and uncle's business went into liquidation.*[105]

Yehuda Leib saw splendid houses and shops standing empty. His rentals evaporated, and even the fortunes of the wealthiest people collapsed and "melted, disappeared like snow in the heat".[106]

The 1904 Cape Town directory lists Louis Schira living at 62 Harrington Street. With little rent coming in, the Schrires now had to rely on their takings from their boarding house and the butchery. But now there was now more competition and people could not pay their bills. Hoping to recoup at least some of his losses, he invested in a newspaper with his friend Nechemiah Dov Hoffmann, who wrote, "A friend of my youth Reb Y L Schrire became my partner with the co-operation of a Warsaw Jew, Mr M. Mathuson. However, owing to financial circumstances, this partnership lasted only 6 months".[107] This was an exaggeration, as *Die Judische Folkszeitung* was actually "first published on 9 September 1905 [and] ... lasted until 11 October 1905".[108]

Schrire was not the only one to lose money in his investments at this time. His friend, Idel Schwartz, a founder of the *Dorshei Zion* society, narrowly escaped bankruptcy after his property deals collapsed by selling everything he owned.[109] Schrire describes the chaotic situation in 1908 where he was impotent in the face of widespread poverty that led to penniless tenants living in his crumbling buildings.[110] His woes were deepened by the spate of sanitary inspections following the episode of bubonic plague of 1901. Because the epidemic was believed to emanate from dirt, infected houses were evacuated, hosed down with disinfectant, cleaned and white-washed, and clothing and household effects were disinfected or destroyed.[111] Thereafter, the City Council employed sanitary inspectors to examine houses and issue warrants for repairs and cleansing. They targeted District Six where Jewish living conditions had been identified (possibly unfairly) by the district surgeon as a contributory factor in the spread of the plague:

> *Dwellings of the Jewish community are much overcrowded and ill-ventilated. These people herd together and overcrowd to an alarming extent. They are exceedingly afraid of fresh air and ventilation, and close every aperture in their rooms, notably when they have any illness. Their mode of living is objectionable and dirty in the extreme. They seldom or ever bath and their bodies are covered with vermin.*[112]

The Schrire properties were in a terrible condition.[113] The sanitary inspector was a regular visitor, and court papers reveal that Yehuda Leib himself was issued with summons after summons. Demands from the City of Cape Town's sanitary inspector included a threat to cut off the water unless they repaired a defective pipe, attended to the defective kitchen floor, repaired and thoroughly cleaned defective and dirty interior walls within seven days, removed accumulation of rubbish from the rears of 39 and 41 Constitution Streets within 24 hours, repaired defective yard paving, repaired a defective flushing cistern, removed an obstruction from the water closet, cleared drains, repaired plaster in the front room, and papered the dining room.[114] Yehuda Leib might have been handy with things like woodworking and toymaking but these repairs were clearly beyond him and the summonses drew account after account from his builders — all presently filed away in the Western Cape Archives and Records Service. With no income coming in from the tenants, and a mountain of debt rising for repairs, rates, taxes and bond repayments, the Schrires took out an additional loan, which only added to their debts.

1906 was a terrible year. In August, social unrest generated by the unemployment resulted in the Hooligan Riots, when shops in District Six were looted. Unemployed Jews participated in the riots and one of the leaders, an East European cigarette maker named Barney Levinson, was arrested but later acquitted of making an inflammatory speech. Jewish dealers and auctioneers were warned by David Goldblatt, a Yiddish printer, to stay at home and not participate in the weekly Wednesday open-air market on the Parade. Another leader, J.H. Howard, in a speech to the crowd, condemned stealing goods, breaking windows and Jew-baiting.[115] As time went on, things got worse: so little rent came in and the expenses were so great that the Schrires found it impossible to pay the interest on the bonds and the loan. Their watchful creditors pounced. Schrire had struggled hard to make a living for his family and instead of contemplating a comfortable future, he now lost everything. The Schrires gave away their belongings before the official inspection, and waited.[116] Three years later, on 4 April 1909, the case came before the Insolvency Court, and Gela Schrire made the following official declaration for the Court records:

> *Insolvent states that .... In August 1904 she purchased the property at the corner of Van De Leeuw and Constitution Street for £2,230 obtaining a bond of £2,000 and the balance she paid in cash. She did fairly well till 1906 when the shortfall occasioned by the loss of rent through non-occupation of premises by defaulting tenants and diminution of rent, she disbursed £200 over and above the revenue she received from these properties. Finding it impossible to*

> *pay the interest on her bonds, she endeavoured to compromise with the bond holders — they refused to do so as one of her creditors took action against her and her estate was placed under compulsory sequestration. She further states that she possesses nothing beyond the properties enumerated herein and she has a husband who, being a chronic invalid, is not able to do anything for himself and she requests leave to be allowed to trade in her own name. As regards the properties, the trustees request to be authorised to dispose of them either by public or private sale.*[117]

Even with their estate under liquidation, complaints continued to pour in, such as this letter dated 7 September 1911:

> *Dear Sir*
>
> *It is already a week since I have sent a letter to you. I had no answer. Do you mean to tell me that you can't afford to repair our house? If you would only call yourself and have to look how it is I am sure that you wouldn't stay here a minute. It is just like people living in a pigsty ... It would be better for you that you can live in a clean house and it will be better for you that you have clean people in your house.*
>
> *Mr Milner* [118]

Who then were their tenants who failed to pay rent or wrecked their premises? Judging by the names of people whose rents were collected afterwards by the court-appointed trustees, most of them were Jewish (Garb, Katz, Levinson [Barney?], Rubinstein and Rutstein); two were Muslim (Norodien and Zaladien); and two were English (Staine and Mr Milner). The builder Weintroub, to whom they owed money for repairs, was also Jewish.[119]

Yehuda Leib lived to see the end of the economic depression and the establishment of the Union of South Africa in 1910.[120] By the time he died, in 1912, Yehuda Leib had witnessed great changes in South Africa. In 1892, a mere 18 months after he trundled on a mule cart from Vereeniging to the goldfields, he was able to return by train. His family could not compete with the rich who had "Electricity for lights",[121] a luxury enjoyed by a mere 20 households when it first reached Cape Town with the opening of the Graaff Electric Light Station in 1895. By 1904, with the opening of the Dock Road Power Station, electricity became available to 1,300 households[122] but not until the 1920s and 1930s did it become common in homes.[123] Poor, but putting a brave face on his fortunes,[124] Yehuda Leib Schrire bequeathed what money he had to his children on condition that they went to live in Palestine. The will was contested.[125]

The Rebel: Harry Nathan Schrire (1895–1980)

Harry Schrire, author of the Memoir, was born in Cape Town in 1895, the youngest child and third surviving son of Yehuda Leib and his wife Gela.[126] The character study that follows is based largely on the memories of his surviving descendants. Like his father, a cantor and a violinist, Harry had a beautiful voice. He sang in the choir of the Roeland Street Synagogue, and at one time aspired to become an opera singer. The family used to entertain themselves with musical evenings featuring Sam at the piano and Harry, Annie and his father singing. While at university in Edinburgh he played the piano in a university parade seated on a truck. In addition to singing, Yehuda Leib would be asked to compose verses in Hebrew for weddings and other celebrations, and Harry, being a talented pianist and a good improviser would do the same in English. Harry was a jovial man with an excellent sense of humour. He also had many friends and was a great tease.

With his father and his mother at *shul*, working in the butchery, or out engaged in charitable work, young Harry was always up to mischief. Although he was 14 years old when his mother was declared insolvent, he seemed unaware of his parents' financial problems. Poverty plays little role in his stories of the pranks and tricks that he and his friends — the Harrington Street Loafers — got up to, quite apart from stealing watermelons, and the Great Saccharine Venture, a failed get-rich-quick scheme. This was a period of peak East European immigration, and his family was involved in assisting the newly arrived immigrants, meeting them at the docks and providing them with accommodation and kosher food for the journey to the goldfields. Harry would later grumble to his children that he often came home to find that his bed had been given to strangers off the boat and that he would go hungry because his food had been shared with them.

He also complained that his mother was never at home but seemed always to be running around with her friend Rebecca Zuckerman, also a keen Zionist, collecting money for worthy causes.[127] Judge David Cohen (son of the Krakenover Cohen), whose family boarded with them, told Gwynne that Gela Schrire was known as one of the first social workers. Both she and Rebecca Zuckerman were tiny women and when they came to a house to solicit donations, Mrs Schrire would climb on Mrs Zuckerman's back to kiss the *mezuzah*.At the following house, they would reverse positions. Dr Edna Bradlow wrote that her five-foot-tall grandmother, Mrs Clain, whom Harry called a "remarkable woman", towered over Mrs Zuckerman.[128] Another old-timer, Ben Fine, told Gwynne that when people saw Mrs Schrire coming down the street, they would pretend not to see her, because they knew she would ask them for a donation, but that when they saw both Mrs Schrire and Mrs Zuckerman coming, they would close their doors and draw the curtains because they knew they were going to ask them for a *big* donation.[129] Both Mrs Zuckerman and Mrs Schrire were presented with (undated) illuminated certificates to thank them for their work. Gela was awarded hers by the Cape Jewish Orphanage, the Board of Guardians, and the Aged Home "... on her retirement from active participation in Jewish Communal Activities" who wished her a contented retirement after her efforts.[130]

Yehuda Leib died suddenly, shortly after his youngest son scraped through Matric at the Normal College, later the Cape Town High School. Harry went on to study for a Bachelor of Science at the South African College School (SACS) at Hiddingh Hall (later the University of Cape Town) in preparation for going overseas to study medicine, as there was no medical school in South Africa at that time. His family supported him to go to Edinburgh in 1913 with his friends Ben Cheifitz and Wulf Rabkin. Cheifitz returned to Cape Town and became a popular general practitioner and Rabkin (known as "Rabbit") became the city's first pediatrician. Unlike them, Harry rapidly lost interest in his studies, and the little money his widowed mother and hardworking brothers despatched to Scotland every month lasted only a few days once he had paid his debts. Instead of studying, he supported himself by singing in a church choir, gambling at billiards and playing the piano in the dark to accompany silent movies.

When the Great War (1914–1918) broke out Harry wanted to enlist. At this point we have conflicting accounts. In one version he volunteered for active service but was turned down, on the grounds that he would be more useful once he qualified as a doctor. This was not soon enough for the impetuous Harry. He persuaded a friend, a surgeon from Panama, to issue a statement that he, Harry, was a doctor who had lost his papers when his ship was torpedoed. On the strength of this, he joined the navy as a "doctor". In another account, the army found itself short of doctors after heavy losses in the trenches and agreed to take on unqualified medical students who had completed a certain amount of training. Again, Harry's friend wrote a certificate to that end. Whatever pretext worked, he joined the navy and became a "doctor". Harry worked at the Dumfries Royal Infirmary, assisting with operations and administering anaesthetics. He was nervous when asked to do an appendectomy but the theatre sisters told him what to do. Later, he proudly told his children how he had saved the life of a boy who was having an operation on his wrist. Harry was giving the anaesthetic, the surgeon turned around to talk to the watching students, and the boy stopped breathing. The panicky Harry

Fig. 11: Harry Schrire, with army tents in the background. Edinburgh, 3.12.1914. (Arthur Schrire coll.)

asked what should be done. The doctor took off his gloves and said, "Oh, don't worry. I'll just write out a death certificate." Harry jumped onto the boy and began pumping his chest until he started breathing again. He also said he worked for 24 hours at a stretch in the hospital during the 1918 influenza epidemic. His son, Arthur, has a photograph showing Harry, debonair in spats, posing in front of a painted backdrop of army tents, holding flowers. It is inscribed to his brother and sister-in-law: "To my dear Max and Rebecca. With best love from Harry, 3.12.1914, With best love for the boys and selves." (Fig. 11).

When the War ended Harry did not return to university. He later told his children that he had been a remittance man and that the family sent him money each month to keep him away because he was the black sheep of the family. When his brothers discovered that he was not studying medicine, Harry received an angry telegram, ordering him home. He boarded the *Norman Castle* on 18 June 1920 to return to Cape Town.[131] Near the Equator he started chatting to a fellow passenger, Lily Finberg, who was emigrating to South Africa with her family, and by the time the ship docked in Cape Town they were in love. Unlike his oldest brother Max, whose marriage was arranged by his parents in London, and unlike Samuel, who was dispatched to Kimberley by his widowed mother on the advice of one of her boarders, Mr Maresky, to marry the jilted, only daughter of a wealthy man, Harry shook off the *shtetl* tradition and found his own wife.

By the time Harry came home, his sister Annie, who had married Hersch Charles Schus, had died, childless, in the 'flu pandemic of 1918. Harry's carefree days were well over. Max put his disgraced younger brother to work at M&S, the shop on Darling Street that he shared with his brother-in-law, Israel Mauerberger. Originally from Lazdey in Lithuania, Israel's widowed father, Joseph Theodore, moved to London and then brought his five children out in turn to join him.[133] When his daughter, Rebecca, married Max Schrire in 1905, she brought her 15-year-old brother Morris (Morrie) to Cape Town to work at M&S. This teenager soon launched a business of his own as Castle Drapers, and later helped finance travelling salesmen employed by M&S to set up shops of their own — Sam Kirsch with Stanhope Drapers, Gus Ackerman with Smart Stores, and Leon Segal with Segal's Smart Store. Morrie supplied the stock for all their shops at a profitable rate to himself. When his wife became pregnant, he was reluctant to go to London on his regular buying trip, and instead he sent Leon Segal, arranging for Leon's 18-year-old brother-in-law to manage Segal's Smart Store. When Leon's wife, Mary, phoned Morrie to complain that the inexperienced young man was not given suitable supervision,[134] Morrie put Harry into the shop to help.[135] Mary was no more pleased to discover that Harry was equally inexperienced, having just "returned to South Africa after several years of unsuccessful study in Edinburgh to become a doctor. He had never been into a drapery store in his life before. I don't think he knew the difference between drapery and costume jewellery". Mary phoned Morrie to complain again. They had a "flaming row during which he told her that women should not interfere in business and she ended up telling him to go to hell." It was not a propitious start for the newly married Harry, but he weathered it with his usual good humour — his daughter Vivienne said he never got upset about anything — later winning over Mary Segal, who admitted that "Harry turned out to be a very nice man eventually and he remained in the business in a different store but at that stage he had no knowledge of any business whatever."[136]

At the end of the Great War, as after the Anglo-Boer War, there was a recession, and many shops found themselves overstocked. Morrie, Sam, Gus and Leon decided to open a shop in the country where they might sell the surplus stock. They opened Ackermans in Stellenbosch, which became South Africa's first chain store. Max and Israel Mauerberger's M&S was also struggling, and they followed suit in 1924, establishing a chain of stores called Bergers, with Morrie, Israel and Max as the directors. They agreed that Bergers and Ackermans would not compete, and if a town already had a Bergers, it would not have an Ackermans.[137]

Harry was sent to manage the new Ackermans store in Stellenbosch, and his first child, Leonard, was born there in 1923. One of Harry's responsibilities as manager was to fetch the wages weekly from the bank. The police advised him to get a gun, as he would be at risk. Although he had been in the navy, he had not been required to learn to shoot. One night Lily shook him awake. She had heard someone crawling around downstairs. Harry grabbed his gun and fired. The intruder ran away but right through the entire pile of his freshly ironed shirts there was a bullet hole. That was the last time he fired his gun. To someone like his father who grew up in Lithuania, it would have been inconceivable for a Jew to own a gun, let alone be allowed to fire it at an intruder.

Harry moved often, spending about four years in each branch of Ackermans. From Stellenbosch he became the manager of the Salt River store, living at De Lorentz Street in Tamboers Kloof, then in Observatory where his son Arthur was born in 1926, and his daughter Vivienne in 1928. In 1932 Harry and his family moved to Bloemfontein. Once more this was a time of economic depression, and the Free State was badly affected with a large population of "poor whites". Vivienne remembered an Ackermans newspaper promotion advertising free loaves of bread to customers. The newspaper published a photograph of Harry throwing down loaves of bread to the large crowd gathered outside the store. His son, Arthur, remembers that his father started pricing everything in such a manner so that each item would provide the customer with a penny change, and would require the teller to issue a receipt — and change. The Bloemfontein bank ran out of pennies, and Harry had to contact the mint to order more. Harry had a strong social conscience and in order to promote a friendly atmosphere in the workplace he organised recreational and social opportunities for his staff including outings, picnics and dances.

Arthur recalled that his father once became secretive and began attending clandestine meetings. When he and Vivienne were older, Harry told them he had been part of a group of activists fighting the Greyshirts, the South African Gentile National Socialist Movement, a paramilitary Nazi organisation with uniforms, discipline and salutes, started by Louis Weichardt in 1933 to promulgate the National Socialist philosophy in South Africa.[138] The Greyshirts spread rapidly among young Afrikaners, and meetings were arranged in small towns to foment hostile feelings against the local Jews and their businesses. Writing about that time, Nathan Berger reported that "... a group of able-bodied young Jews ... took upon themselves the task of disturbing and breaking up gatherings by the Greyshirts. Serious clashes took place between the Jewish avengers and the Hitler propagandists and bloodshed and arrests were a regular feature".[139] Harry was part of just such a group put together by the Bloemfontein Jewish businessmen anxious to protect their shops.

By 1936 Harry Schrire was promoted to manage the Port Elizabeth branch of Ackermans. For holidays his family would go to Carnarvon, where Lily's brothers Henry and Philip Finberg were general dealers. They owned Finberg Stores while another brother, Dave, ran a shop in Touws River. Harry manned the store while the Finbergs went on holiday. In 1939 he was transferred to Cape Town, where he managed the Wynberg branch of Ackermans. His family lived in Muizenberg and later in Rondebosch. When Ackermans was taken over by Greatermans, Harry left the company and went into a wholesale business in District Six importing textiles with Joey Mauerberger. But it was not a success. Harry bore most of the responsibility for the business, and shortly after they started it the government instituted import permits that they were unable to obtain. Harry then worked for a firm of liquidators, taking inventories at bankrupt stores until he retired.

To the end, Harry remained great company. He would take his grandchildren to the docks and tell them long stories about the mail ships, inspiring them to travel when they grew up. With a little encouragement from his children, he took up a pen in his old age to compose the reminiscences of his childhood in District Six that form the Memoir. Although there is some overlap between Yehuda Lieb's Diary and Harry Schrire's Memoir, neither read the other's work: Yehuda Leib died more than 60 years before Harry penned his Memoir, and his library, together with the notebooks containing the *Tolada* poem and the Diary passed from his son Max to his grandson Toddy. Together these works provide a view of Jewish life in South Africa, and more specifically in Johannesburg and Cape Town at the turn of the twentieth century.

FOOTNOTES

1 For a crisp and comprehensive overview of the history of South African Jewry, see Richard Mendelsohn and Milton Shain, *The Jews in South Africa. An Illustrated History* (Johannesburg and Cape Town: Jonathan Ball Publishers, 2008). For a genealogy of the authors of the Schrire manuscripts, see Appendix I, this volume. For foreign words and expressions, see Glossary, this volume. For the original manuscripts and further information, go to www.rebandrebel.com.

2 Including handwritten notebooks, published works and religious tracts (see Appendix II, this volume).

3 Carmel Schrire, *Digging through Darkness: Chronicles of an Archaeologist* (Charlottesville and London: University Press of Virginia, 1995), p.17.

4 Gwynne Schrire, "Adapting to a New Land: The Greener in Cape Town 1900", *Jewish Affairs,* 1990, 45:5, pp.42–46; "Mostly *Smouse*? South African Jews and their Jobs a Century Ago", *Jewish Affairs,* 2000, 55:1, pp.9-15; " 'A Stranger in a Strange Land': Immigration Problems and Community Assistance in South Africa a Century Ago", *Jewish Affairs,* 2002, 57:4, pp.30–34; "Avraham Meir Solomon, Abba Eban and Early Cape Zionism", *Jewish Affairs,* 2003, 58:1, pp.27–52; "Jewish Life in District Six before World War 1: A Memoir", *Jewish Affairs,* 2008, 63:2, pp.22–28.

5 *The Jews of District 6: Another Time, Another Place,* exhibition catalogue, South African Jewish Museum (Cape Town: Jewish Publications, Isaac and Jessie Kaplan Centre for Jewish Studies and Research, University of Cape Town, in association with the South African Jewish Museum, 2012).

6 Eliezer Ben-Yehuda (1858–1922) revived the Hebrew language to replace Yiddish and other regional dialects as a means of everyday communication, coining new Hebrew words for objects such as doll, ice cream, jelly, omelette, handkerchief, towel, bicycle. For Jack Fellman, "Eliezer Ben-Yehuda and the Revival of Hebrew", see www.jewishvirtuallibrary.org/jsource/biography/ben_yehuda.html.

7 Ezra Mendelsohn, *The Jews of East Central Europe between the World Wars* (Bloomington: Indiana University Press, 1983), p.215.

8 http://aleph520.huji.ac.il/F/PCEVAB38BRLKV2B4VHDV2F7PT97USDPX9XDY52S14GYS2UXMBN-03917?func=find-acc&acc_sequence=000128533. It is catalogued as a "Lied". With thanks to Dani Schrire.

9 The first Hebrew novel, *Ahavat Tsiyon,* by Abraham Mapu, was published in Vilna in 1853. Yehuda Leib Schrire, *Shoshanah Novelet* (Warsaw: Warsaw Typography, Alexander Ginz, 1879; see also Appendix II. 6 , this volume).

10 *Der Afrikaner Israelit* (1890) was the first Yiddish weekly in South Africa. It ran for six months and was followed by *Haor*, which had a Hebrew supplement, *Haohev*, and lasted longer (1895-97). Then came *Der Yiedische Herold* (1896-98), whose name was changed to *Der Afrikaner Telegraph* (1898-1902). These were followed by *Die Judishe Folkszeitung* (1905) published by Hoffmann, Schrire and Matuson, and the fortnightly Hebrew *Kinnerel* (1905) that became a Hebrew supplement to Hoffmann's new venture, *Die Afrikaner* (1909-14). See Nechemiah Dov Hoffmann, *Book of Memoirs: Reminiscences of South African Jewry*, translated from the Yiddish by Lilian Dubb and Sheila Barkusky (Cape Town: Jewish Publications-South Africa, Isaac and Jessie Kaplan Centre for Jewish Studies and Research, University of Cape Town, 1996), p. 39; Joseph Abraham Poliva, *A Short History of the Jewish Press and Literature of South Africa From its Earliest Days Until the Present Time* (Johannesburg: Prompt Printing, n.d.).

11 Hoffmann, *Book of Memoirs*, p. 39.

12 Hoffmann said that he was compelled to abandon *Kinneret* "... because the enlightened people themselves were unable to support me," Poliva, *A Short History*, p. 28.

13 This was the St. John's Street's *Griene Shul*, built in 1892 by a breakaway, more Orthodox group of Jews from Kelme who tried to reproduce a Lithuanian *heimland* synagogue decorated with original Lithuanian-style Jewish handicraft and an ark like that in their *shul* (Mendelsohn and Shain, *The Jews in South Africa*, p. 51). The Jews from Šiauliai went to the other synagogue built on Queen Street in 1888, called *Der Englishe Shul* (see "The Jewish Community of Oudtshoorn", www.seligman.org.il/oudtshoorn_jews.html; Harry Schrire, Memoir, this volume, p. 160; Appendix III.4, III.5, this volume).

14 Yehuda Leib Schrire, *Tolada*, this volume, p. 105, stanza 23.

15 Schrire, *Tolada*, this volume, p. 105, stanza 22. This was the Park Synagogue. See Richard Mendelsohn, "Oom Paul's Publicist: Emanuel Mendelssohn, founder of the first congregation", in Mendel Kaplan and Marian Robertson (eds.), *Founders and Followers: Johannesburg Jewry 1887–1915* (Cape Town: Vlaeberg Publishers, 1991), p. 81; Joshua I. Levy (ed.), *The Writings of Meyer Dovid Hersch (1858–1933): Rand Pioneer and Historian of Jewish Life in Early Johannesburg* (Johannesburg: Ammatt Press, 2005), p. 90.

16 Solomon Rappaport, "Rand Jewry – 1893", in Levy, *Writings*, pp. 100-01.

17 Richard Mendelsohn, "Oom Paul's Publicist", in Kaplan and Robertson, *Founders and Followers*, p. 80.

18 Meyer Dovid Hersch, "Our Jewish Brethren in South Africa", in Levy, *Writings*, p. 90.

19 Richard Mendelsohn, "Oom Paul's Publicist", in Kaplan and Robertson, *Founders and Followers*, p. 81.

20 Yehuda Leib Schrire, Diary this volume, p. 71. Mendelssohn and his congregation, although nominally Orthodox, had abandoned many of the Orthodox practices including observance of the Sabbath and dietary laws, while at the same time keeping the High Holy Days and rites of passage.

21 Morris Abrahams, *The Jews of Johannesburg 1886–1901* (Johannesburg: Scarecrow Books, in association with the Jewish Board of Deputies, 2001); Leibl Feldman, *The Jews of Johannesburg (Until Union – 31 May 1910)*, translated from the Yiddish by Veronica Belling (Cape Town: Jewish Publications, Isaac and Jessie Kaplan Centre for Jewish Studies and Research, University of Cape Town, 2007).

22 Rappaport, "Rand Jewry", in Levy, *Writings*, p.96.

23 Published in Hebrew in *Hatzefirah* in Warsaw.

24 Nechemiah Dov Hoffmann, *Hatzefirah 191*, vol. 18, 1891, letter 9, in Israel Abrahams, *The Birth of a Community: A History of Western Province Jewry from Earliest Times to the End of the South African War, 1902* (Cape Town: Cape Town Hebrew Congregation, 1955), p.146.

25 M. Ben Yishai (Meyer Dovid Hersch), "Historical notes on the Jewish community of Germiston and district from documents and reminiscences of a pioneer", in Levy, *Writings*, p.167.

26 Feldman, *The Jews of Johannesburg*, p.42.

27 Richard Mendelsohn, "Oom Paul's Publicist", in Kaplan and Robertson, *Founders and Followers*, pp.76-79.

28 Schrire, *Tolada*, this volume, p. 108, stanza 35.

29 See Marian Robertson and Mendel Kaplan, "The formation of the Johannesburg Jewish Community 1887-1915: An overview", in Kaplan and Robertson, *Founders and Followers*, p.28. Rev. Philip Wolfers was the rabbi from 1892 till the end of the year according to Abrahams, *The Jews of Johannesburg*, p.47.

30 Hersch, "Our Jewish Brethren", in Levy, *Writings*, p.90.

31 Schrire, *Tolada*, this volume, p. 108, stanza 35; Schrire, Diary, this volume, pp. 69-70.

32 Hersch, "Our Jewish Brethren", in Levy, *Writings*, p.91.

33 Schrire, Diary, this volume, pp.73ff.; Morris Abrahams, *The Jews of Johannesburg*.

34 Schrire, Diary, this volume, p.70.

35 Abrahams, *The Jews of Johannesburg*, p.8.

36 Ibid., p.11.

37 Hersch, "Our Jewish Brethren", in Levy, *Writings*, p.91.

38 Abrahams, *The Jews of Johannesburg*, p.19.

39 Ibid.

40 Hersch, "Our Jewish Brethren", in Levy, *Writings*, p.88.

41 Abrahams, *The Jews of Johannesburg*, p. 21.

42 Hersch, "Our Jewish Brethren", in Levy, *Writings*, p. 88.

43 Gwynne Schrire, "Litvaks who Returned to Europe and Why", *Jewish Affairs*, 2008, 61:1, pp. 7–14. In 1882 the re-emigration rate from the US was 29%, and although it fluctuated with the economy, it usually averaged out between 7–10%. The London Jewish Board of Guardians and the South African Jewish welfare organisations paid only part of the return fare. For a discussion of this situation in America, see Jonathan D. Sarna, "The Myth of No Return: Jewish Return Migration to Eastern Europe, 1881-1914", *American Jewish History*, 1981, LXXI:2, 256-68.

44 Gwynne Schrire, "Adapting to a New Society: The Role of the Cape Town Jewish Philanthropic Society c. 1900", *Proceedings of the Eleventh Annual Conference*, South African Association of Jewish Studies, Department of Hebrew and Jewish Studies, University of Natal, Durban, 1990, pp. 26–36.

45 Schrire, *Tolada*, this volume, p. 112, stanza 48.

46 Schrire, Diary, this volume, p. 91.

47 Ibid., p.16 (or 19).

48 Schrire, "Stranger in a Strange Land", p. 33.

49 Abrahams, *Birth of a Community*, p. 77.

50 Schrire, *Tolada*, this volume, p. 114, stanza 56.

51 His wife (1855-1934), whom the family knew as "Gela", is listed as "Gelia" by the Russian authorities in the Dieveniškės census, "Gerte/Gele" in our genealogy, "Gerte" in her court case, "Gertrude" on her tombstone and "Gila bat David" on the Cemetery Maintenance Board website. The children who came to Cape Town with her were Moshe Mordechai (Max) (1881–1953), Samuel (1889–1949), and Annie (1891–1918).

52 Schrire, *Tolada*, this volume, p. 117, stanza 69.

53 Abrahams, *The Birth of a Community*, pp.109–110.

54 Louis Herrman, "A History of Capetown Jewry", in Morris de Saxe (ed.), *The South African Jewish Year Book. Directory of Jewish Organisations and Who's Who in South African Jewry 1929, 5689–90* (Johannesburg: South African Jewish Historical Society, 1929), p.69.

55 Hoffmann, *Book of Memoirs*, p.39.

56 Abrahams, *The Birth of a Community*, p. 109.

57 Schrire, Memoir, this volume p.165; Herrman, "Capetown Jewry", in De Saxe, *South African Jewish Yearbook*, p.69.

58 Hoffmann, *Book of Memoirs*, p.29.

59 Schrire, *Tolada*, this volume, p.118, stanza 73.

60 Ibid., p.115, stanza 60.

61 Ibid., p.115, stanza 61.

62 Ibid., p.118, stanza 74.

63 Nigel Worden, Elizabeth van Heyningen, and Vivian Bickford-Smith, *Cape Town: The Making of a City — An Illustrated Social History* (Cape Town: David Philip Publishers, 1998), p.158.

64 Ibid., p.174.

65 Western Cape Archives and Records Service, mortgage numbers: 1896-S556 (DOC vol (4/1/460); 1897-1536(4/1/524); 1898-4932 (4/1/620); 1900-149 (4/1/708); 1900-1150(4/1/708); 1904-507 (4/1/1011); 1904-508 (4/1/1011). Thanks to Professor Deborah Posel for this insight.

66 Western Cape Archives and Records Service, 1898, CO 4311, 56.

67 Paul Cheifitz, in litt., 6 June 2010.

68 The death certificate is Western Cape Archives and Records Service, 1912 MOOC vol. 6/9/701 ref. 2880. The entry number is 1238 and the date of death is 9 October 1912. Thanks to Paul Cheifitz for this reference.

69 This date is apparently wrong. Schrire's diary ended on his arrival in Cape Town on 12 November 1893, so there is no way that his wife could have arrived earlier, in April of that year. Harry Schrire confirms that the family arrived in 1894 (Memoir, this volume p.158).

70 Western Cape Archives and Records Service, 19-9, MOIB 2/3251/991.

71 Cecil Helman, 12 June 2002, pers. comm.

72 Hoffmann, *Hatzefirah 191*, vol. 18, 1891, letter 9, p.146.

73 Schrire, *Tolada* this volume, p.117, stanza 70.

74 Ibid., p.118, stanza 72 .

75 Israel Abrahams, "Western Province Jewry 1870-1902", in Gustav Saron and Louis Hotz, *The Jews in South Africa: A History* (Cape Town: Oxford University Press, 1955), p.35.

76 Myer E. Katz, *Jewish Education at the Cape 1841 to the Present Day: A Survey and Appraisal in the Light of Historical and Philosophical Perspective*, PhD thesis, University of Cape Town, 1973, footnote p.70; *The South African Jewish Chronicle*, 28 November, 1947.

77 *The South African Jewish Chronicle*, 28 November 1947.

78 Herrman, "History of Capetown Jewry", in De Saxe, *South African Jewish Year Book*, p.69.

79 Louis Herrman, *The Cape Town Hebrew Congregation 1841–1941: A Centenary History* (Cape Town: Mercantile-Atlas Co Pty Ltd, 1941), p.74.

80 Abrahams, "Western Province Jewry", in Saron and Hotz, *The Jews in South Africa*, p.33.

81 *The South African Jewish Chronicle*, 28 November 1947.

82 Schrire, Memoir, this volume, p.170. Dave Cohen, the son of M.J, became chairman of the United Communal Fund; member, Western Province Zionist Council; chairman, Israel Maritime League; national vice-president, South African Jewish Board of Deputies; chairman, SA Legion of the BESL, the Discharged Soldiers' Rehabilitation Committee and the Governor General's War Fund. See Gwynne Schrire, *South African Jewish Board of Deputies (Cape Council) 1904–2004: A Century of Communal Challenges* (Cape Town: Citi Graphics, 2004), p.55.

83 "No. Master Harry did not *daven* [*gedaven*] his prayers" (Afrikaans).

84 Literally, "late lamb", meaning the last (possibly unexpected) child (Afrikaans).

85 He took delight in leading the *seder* for his grandchildren, banging the table so hard when he recited "And the Lord took the children of Israel out of Egypt with a strong hand", that all the glasses would shake and the cutlery rattle, copied with glee by the grandchildren and watched with anxiety by Arthur Schrire's wife (Sylvia Schrire, 2011, pers. comm.).

86 The Roeland Street Synagogue was the first one to challenge the supremacy of the long-established Cape Town Hebrew Congregation (1863). It attracted less affluent Lithuanians who were keen Zionists, an affinity that Rev. Bender of the Gardens Synagogue regarded as being disloyal to the British Empire.

87 Marcia Gitlin, *The Vision Amazing: The Story of South African Zionism* (Johannesburg: Menorah Book Club, 1950), p.43; Abrahams, *The Birth of a Community*, p.104; Saron and Hotz, *The Jews in South Africa*, p.37.

88 Gitlin, *The Vision Amazing*, p.48.

89 Abrahams, *The Birth of a Community*, p.104.

90 *The South African Jewish Chronicle*, September 1903. "Jargon" means vernacular language or Yiddish here.

91 See Gwynne Schrire, "Immigration Restriction, Plague and the Jews in Cape Town, 1901", *Jewish Affairs*, 2008, 63:3, p.3, 16; Elizabeth van Heyningen, "Cape Town and the Plague of 1901", *Studies in the History of Cape Town,* 1981, 4, pp.66-107.

92 Van Heyningen, "Cape Town and the Plague", p.69.

93 Ibid., p.77.

94 Schrire, *Tolada*, this volume, p.119, stanzas 77-79.

95 Ibid., p.120, stanza 80.

96 Ibid., pp.120, 122, stanzas 83, 89, 91.

97 For Max Schrire's Boer War photographs, see Western Cape Archives and Records Service, Schrire Collection, SH1-27.

98 Schrire, *Tolada*, this volume, p.128, stanza 114.

99 Elie Kedourie (ed.), *The Jewish World: Revelation, Prophecy and History* (London: Thames and Hudson, 1979), p.298, plate 40; Letter from Theodore Herzl to Rebecca Mauerberger, 13 June 1901, The Nahum Goldman Museum of the Jewish Diaspora, Tel Aviv, Neg. no. EXH. 42.3c.29.11; Schrire, *Digging through Darkness*, pp.17, 226.

100 Schrire, *Tolada*, this volume, p.129, stanza 117.

101 Thanks to Paul Cheifitz for the shipping list, 22 February 2012.

102 Gustav Saron, "Jewish Immigration 1880-1913", in Saron and Hotz, *The Jews in South Africa*, p.95.

103 Meyer Dovid Hersch, *Hatzefirah* 82, April 1903, quoted in Levy, *Writings*, pp.137-38.

104 Worden, Van Heyningen and Bickford-Smith, *Cape Town*, pp.26, 33.

105 Max Sonnenberg, *The Way I Saw It* (Cape Town: Howard Timmins, 1957), p.85.

106 Schrire, *Tolada*, this volume, p.130, stanza 120.

107 Hoffmann, *Book of Memoirs*, p.55.

108 Poliva, *A Short History*, p.28.

109 Bertha Solomon, *Time Remembered: The Story of a Fight* (Cape Town: Howard Timmins, 1968), p.32. See Gitlin, *A Vision Amazing*, p.47 and Schrire, Memoir, this volume, p.176.

110 Schrire, *Tolada*, this volume, pp.133-134, stanzas 134-137.

111 Van Heyningen, "Cape Town and the Plague", p. 80.

112 Wynberg district surgeon, Dr Claude Wright, 1902 Report on Public Health for the Year 1902, quoted in Milton Shain, *The Roots of Antisemitism in South Africa* (Charlottesville and London: University Press of Virginia, 1994), p.45.

113 Schrire, *Tolada*, this volume, p.129, stanza 119.

114 Western Cape Archives and Records Service, Insolvent Liquidation and Distribution Account, MOIB 2/3/85/337, 1908; MOIB 2/3251/991, 1909; MOIB 2/3354/96, 1910; MOIB 2/3376/335, 1911; MOIB 2/3501/434, 1913; MOIB 2/3679/754, 1914.

115 Robin Hallett, "The Hooligan Riots, Cape Town: August 1906", *Studies in the History of Cape Town*, 1979 , vol. 1, pp. 42–87.

116 Schrire, *Tolada*, this volume, p.134, stanza 139.

117 Western Cape Archives and Records Service, Insolvent Liquidation and Distribution Account, MOIB 2/3/85/337, 1908.

118 Western Cape Archives and Records Service, Insolvent Liquidation and Distribution Account, MOIB 2/3376/335, 1911.

119 Western Cape Archives and Records Service, MOIB 2/3251/991, 1909.

120 Schrire, *Tolada*, this volume, p.137, stanza 148.

121 Ibid., p.136, stanza 144.

122 Jane Carruthers, "G. H. Swingler and the Supply of Electricity to Cape Town", *Studies in the History of Cape Town*, 1984, vol. 5, pp. 88, 214.

123 Vivian Bickford-Smith, Elizabeth van Heyningen, and Nigel Worden, *Cape Town in the Twentieth Century: An Illustrated Social History* (Cape Town: David Philip Publishers, 1998), pp. 67–70.

124 Schrire, *Tolada*, this volume, p.136, stanza 145.

125 Paul Cheifitz located the will, written in Yiddish, in the Western Cape Archives and Records Service, 1912 MOOC vol 6/9/701 ref. 2880.

126 The reminiscences of Harry Nathan Schrire (1895–1980) were dictated around 1978 and transcribed by his daughter Vivienne Stein and son Arthur. They were later used by Gwynne Schrire in "Jewish Life in District Six before World War 1: A Memoir", *Jewish Affairs*, 2008, 63:2, pp. 22–28. The information in this section comes partly from there and also from interviews conducted in 2011 with the transcribers.

127 Rebecca Zuckerman's husband, Moses, was the founder of the *Bnoth Zion* Association. She became its third president and later Honorary Life President until her death in 1958. She was the mother of Solly, Lord Zuckerman (1904-1993).

128 Edna Bradlow, "Rachel Clain: A Jewish Immigrant's Story", *Jewish Affairs,* 2011, 66:2, pp. 25, 26. See also Schrire, Memoir, this volume, p.176.

129 Ben Fine, 1976, pers. comm.

130 See Appendix IV, this volume.

131 Ancestry.com. *"UK, Outward Passenger Lists, 1890-1960"* (database online, 2012). Original data — Board of Trade: Commercial and Statistical Department and Successors, Outwards Passenger Lists. BT27. Records of the Commercial, Companies, Labour, Railways and Statistics Departments. Records of the Board of Trade and of successor and related bodies. The National Archives, Kew, Surrey, England. Harry Schrire is listed mistakenly as "Schure". Thanks to Paul Cheifitz for this reference.

132 In Cape Town, 122,720 people contracted influenza. Among the 6,345 who died, 1,456 were white of whom 79 were Jewish. See Howard Phillips, "Black October: Cape Town and the Spanish Influenza of 1918", *Studies in the History of Cape Town,* 1979, vol. 1, pp. 88-106. A special "Memorial Service for Members of the Jewish Community who died during the Epidemic" was held in the Great Synagogue, Cape Town, on 24 November 1918. A memorial brochure with the order of the service was printed listing the names of the Jewish dead, including nine Cohens and Mrs Annie Schus.

133 Mendel Kaplan assisted by Marian Robertson, *Jewish Roots in the South African Economy* (Cape Town: C. Struik Publishers, 1986), p. 308.

134 Mary Segal became chairman of the *Bnoth Zion* Association in 1936, making *aliyah* when she was 80. She passed away in 1989 at the age of 92.

135 Kaplan, *Jewish Roots*, p. 314.

136 Ibid., pp. 14, 116.

137 Ibid., pp.318-319.

138 Gideon Shimoni, *Jews and Zionism: The South African Experience* (1910-1967), (Cape Town: Oxford University Press, 1980), pp.110-114.

139 Nathan Berger, *In those days, in these times (1929-1979)* (Johannesburg: Kayor Publishing House, 1979), p.64.

2. DIARY of REB YEHUDA LEIB SCHRIRE, 1892-1893[1]

Translated by Michal Solomon; transcribed, edited and annotated by Gwynne Schrire and Carmel Schrire

Editors' Note: The Diary (see Appendix II.13, this volume) is contained in a small, tattered notebook, whose unevenly trimmed cover suggests it was handmade. It measures 18 x 11.4cm, or (7 x 4½ in). Its contents were originally identified by Andrew Plaks and later by Devis Iosifzon (*in litt.*, 14 November 2011). The notebook has two main entries, which we have divided into three parts. Part 1 is 56 pages long and has not been translated. It includes 48 pages of text that deal mainly with the story of Joseph, Mary and Jesus, and ends with eight pages of what might be Yiddish poetry. Parts 2 and 3 were written at the other end of the notebook by turning it upside down. These comprise the Diary that we have translated in full below, adding punctuation, subtitles and paragraphs for ease of reading.

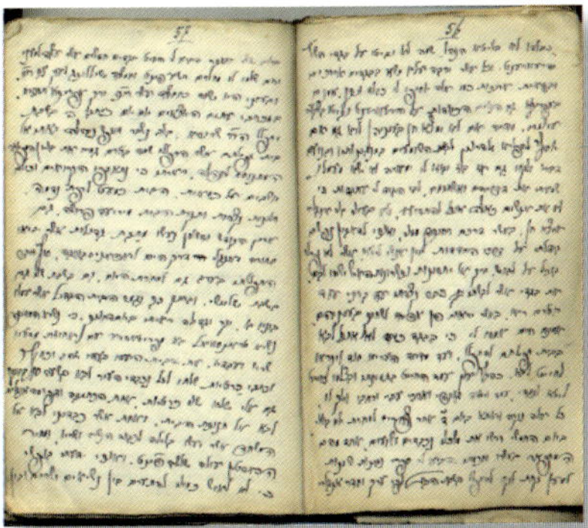

Fig. 12: Pages from the Diary of Yehuda Leib Schrire, showing cursive Hebrew script. (C. Schrire coll.)

The Diary of Yehuda Leib Schrire contains 94 pages, 82 of which are paginated (Fig.12). It is handwritten in cursive Hebrew, and is an account of his travels from Lithuania to South Africa. Apart from a Yiddish poem on a separate page, the language is pre-Ben Yehuda Hebrew and, as such, lacks the vocabulary of modern Hebrew. The translation seeks to achieve two things: to retain the period feel of the text rather than rendering it into colloquial language which might not have done justice to the original; to avoid making the writer appear childish or foolish in his use of terms for which his Hebrew had no words. We have tried to resolve this issue by simply translating his more opaque colloquialisms in brackets where needed.

The Diary is not a daily log but rather a recollection of his past. The timeline of the narrative runs for about 19 months, from 21 April 1892, when he prepared to leave Europe, to his landing at the Cape and his subsequent arrival at Johannesburg on 8 August 1892. It continues beyond the date on which he left Johannesburg, 1 November 1893, and ends with his undated return to Cape Town (see Figs 1, 3, 4, this volume). Its intended audience is not entirely clear. Yehuda Leib expected his Diary to be read by a "reader" or "dear reader", noting that it was specifically penned for himself and his sons, which may be why he transcribed it neatly some time around its latest recorded date of 1894.[2] In other words it was not written for publication, which may be why he freely describes his feelings, attitudes and experiences with a freshness, excitement and spontaneity so often lacking in more formal narratives.

Translator's Note: It has been a great privilege to me, as an Israeli, to work on this unique document that demonstrates the early development of the modern Hebrew language. I found it very touching to read the handwritten Diary of Yehuda Leib Schrire and to see how he struggled to invent his own words for concepts that did not exist in the *Tanach* and *Talmud*. The Hebrew diary should prove of great value to researchers studying the development of modern Hebrew. The English translation provides a vivid portrait of the initial shock experienced by East European Jews when they encountered the more relaxed religious attitudes of earlier settlers.

****

Why I left Neustadt

On the 24th day in the month of *Nissan* after *Pesach*[3] I left my house and abandoned my inheritance to travel to my birthplace[4] near Vilna, my childhood home, in the town in which my forefathers had lived for many years, to have pleasure in the company of my dear parents who are dearer to me than my life, may G-d be above them (see Fig. 1 , this volume). The purpose and the idea in my heart was to finish the craft of *shochet* and *bodek* which I had learned when I was still a *shatz* in Zizmar.[5] Since then nine years had passed during which I had been employed, at first working as a *shatz*, but I was not doing the holy work of *shochet* and *bodek*. This is why I was returning this time to continue to study the craft to become a *shochet* properly.

I observed that my loved ones, my friends, my acquaintances, and the ones who appreciated me, saw that my road to go to Africa was correct. My wife's brother[6] had already been living there for a few years. He wrote to me and told me to be prepared for the journey because in a few days they were going to send me expenses for the journey to bring me to Johannesburg in South Africa to work there as a *shatz* and maybe as a *shochet* and *bodek*. My ears had picked up [I had heard] that Africa is a land of freedom and most of its inhabitants follow their eyes and their hearts and eat non-kosher vermin. That is why he told me to finish the qualifications for the *shechting* and to bring with me letters of certification from the Russian rabbis.

What is more, when I had seen with my own eyes how the community leaders and managers had destroyed the town — instead of Neustadt, "New Town", it should have been called "Town of Destruction", like *Chazal* who said [?Aramaic]. Its rabbi fought a fight. He looked for schemes and he did not pay attention to the complaints of the people who were grumbling and protesting to him. They did not want to believe in him or to follow him as a rabbi. He, of course, was able to make plans for community concerns that would not take away their bread and *parnosse* and the bread of their homes, and the community looked to him to fix things so that everything would be at peace. Unfortunately he did as he wanted with a very smooth tongue, and he led them astray. He only managed to get out his own salary from this, taking it from the hands of the butchers. He made it harder for them and laid his hands on them so that they were not able to make decisions on certain questions. He also went after the cooks. This added to the price of *shechita* and he blamed them. All the people of consequence in the town called him "Jerubbaal",[7] but he just followed the advice of the *rebbitzen*, and only she. She was born to her parents, scum of the earth and nameless. He did not listen to the words and complaints of the community and he did as he wished.

To the disappointment of the whole town who loved and honoured me [I decided to leave] as a result of all these arguments and fights and lack of order. They saw from my plans that I was going to travel to another place to finish my studies as a *shochet* and *bodek*, but they were not able to help or force the hand of the rabbi to get him to add me to [those who worked at] the abattoir [so that I could not] finish my studies there. To avoid the complaints made to him and to distance himself from the responsibility of not allowing me to study there, the rabbi gave different answers to everyone — and to himself — who asked him about my studies. Nevertheless it is true anyway that the *shochtim* themselves told some of the important people that the rabbi had told them very strongly that they were not to allow me to have a right among them in the matter of *shechita*, so that I would not be as a Satan to him in the future. This was his word, as he held a grudge and took revenge like a snake on any person who came and went among the students. More than that, the rabbi was afraid that an upright well-spoken man would draw the heart of the people after him, and they might follow him instead. The people could not tell him that openly but could only listen to words from his holy mouth and the rabbi was like a bubbling fountain. But the community got comfort from their belief that when I had finished as a *shechter* and got my qualification, they would all arise as one and fight the fight with a strong hand and employ me as a *shochet, bodek* and cantor.

But for myself I knew that they just believed in it for nothing, and not once, but twice, I figured out the spirit of the crowd. I knew that in their houses they would join together in a group and talk on and on and on and on. This one will get upset and that one will get hot and this one will curse and that one will raise his fist [just] as though it were proper to hit the head of the rabbi and *rebbitzen* — but the wind would carry away their words like the waves of the sea before the winds of the storm, though when the wind drops, the sea returns to the same quietness shining like a [smooth] mirror. That is how the spirit of the mob would slowly disappear. All of this I knew even before I determined in my heart to travel to Oshmanya, and that is why I was not attracted to the idea of fighting back and I was strong in my determination to leave.

I told my loyal wife that I was not going to leave her only for one month because I believed that who knew what one day might bring? Maybe they would not send me expense money from Africa and I would then have to travel in Russia to look for a different place and a different town in which to make a living. Who knows if it would be possible for me and if I would be successful in finding a good house and an honoured position in one month? Furthermore this is a very bad time for Jacob. It is a time of trouble and the people of Israel are running for their lives as before a sword. Some from here are going to America and some to Africa and the ones who stay, to their unhappiness, live in great poverty and a lot of torments under the foreigners who rule them very harshly. They are very happy when they manage to find enough bread to satisfy their stomachs. How can I hope to be a *shatz* to them when they do not even have money to buy bread? They are dirt poor and are so oppressed that they have no hope of bringing a *parnosse* to me for my house with honour.

I told her everything that was in my heart and that the coming days would be better than the first days when I was only a *shatz*. When I would be a *shochet* as well as a *bodek* I would find a good place with G-d's help. The two are better than one. The *shochet* and the *chazan* are like two twins and it will be possible to find enough bread for a living. Nevertheless I told her that if the letter came from Africa she must send me a telegram on the day she hears so that I will know how to plan things.

In the darkness on Sunday night I took a good bye blessing from my beloved wife who cried secretly, and from my elder son[8] who both went with me. Only my little son[9] and daughter[10] were already fast asleep and they could not talk to me. Tears choked me and I went on the carriage which moved heavily because of one weak horse walking slowly and looking from one side to the other as though he himself were also thinking that he was travelling on a bad road full of mud with muck up to his knees and he had taken it on himself to carry three people on the way to Raseiniai[11] with a driver who kept exhorting him to trot faster.

I was sitting trustfully and quietly, dejected and with a broken heart. I took it into my heart to examine my situation because my pockets were empty and I had only two *shekels* and I still had to pay the driver one *shekel* for the trip. How would I get to my birthplace? I passed [?] 50 *versts*[12] and I knew days of trouble and toil were waiting for me. I also figured that it was not good for a person to sit in the house of his parents when he was an adult, to eat the bread of charity from the hands of his parents who worked by the sweat of their brows to earn their bread. It is shameful for a person like me to ask for charity from poor people who are not [even] able to fulfil their own needs. So I was very upset and my heart broke from the shame when I told myself that it would not only be for one day or two days or 10 days or 20 days that I would have to live with them. Who knew if the *shochtim* and the rabbis would not lay a heavy burden on me and increase the fees? From where would I get even one copper coin? Very heavy groans came from the depths of my heart, even tears came out, running down my cheeks. Luckily I controlled my emotions and without bitterness, but I was angry. It was my way in times of stress to smoke double even though I knew that the end of this pleasure would eat half of my flesh. It was only because I became addicted to this wretched desire in my youth and I could not stop myself or turn away from this bad habit. This is the way of every lust and habit — a person who is addicted at a young age cannot easily get away from it. As *Chazal* said: "If you make a sin, you lose a year from your life."

On the afternoon of the third day I came to Raseiniai. I paid the fee for the wagon and was left with 50 kopeks in my pocket. I did not speak to anyone and I did not disclose to anyone that I was a *shaliach tzibur (shatz)* because I thought I would be a joke if I arrived on a Tuesday, it being the custom for cantors to come on Thursdays. They rest for a day or two and then they do as they choose. So I asked the owner [of the boarding house] for a room alone to rest from the troubles of my journey. I lay down and slept till dawn the next morning. I saw all my acquaintances and they all predicted that in every town only one member of a family was left and that was what was going to happen [everywhere] because anyone who had the opportunity to move and travel was hastening to do so to escape from the fear of bad times.

Giving up all hope I prayed on *Shabbat* and they liked me and the people of the town gave me ten *roubles*. On the second *Shabbat* I was in Oshmanya.

Back in Oshmanya

On the Thursday evening I came to the house of my elderly parents[13] who knew nothing about the fact that the African journey had found a nest in my heart. They hugged me and kissed me with burning lips but I did not want to worry them or tell them the goal of my plans because I knew that we had once been five brothers[14] to our parents, may they live (Fig. 13).

Fig. 13: Yitzchak ben Shmuel (Itsko), father of Reb Yehuda Leib Schrire, in Oshmanya. Inscribed on reverse in Hebrew by his son "My father, my teacher, Yitzchak ben Shmuel Schrire, born in the year 1821".
(C. Schrire coll.)

One of us went to Kharkov[15] when he was a teenager. Over there he did well and took a wife and had children. Suddenly we heard that his wife had betrayed him and has given her love to strangers, and she added to it murder because she poisoned his drink and he died. Another brother was good and honest, coming to me and I was protective to him and gave him the fear of G-d. He died in his youth to my great distress and he also left behind a single son. One died when he was a small child. The youngest of the brothers went to America and we lost trace of him. For one of my brothers the wheel of fortune turned this year and he went downhill and his business deteriorated and could not support the needs of his family. He also went to America and now there is no memory of him. So now I was the only son around, the first and the last. So how could I worry them and throw salt on their wound and on their pure hearts and tell them that I am also going to leave *(be'ezrat Hashem)*? That is why I kept it from them and I believed that in the days to come slowly, slowly, I would let them know: and so it was.

Six weeks I sat with them and finished the [course] work of *shochet* and *bodek* well and I took with me letters of recommendation. In the following days I told my parents about the poverty and oppression that I saw day by day and I presented them with the good hope shining on me from Africa, and like a little child I cuddled in their love. So finally the days passed that I stayed with them and the letter came from my wife that the people from the sons of Johannesburg had sent 250 *roubles* there for the expenses of the journey to hurry me to come to them. With my heart crushed to smithereens, with eyes watering from tears, with my mother's kisses burning, I held my mother and her face was wrinkled with sorrow and old age. My father turned aside, cried, and held me. He turned to her and said, "Stop crying, go home, and do not worry his soul". But she could not control her spirit because of the crying voices she heard from all sides from people who came to bid farewell — men and women, children and the elderly.

My father and I went up together to the wagon and the master of the horse sent his whip down on his loyal slaves to speed them through the streets of the town. A whole hour we sat in silence and did not say anything until we came to the railway station and our train. I said goodbye to my clever and honest father: who knows if it is not going to be forever? My mother-in-law was also sitting and crying in the corner of the house because she was travelling to her young daughter in Smargon[16] and a few days before that I was there.

I departed with lots of tears and we were still looking at each other with tears in our eyes. A great *teruah* was heard with smoke and running and fire glittering. Here, dear reader,[17] pay attention to contemplate this last awesome moment. One moment I looked at my father eye to eye, old age on him, the tears in his eyes penetrating into my heart, his eyes leaking water as he carried my bag to bring it to the compartment, hurrying up the steps for fear of missing the time and me in my hurry and anxiety. I took it from his hand and I couldn't look at his sad face because I was afraid our eyes would meet. A long hot kiss, and without words my father went down from the steps of the carriage, the door was closed strongly by the hands of the station master, and I hurried to look out of the window and I still saw my father watching as the coach passed by him, wrapped in tears, with his hands uplifted. The sound of the machine and the smoke stole from me the last comfort of seeing each other for the last little bit.

For about a whole day I sat at my place in the compartment with men and women. Most of them were going to America. Children and women wore torn clothes and lay down barefoot on bags, their clothes around me. This one stands and this one eats and that one drinks. My heart was torn to pieces from what I could see in front of me. I could see the faces of my beloved parents, their tears, their moans, still sounding in my ears. I put into my heart this awesome idea. How great is the love of parents for their offspring and their kindness that they extended to me from the first time I could remember until this day, and now I have left their house in their old age and G-d knows if I will ever be able to see them again. Alas! If I could only hug them with my right hand and take them with me. I would give everything I had but unfortunately even more than that, I am going to the edge of South Africa. How many will be the years of my toil and wandering? Until all these wonders only *Hashem* knows if I will ever see my dear father whom I love so much? Will I see the face of my poor mother who was left lonely and alone and complaining about her fate because I was taken from her?

These ideas and thoughts filled the chambers of my heart till midday and I could not pay attention to the lack of order in the compartment and slowly, slowly, these terrible thoughts passed. After a very strong rain cloud passed, a new hope came that I should soon be able to see the face of my loyal wife and my dear children whom I had not seen for eight weeks. I could not wait to see them. Two days passed and on the third day, *Erev Shabbat Parshat Shalach*,[18] I came to Neustadt and I found my family waiting for me in the street and they fell into my arms. My eldest son heard at school that I had come and he also ran to me and fell into my arms with a crown of kisses and we welcomed each other.

The departure

I stayed at home for three weeks. I went to Memel[19] with my wife. She prepared everything I needed for the journey. With her own hands she prepared *latkes* and rusks to take on the boat. I took a chest full of books, science books, and *drush* books with me. Six days before my trip I sent a chest of clothes to Hamburg. That, not counting my sack full of food that I took with me in the railway train.

Three boys travelled with me to Africa. Each one prepared for themselves for their needs and on Sunday we were ready to part from the soil of Russia to cross the border. I got up early at dawn on Sunday morning and prayed to G-d from the depths of my heart. I also parted from all my beloveds and acquaintances with penetrating eyes and I looked at the shape of the synagogue that was built so beautifully and gloriously opposite my house, and in my heart I said: "Alas! For eight years and three months I have been employed in the synagogue as the *shatz*. How many drops of sweat came off me and how many times have I enjoyed the pleasant echoes on the ear and now I am preparing to part from this great and holy house."

All the days of my life its stones had been sweet to me, the walls, from the foundations to the roof, were all dear to me. Holy feelings found ways into my heart. I kissed the *mezuzah* of the doorway of white stone as cold as frost and I imagined in my soul that the stone was also mourning and crying and a holy silence filled my ears. I hurried to leave to go home and now men and women came together. This one wants to send a letter and that one wants me to be a mouth for her to wake the mercy of her relatives to send for her. The most moving for me to hear was the crying of one who was spreading her arms to me, begging with bitter tears that I should wake the mercy of her husband who had left her and her sons in poverty, great need and hunger, while he was wasting his money like dust to run after every lust and fancy in the bosom of non-Jews!

So I stood in the middle of all this crying and horror and looked at the walls of my house and sometimes at my sweet wife, who was covered in tears, and all the ones around me clutching the edges of my clothes. Also my little daughter was watching me and smiling at me. Carrying with me their looks full of tears, I cried a bitter cry and the sound of the horses blocked the sight because the owner of the wagon that was to carry the passengers to the railway station came to my house. He and his helpers hurried and took all our bags and put them inside the wagon and I knew that my weak spirit would not let me restrain myself, so I hurried and went outside and did what they wanted and went to the street that went to the border. Over there I met many people standing there waiting for me in a little wagon to take me with them to cross the border to the house of Rubinstein where we would meet the passengers who would be accompanying us. He had organised our belongings that had become disorganised through the handling of the officials at the border. Rubinstein himself was going with us to Hamburg to accompany his young son who was going with me to Africa. We went up to the house of L. Segal at the edge of the street and over there were gathered all my acquaintances and friends and my wife, two sons, and little daughter and the maid who came together with everybody. I told my loyal wife to give my little son and little daughter a small coin so that they could go and buy candies so that they would not be there at the last minute when I parted from them. My eldest son of 12 years old — may he live — will travel with us till the Rubinsteins' house. I nodded my head to all who had gathered around because I could not speak and I hurried to get out of the way with my two friends and in a quarter of an hour I was in the Rubinsteins' house and was organised with the clothes and the food separated and everything in its correct place.

I asked my wife not to come with me to the railway station because what would it do for her to see this big steam machine [train] stealing her husband from her arms? It would be better for her to go back home and play with her little children so that they will not cry, and only my eldest son would travel with me till the station. She cried and begged me not to stop writing and I promised her that with G-d's help I would fulfil her wishes. With a broken heart and a trembling spirit I controlled myself. I sat on the wagon that stood ready. I heard the sound of the people blessing me and I also heard her crying voice begging for letters. Time after time I turned my eyes and head backwards to look at her. Alas! Poor me! "I left her with nothing in a foreign land," I said to myself, "Only 10 marks that I had begged her, that I convinced her, to take from my hands. She has to find ways to feed herself and her dependents until G-d will make me successful and able to send her some money. But some months will pass before G-d will make me arrive in Africa and before I find my hands and feet and thus, poor me, what will she do?"

The idea shook me and it was only when I saw my son sitting opposite me and as a young boy enjoying the galloping horses and the beauty of nature that I found a little comfort from my sorrow. It came into my heart to disclose to his ears that he should be diligent in his studies and listen to his mother who has been left alone. Only when I started talking both he and I melted like wax with our tears and so we sat quietly until Baniel [?], the station house. I came to the head of the railway official who gives the trip documents and I took a letter to Berlin. My son was going after me counting my steps because his heart was telling him that very soon he would be going and would not find me. I gave my son a bread roll and sweets as I knew that up till now he had not eaten anything, only he did not take it from me because he was full and could not eat. I understood that he could not eat because his pure heart was full of sorrow. I begged him to take it from me but the sound of the bell rang and each one of the passengers hurried to take his bags and get into the railway carriage.

The journey through Germany

We were five people — me, the three boys travelling with me, and Rubinstein travelling with his son to Hamburg. The last minute arrived, I kissed my son who was dearer to me than my life, and he raised his voice crying bitterly and kissed my hand. I went up into the carriage and he, melting with tears, stood on the ground looking at the compartment. The train conductor closed the door with him crying "Father! Father!" I looked at him through the window with a melting eye and a torn heart and the horses of fire started to rush past my eldest son's face. In vain I looked for him where he had been but the carriages went past like the wind and I could not recognise him. Then my eyes opened and I cried without stopping and I felt a little better.

The compartment was full of people and there was no room to sit. We sat on our bags on the ground and my eyes turned to the door through which I had climbed. I saw the number of the compartment — 2354 — was written in a black colour above. At 4 p.m. on Sunday we sat in the train again and towards evening we came to Insterborg.[20] We waited over there until 11 p.m. for the connection to bring us to Berlin. At 3 p.m. on Monday we arrived in Berlin. We climbed down and laid our bags on the station platform.

Who can describe the glory of Berlin? Its beautiful wide streets, its great and fortified walls, the beautiful view of the metropolis, city of the King of Prussia, grace on every step and stride, her gardens and bridges amaze every eye. The machine tracks going from one side of the city to the other with trolley wires on the walls of the street and on the roofs of the houses and every five [?],the passengers can sit in the carriage and travel to any place they want and the machines and the tracks run and do not touch each other. This one is coming, this one is passing, this one is returning. The tram stops are built of glass with glass roofs in a wonderful way so that the passengers can go up and down marble steps with wrought iron columns and he who enters the station houses would be amazed at this wonderful building and the grace of the sight.

The whole day and the next full day we went to see the streets and paid very careful attention to all the glory of this town and at night at 10 p.m. we travelled to Hamburg and the train station. When I came to the carriage I again met up with people from my home town Oshmanya who were travelling to America. I didn't have enough space to sit because it was so full and when one person got up, other people hurried to take his seat. And so we sat on our bundles until the light of the morning.

We crossed the most wonderful bridge in Europe, this is the Dessau Bridge. Many towns are built beautifully, captivating to the eye and to the hearts of the passengers who are looking out of the windows. I forgot everything that was with me, my situation, the past, and the future and my eyes and heart were only on the new things passing in front of me like shadows. I have always tried to examine those things that exist in nature and there is a great inclination for each person to see and be inspired to see new things. Then he will forget his toil and sadness and grief and occasionally even hunger will not waken his master's stomach to disturb his interest. At midday we saw the station close to Hamburg. Ships covered the face of the water from all sides and countless iron machines hooted and whistled; hundreds of steamboats passed from one side to the other like a living wind that was ruling over it.

The passengers started to organise their bundles. The ones who lay down got up and the ones who sat down got up and everyone was busy working. At 11 in the morning on Wednesday we arrived in Hamburg. With a *teruah* and a lot of smoke and a torch of fire the machine went up into the gates of a large awesome station. Pushed and shoved and nervous we got off the coach and here Kottel came to collect me to [take me to] his house. Here, too, we laid down our bundles over there and went to town. A wonderful sight at every step: steam machines [engines? trams?] going on either side of the water. On the opposite side are the railways and hooting and tooting and the hands of the people by the thousands putting stuff on and taking stuff off and stacking and taking apart.

So we went down from the top of the mountain until we came to the train station that was going to Altona. We sat in the compartment and came to the house of the man who was taking me there. We stayed a whole day in Hamburg. We went to the shops and we bought forks and spoons, knives, wine and cones of sugar. We came to the conductor and for the price of 260 marks we bought boat tickets for each person and I spent the sum of 20 marks on necessities for the journey, for my meal, and for my luggage that I had left at the station.

In the evening we all went to the station that was going to Vlissingen,[21] a region in Holland. The conductor sent us to travel by train and from Vlissingen a large boat would take us. That night Mr Rubinstein parted from us, the father of the boy, and returned to his house and we were left like a flock without a shepherd, and like strangers in the land, and the three boys listened to me. They were obedient and honoured me the same way as if they were still with me in their homes and they had full trust in me that I would lead them because they were much younger than me. When I saw that the man who was like eyes for us returned to his home and in a day or two would join his wife and loved ones who would hurry to come to him and ask about everything that had happened, this time my mood also darkened and my eyes were not dry.

"Alas!" I said, "When will I be able to see my sweethearts? Alas! From day to day and from minute to minute I am getting further and further from them and only *Hashem* knows the depths of the feelings in my heart."

At 11 p.m. on Thursday night we climbed onto the train. With much toil we carried in our bundles and the journey started with great speed because the English and Prussian machines go much faster than the Russian machines and furthermore it was an express train, second class. Four times we heard announcements telling us to go and take our parcels because the coaches were going to change, and every time with great toil we took every item from its place and brought it down and then put it into the new compartment.

Some passengers tricked us. Suddenly they called out in a commanding way "GET DOWN! GET DOWN!" We hurried with both hands to pick up our bundles and there was loud laughter from the train staff. "Where? What? Go back to your places!"

Vlissingen in Holland

After midday we saw the train station yard and the border of the land. From afar we saw the big boats moving fast. Beyond a piece of sea there was something built from stones and iron bridges built on very strong foundations and large stones from the bottom of the sea extending five times the height of a person and people were passing buckets from one person to another.[22] Big steam boats were standing and hooting with a great and powerful *teruah* as if they were ready to swallow everyone who came close to them and other tracks [?] were running like crazy from the other side from where we had come.

The passengers went down and carted their belongings. They were walking around like lost sheep. Everywhere you went, in every corner, were bundles and clothes and dishes and bags and crates and their owners were looking at them with seven eyes[23] and did not know where they were. None of us could understand the language of Holland spoken there and with great anxiety we waited for the agent of the company who would come to receive the passengers sent to them. My three boys and I stood together and from afar we saw a young man coming closer. He came to us and spoke the English language but I told him that none of us understood his language and he should speak Ashkenazi[24] and then we would know and understand his wishes. In a broken language as well as sign language he asked each one of us to give his ticket to him. He took the documents into his hand and said our boat would be ready to take us midday the following day. He went and loaded all of our luggage onto a small wagon to take it to the big station. So we loaded all our belongings on the wagon. Twenty-five Jewish people were with us along with people of other religions and languages. All as one called "HOORAY!" Some pulled the wagon instead of horses, some helped load, and most of them pushed the wagon from the back. One was happy and cheering and one was moaning from anxiety. All gathered and went to the shed. The agent told us to place our luggage in the right order so that each person could write his address on it, the doors were closed, and the entrance guard placed a watchman to guard them.

Then the agent told us to follow him to the town, an hour's walk. He told us his company would put us up for the night with a meal. He went ahead and we followed like sheep. We crossed an iron bridge under which boats passed.

We went a distance until we came to the town. The agent brought us to a Dutch hotel but that did not have room for us all together so 18 people were separated. My friends and I did not part from each other all the days.

Over there in the hotel we were given soapy water to wash our face and hands. They set a table and gave us a loaf of bread and butter and coffee. I could not eat because I was not used to eating *goyishe* butter but I took out my own bread from my bag and a piece of cheese which I had taken with me and I ate. Every person sat at his place to write a letter home. When I finished my letter I took one of the boys with me and I went to town and prayed *Minchah*. Whatever I had in my pocket I put in my small bag which I gave to the two remaining boys because the Holy *Shabbat* would start very soon.[25]

We went through narrow clean streets facing the lighthouse shining from the sea and we saw the mountain[26] from afar and on it were flags of different colours. We went upon the mountain and this is how the mountain works. The distance from the town to the top of the mountain is about half a *verst*. All the way it was going up and up and up on a slope paved with smooth stones so that even wagons and horses could go up the road. On top of the mountain is a wide square with an iron rail the height of a man surrounding it so that no one could fall off it into the sea. The walls of the mountain on the other side were built of strong stones from the foundation to the top like the wall of a fortification.

As we went up there we neared the rail where the Baltic Sea[27] was stretching round from the one end of the sky to the other end, the whole horizon all around and much deep water. The noise of the waves sounded loudly and forcefully with foam on the top of the water like a foaming pot. The force of the water hit the mountain wall and the waves washed very strongly backwards and then forwards again. When I turned to the other side facing the town, I did not feel any wind. The air was tranquil and quiet and when I turned to the sea I saw the waves shining like gold and sparkling with precious stones from the sun's rays before she collected up her light and a cold wind blew on me. I was afraid that the wind would blow my hat from my head into the sea so I held it with both hands until the brim tore off. We saw small boats sailing on the waves of the sea like white ducks and the masts of the big boats were standing numberless like the cedars of Lebanon.

"Alas!" I said to the boy who was standing next to me amazed. "Tomorrow we too will be in the heart of the sea over there under the end of the horizon and the sky between the waves full of noise and turmoil moving like a drunkard."

The boy started to cry. My eyes too were filled with tears, full of emotion and anxiety and we returned to the shore to go back to our hotel.

The sea gathered its light. *Shabbat* with its holiness had not yet come to Vlissingen because we had not yet seen any of our people the whole time. With a broken heart I prayed the evening service at the back of the house behind the doorpost.[28] I took a glass of wine for *Kiddush*. I could not say a word from my lips because the memory of my dear ones came to me. A week ago I had come from the synagogue and my wife and household and everyone were sitting around me and I was like a king sitting at the head and now [I was] within this hotel full of guests, Dutch, English, drinking, eating, playing and laughing. The owner of the hotel too was not Jewish and mocked the Jewish guests and watched our movements. I ate a small piece of cake that I had taken with me secretly to use for a *Kiddush*. I had hidden it from their eyes because I did not want them to say the people of Israel were always hungry.

To my great joy the owner of the hotel beckoned us to follow him and he would give us a place to sleep. We followed him together up onto the roof and from there another ladder was standing [for us] to climb to a top room which was a bedroom. There we found beds made up with white sheets, pillows and blankets on each bed, each bed identical as though made from the same stamp. They were small rooms and in each room were two beds, a table, soap, water, a comb and a mirror, everything put orderly in its place. I lay down and slept.

I got up in the morning and about 10 more people were praying *Shabbat* service in the hotel and we went outside. Opposite our hotel I noticed a man go out holding hands with his wife. Their faces were Jewish faces, only [he had] a pipe in his mouth and a thing for the protection from rain [umbrella] in his hand. From afar they also looked at me. I said to the boy who stood next to me: "Please go and follow him and look where they are going because their faces are the faces of Jews but their doings are the doings of *goyim*."[29] Fifteen minutes later the boy came back and said: "You saw well. Let's go to the synagogue because they went there too." I also followed them until I came to the place.

This bit of good news spread fast and all the passengers, about 20 of them, agreed to go there. We went with the boy as a guide and in a narrow street we saw a house built well. Slowly we opened the doors of the house and inside was a holy quiet silence. The Holy Ark was on the east side and on it in golden letters was shining "*Shiviti Adonai lenegdi tamid*".[30] Inside the house was a small *bimah* and on the *bimah* stood a cantor and the rabbi *davening*. His clothes were like those of a choir cantor. To the right and left of the *bimah* were long benches. About 15 Dutch families in small groups that lived there were there with children, covered in prayer shawls around their necks to pray. When we came in — about 20 people in all — they turned to face us and one of them pointed with his fingers to us to sit on the benches on the western wall. I heard the cantor singing softly "*Yishtabach*". His pronunciation was like that of the Ashkenazi. Everyone was silent and on the hymn "*Hakol yoducha*" the cantor started one sentence and the congregation followed on in an organised tune until "*Yotzer hame'orot*". Then we all quieted down and only the cantor was praying until "*Shema*". Everyone turned to face to the east and stood up. After "*Shema*" they all sang "*Ein Kamochah*" and "*Vayehi binso'ah ha'aron*" and they took out a *Sefer Torah* and they called out to the *kohen*.

Now suddenly one of our people came inside and told us that the agent of the company was standing and waiting in his wagon to take us to his ship. We hurried to return to go to our hotel. Everyone took his little bundle and clothes out to the six-wheeled wagon and its two mighty horses. Many of our brethren already sat in it and did not pay attention to the holiness of the day but I, G-d forbid, did not take anything to put in it and did not listen to the words of the agent, and the rest of the evil doers, who told me to sit in the wagon and laughed at me.

"Do you know that the journey is a two hour walk, and for a handicapped person like you,[31] it will take four hours?" said the agent. "What about these people in the wagon? They are also Jews."

"When is the boat that we are going to go on due to depart?" I asked the agent. "Today. In the evening," he said and looked at me as though I were a simpleton. "If so," I said, "you have nothing to worry about because I have until the evening to walk there. I shall go there slowly."

He smiled a cynical smile on his face and turned and went. I found three honest people who came with me and we walked according to my ability. Drops of sweat poured from me, and my hands were wet with water, but in my heart I was happy because I was honouring *Hashem* and the Sabbath when I went walking about two Russian *versts* on my pathetic legs. We came to the place where the agent had told us to sit. All the passengers had come there already as well as our luggage and bundles which had been brought from the shed where we had placed them the day before. We sat there for about three hours until about 4 p.m. when we saw a big, awesome ship approaching close to where we were sitting.

The name of the boat was the *Dunbar Castle* (Fig. 14).[32] The Castle Line Company has 22 big ships going to Africa, America and Australia. Each one makes its way four times a year. As well as these ships, they have different places where these boats are being built, including in Vlissingen. We saw a big ship being built by the hands of 580 workmen. This sight was wondrous to the eyes of the beholder. It was being built on the 25th story above the workshop and it was leaning on columns of steel supported by stone columns. There all the workmen were busy at their work with iron hammers and the hammering sound deafened the ears of the passersby. These people worked on this job for four months and once they brought her to sea on machines on wheels that were meant for this, they would start a job that would last for another six months until it was all done. Whenever we passed through that street, we raised our eyes to the sky to see the multitude of workers doing their work diligently on the rods [scaffolding] on top of the walls.

On the *Dunbar Castle*

The ship that came to pick us up had a depth of 130 fathoms and its width inside was 16 fathoms[33] and yet this is not one of the boats that would be counted as a passenger boat, but for cargoes. But it still had in the lower part 32 [?] and there

Fig. 14: SS *Dunbar Castle.*

was a place for passengers in all the three other storeys, as well as very deep holds below deck. In these would be found a treasury of food and heavy cargo. The place of the engine that they fire with coal day and night is very deep. Two people work there for two hours and when they come up from the belly of the ship, they look like devils with all their bodies and vests black from coal dust. They change every two hours and others take their place and go down underground.

With its sailors and officers, the rowers, the captain of the ship, three officers, a doctor, bakers, cooks, waiters, managers, workers, animals, birds — the number of people on the staff of the boat was 63. The smoke chimney [funnel] that is standing in the middle between two masts is as high as 5½ fathoms reaching 4 fathoms above all the houses built on the top. From its mouth, the smoke comes out like a furnace. Its outside walls are of very thin iron sheets, the thickness of two fingers and with iron pegs solid and tight one to the other. A small bell sounds its voice on the hour every hour, and from the other side opposite to it at the edge of the ship were people with a machine made to cast the anchors with a very big bell. From 6 p.m. to 6 a.m. the second bell will also sound the number of hours. One person who stands the whole night on his watch calls out the number of the hour loudly. The whole ship is smeared with tar from its head to its end.

Stocks of food — meat, fish, flowers, fruit, chickens — live and butchered — as well as stacks of rope — very thick new ropes and old ones made of linen — grass and iron rods and a well of sweet water to drink. Between the decks are eight small steps, big and small. Each cellar has two machines and the big machine will send its heat through a hollow iron tube. Sixteen iron chimneys painted red like blood are inside: their mouths are like the face of big *shofarim* through which the wind blows and cools the air below and they turn easily whichever way the wind blows. In addition to water wells for work, wells for washing clothes stand there. When they push the feathers [spokes] of the wheels, their mouths open and a huge gush of water covers the face of the ship.

There are places for excretion through which clean hollow pipes pass with water to wash away all vomit and faeces. In the Third Class cabin into which we went down, there were 72 people, 26 of whom were Jewish. In the Second Class cabin there were 54 people and in the first class only 32 people — 158 passengers not counting the staff working on the ship, 63 — altogether 221 men and women and children. The company agent showed us our places and beds to sleep in. There are 32 bunks on one side and 32 on the other. On each side there were 16 down and 16 up. That is what I saw in the Third Class cabin to which we were brought.

I did not visit the other cabins. This is the system of the boat, the *Dunbar Castle*, which we boarded on Saturday at 5 p.m. Over the horizon at Vilna it was already time for sunset — on this day it was 8:35 p.m. there but here in Vlissingen I saw on my time show-er [watch] that it was 7:45 p.m. The sun had already set and great stars were seen from afar.

From 4 p.m. in the afternoon until 11 p.m. they emptied the wagons that we had carried from the railway station. There was very heavy cargo, big bulky boxes, iron rods, carts full of different merchandise, barrows full of salty fish as well as other goods that were in them. Altogether the strength of the ship was able to carry 5,000 tons, so the ones who knew told me. We heard that at 1 a.m. the boat would set out on its journey and all the passengers who had been standing anxiously all day long already lay on their bunks, each one resting from their toil (see Fig. 3, this volume).

Only I could not control my curiosity to watch the movement of the ship from the beginning. That was why I went out onto the deck to see what they were doing. They took off all the very thick cables with which the boat was tied and one light steam machine tied to our big ship started going out very slowly to take her out of the harbour and lead her to the open sea. One of the sailors on the ship who knew the Ashkenazi language told me that it was a year and a half since the boat had come to the harbour, where, with much toil and trouble the staff had tried to take her out and bring her in. That was why the big boat had been standing in the open sea about 2 *versts* from the shore all day.

Miracle of miracles, the sight was wonderful. The shining moon spread its glow on top of the water and the silent wind hit the little waves passing from the two sides of the boat strongly and the boat passed through the white waves that were shining with phosphorescent light. And the waves were turning back with foam and bubbles and the strength of the wheels of the machine was hitting the waves and pulling the ship forward. From its two sides shone electric lights set in iron lanterns for protection. Many people ran from the two sides of the deck, from the one to the other, this one yelling loudly and that one ordering the other to do something. They were all talking in the English language and all of them were coming and going, the managers and the bosses from the harbour.

From afar I could see the lights of Vlissingen moving farther and farther away from me. They turned aside [?] and so I stood amazed and overwhelmed until all the traces of the town and the electric light of the town were gone and only the whiteness of the moon shone on the waters. I also heard the mighty water gushing out of the sides of the ship, and the sound of the machine [engine] doing its work did not stop day or night. So I stood for a whole hour and then I went down to the place where the people were sleeping under the deck and I slept.

On Sunday at midday the captain brought in a board on which was written the distance that the ship had covered. That was what they did every day so that the passengers would know what distance had been covered each day. With all my might I tried to find the place where the officials who knew the ways of the ship were. How did they know how many *passaot*[34] the ship covered every day? To my great joy I got acquainted with one of the passengers because he knew how to play the flute and I took my violin with me as well as some books of nature. That is why we became friendly with each other. This man also knew the Ashkenazi language and he knew the ways of the ship well. I asked him how they knew the distance from place to place. He explained to me that the captain of the ship could tell the distance covered each day from two things. The first thing he showed me was that on the other side of the ship in the place where the oars were kept was tied a very large rope leading into the water. This rope was tied on the other side to a machine that showed the time. The movement of the water moved the edge of the rope leading to the clock and the movement of the machine, which was marked with perpendicular lines of measurement, marked hours and had an hour liner. He also showed me that the wheels of a big machine in the middle of the ship standing by the compass made an impression. Every time the wheel turned a full circle it made a mark on the small machine and since the ship's officers know the length of the circumference of the wheel, they could make an exact calculation every day of how many times the wheel had turned. For example if the circle of the wheel went up 30 feet and the wheel turned 800 times, it would add up to 30 x 800 totalling 245,600 feet [sic]. They count this total sum in English *passaot* — each *passa* being about 14 Russian *versts* or 2,000 *arshins*.[35] The boat made 116 English *passaot* from midnight till midday.

The work went better and better, the sailors were hurrying to climb up and down the rope ladders like locusts to spread the sails and the masts and to pick up the spread out sails. At midday on Monday the boat made 268 *passaot* and in the evening a stormy wind made the sea look like boiling mountains and valleys on the face of the water, and the ship started to move as though drunk. From afar the waves ran like mountains and foam raised the ship from one side to the other. We could not stand on the deck of the ship anymore because we fell onto each other and from moment to moment the waves of the sea started casting giant waters onto the deck.

The passengers went down under the deck and the cry of the passengers went up to heaven because they believed in their souls that the end had come. The bunks on which they lay down started to turn from side to side and the tables and chairs overturned. All the crockery and glass dishes — the bowls and plates — broke to smithereens and their crates and bundles were shaken and moved from one end to the other. In a split second seasickness, like a destroying angel, hit them to devastate them. This one was vomiting from his bed and that one opened his mouth to vomit. Great sounds of moaning and crying could be heard. Not one of us could stand on his feet to relieve his friend's symptoms by passing one another water or vinegar. Everyone was lying down sick and the boat was in turmoil because of the strong stormy winds. How horrible that night was! We saw with our own eyes how death was coming closer. In a little while we were all going to be food for the sea! That was going to be our graveyard! Every person asked his fellow to have pity on him and give him some water or vinegar to revive him, but it was in vain because his friend was also lying down like a beaten corpse, his mouth vomiting whatever he had eaten with great pain. A little bit of green water [bile] was washing down from his mouth and nose.

If we only had known ahead that in another day this danger would have passed, then we would have been able to take this sickness with a stronger heart, feeling more secure; but fear broke our hearts and melted our spirits and we believed these were the last days of our lives. Every time when we listened to the steps of the ship workers on the deck over our heads yelling to each other in their own strange language and to the sounds of the gushing waters which rose and reached the deck of the ship, we said "We are doomed! Our end has come!"

In every nook and cranny people were lying, moaning heavily, dirty with vomit, and very deep groans were coming out of everybody's heart. Some were clutching their chests confessing their sins as if preparing for death. A few only looked on with eyes full of horror as their broken dishes were thrown around in front of their eyes and could not lift their eyes from where they lay. You could say that only I and four other people did not get sick like them. I only got a very big headache and I stood on my feet at the door of the room leading up to the deck until the middle of the night so that I could breathe in the cold wind, and when I got tired of this, I went to my bunk and lay down. There came to my heart and my thoughts the memories of my dear ones, the sweetness of my life. I believed that very soon I would hear the voices of the sailors calling to us to run to the small boats because that was what I had heard from passengers — that in times of trouble one could escape on small boats to wherever the wind would take them.

Many of these would find their graves below the waves of the sea which could turn the lifeboats upside down.

In the second bed below mine lay a Dutch man, the one who played the flute. He laughed at our misfortune. He said this was how you were supposed to feel when seasickness hits and the boat turns from side to side. When the sea quiets from its anger, all the sick ones will get up and ask for food. He explained to me that until now there had been no reason to be fearful. The ship was making its way and it was only the power of the wind that was raising and lowering the ship as though it were drunk. If the captain thought disaster was coming, he would have already lowered the lifeboats and given the command for each person to take the coats of armour [life jackets] under every person's head.

I did not yet know that under each passenger's blanket there was a life jacket. Even though my head was dizzy, I still moved my blanket and took out my life jacket and saw that it was made out of square pieces of cork trees sewn together on a strong piece of material like a woman's apron with six strings of linen attached to it, two to tie around one's neck, two on one's body, and two under one's knee, so that all one's body from the face and neck until the knee would be covered with a thick dress from a cork tree the width of three fingers, and if one were to lie in the water with one's face down, one would not sink into the depths of the sea. Under everybody's blanket was a folded garment like that. Sleep closed my eyes and I slept, fatigued.

When I awoke early in the morning, I got up from my bed and I could not walk without leaning on the sides of the ship. With much effort I went up onto the deck to sit at a place where the wind blew. The sea still turned like crazy, raising the edge of the ship up and lowering the edge of the ship down. I saw the three boys who were travelling with me from my home lying on the ground and vomiting non-stop. I gave them a little vinegar mixed with water but they could not even taste it.

Tuesday was the day of [our travels] and it was a fast day. The 14th of *Tammuz*[36] — all that day no one ate a thing, because their strength had gone away, and by the evening the fear had gone away. The anger of the sea had calmed down, the wind passed and the sun started to bring healing on its wings. All the passengers gathered on the deck to enjoy its pleasure and renew their strength. This day the ship made 244 *passaot*. All night we lay on the deck of the boat and we did not go down to the place where we were supposed to lie on our allocated bunks because whenever someone got under his bedcover, his head would spin and would move back and forth like a drunk and he would start to vomit.

Las Palmas in the Canary Islands

Midday next day we saw from afar two ships going the opposite direction. Also fish flying like little birds. That day the ship made 236 *passaot*. On 19th *Tammuz* the ship made 269 *passaot*. The heat started to increase. 20th *Tammuz* we again met two boats and a good wind was blowing behind us until the sails on the boat were raised and the boat did 268 [*passaot*]. We heard that tomorrow on *Shabbat* we were going to see an island, Las Palmas, one of the Canary Islands.

With impatient eyes we waited to see the edge of the sea. The boat made 276 [*passaot*]. At 4 p.m. we saw from afar tall mountains rising out of the sea. In the beginning I thought they were clouds covering the face of the sky and it was only when we came closer that we could easily see that these were all mountains and hills. The boat approached the foothills of the mountains and huffed and puffed through the sea [word missing]. On the top of the mast a red and white flag was raised. Like the thirst for water, so was my soul longing to see people walking on dry land. With seven eyes I examined the solid mountain very closely. On it was built a tower. Only because of its height and because it was so tall, the little houses looked to the eye like a child's toy. On the foot of the mountain big letters in the English language appeared stuck on the soil which said CANARY ISLANDS and on its mountain the year "47".[37] Bit by bit the boat continued moving and I saw a big town on the slope of the mountain and on the other side were railway trucks and a wagon tied to horses. We saw passers-by walking on the streets of the town on a paved road.

Many boats were standing there. From our boat the sailors also threw big iron anchors, and one of the slaves of the boat stood on a special place from which the officers of the ship stood when they were on guard on their watch.[38] This was far higher than all the other boats that were not far from us. He had a metal rod in his hand and a very strong long cable. Well-known measurements were marked on the cable and he threw the pole into the sea three times to measure the depth of the place. Each time he raised his voice and said a few words whose meaning I did not understand and then the boat settled 300 *amah*[39] in length from the town.

Well, from each side and corner you could see small boats and fishing boats coming nearer and nearer and the people, the inhabitants of the island, Dutch natives, their faces a mighty black, and Portuguese. They approached our big ship with their small boats. The slaves of the ship threw ropes down to them and they climbed upon the deck from each side like locusts, and they brought with them baskets of grapes, coconuts, pears and bananas growing on one branch, tasty to eat and lovely to look at. Cigarettes, cigars, tobacco leaves in the shape of bricks, also different birds like canaries and parrots in cages made from reeds that grow on the edge of the shore. Many of the passengers went down on little sailboats into town. They brought back chairs for sitting in and woven things made from a thick straw, woven in exquisite taste.

A whole ship full of drinking water was brought and it was transferred into the well on our ship, the *Dunbar Castle*, with a long hose. Four people turned a strange-looking artificial wheel which emptied the water all the way to the end. Six small boats brought coals and on each boat black people were aboard, looking like devils from the soot like black ink — only their eyes and white teeth looked like white wool. The machine that was made to load and unload heavy cargo started to do its job with a great noise and people's hands were full of work, taking out and bringing in the coals to the treasury of coal, and within a minute the boat standing in the middle of the sea had turned into a busy market street. The tired passengers opened their eyes and gave everything they had to refresh themselves with new fruit. One buys, one sells, one will point with his fingers and one will feel with this hands, one eats and one is about to start eating.

About 50 black slaves [labourers, workers] were working very efficiently loading the coals, and the soot and dust were going up to the sky covering the faces of those standing by. The sun was about to go down and the evening was starting to darken this wonderful sight. The voice of the officer sounded for them to separate from the community because the ship would soon be starting on its journey. Darkness covered the face of the earth and big lanterns were lit. The newcomers started to descend in a great hurry, one would crawl like a snake on the ropes of the boat going down and one would jump into his little ship, one would get up and one would drop, and in a few minutes all of the foreigners had disappeared.

One boat brought four oxen and eight sheep and all kinds of food — eggs, fruit and vegetables — full to the brim. That boat approached the ship and in a blink of an eye they lowered a thick rope and tied it to the horns of an ox, the machine raised the ox and brought it onto our boat. They did the same thing to all the animals on the boat. An iron grid from the big boat was built into the side of the second machine which took out the anchors, and the boat started to move. From afar we could see the lights of the lanterns in the houses of the town, shining like candles. It moved further away from us, although from time to time you could still get a glimpse of it, until it disappeared.

The Dunbar Castle continues her journey

On Sunday the ship made 211 *passaot* because yesterday it had stayed at Las Palmas for six hours. A ship going to Australia passed us and the passengers raised their hats and shouted "HOORAY!"

On Monday the ship made 265. On the same day we saw big fish the lengths of a few *arshins* and heads of strange creatures lifted their heads from the water. The wind was behind us and the heat was growing. On Tuesday there was great heat. The flying fish fell on top of the ship and two found alive fell by my feet. The ship made 258. Wednesday the ship made 241. I saw terrible sights and the heat started abating. Thursday the ship made 252. A big strong wind and also strong rain. Friday 258 *passaot*. The air was cold and at midday a counter wind started. They took down the sails and the cover of the boat made from oilskin. On that day I butchered an ox and we ate kosher meat because they gave us new dishes and I took a new pot, also four spoons and a knife I had brought even before I got onto the boat. *Shabbat* the ship made 259, the air was very cold and it was a head wind. Sunday 245, Monday 246. I butchered a sheep. The air was cold and an opposite wind. Tuesday 236, Wednesday 236. A stormy head wind. Thursday 245 with an opposite wind. I butchered another sheep. Friday 241, stormy rain, a flood of water and the ship started to move like a drunkard.

Saturday 239, a storm came opposite us and the waves of the sea washed the deck of the boat. At 2 p.m. everyone sat under the cover because they could not walk on the deck and only I had to go there, so I put on a thick garment and with great trouble I approached the edge of the ship to pass water, when suddenly a huge wave washed over the deck and the water was as high as my knees. If I had not been holding on so tightly to the chain that was there, who knows if the water would not have taken me with it? As it happened, the chairs and a wooden chest on deck disappeared with the water, and were gone in a second. I went below deck to change my clothes, shirt and shoes, and I thanked G-d for the grace that He had shown me.

On Sunday we did 208 *passaot* with a strong head wind and the ship's movement was terrible. On Monday I slaughtered and again by dusk we had covered 234 *passaot* and the sea rested from its anger. On Tuesday we did 243 *passaot* with a good wind, Wednesday was a very good wind. I slaughtered mutton and each time I slaughtered we were given a pound of kosher meat for each of the 26 people. Only when it was mutton were we given the internal parts. We made 256 *passaot* and the wind was very good and the sea seemed as though it were a polished mirror. That same day we heard one of the ship's officials saying that we would reach Cape Town that same day, in the evening. The good news made us relax and we watched out the whole day. We saw white birds and wild geese passing the ship on both sides and then resting on the water, some flew high and others came in their place as we came within 80 nautical miles of Cape Town.

At 12 noon we saw a ship passing us on our left, also bound for Cape Town. At 1 pm we saw through our seeing tube [telescope] the beginnings of tall mountains, the Table Mountain that stands in Cape Town. The sun went down and the evening's light shadowed our destination. We could only see light from a lighthouse in the distance. None of the passengers on board would go below deck. At 7 pm we reached the mountain chain. Then we saw the mail ship leaving Cape Town bound for Europe and the captain told us all to cheer "HOORAY!" He released fireballs of different colours into the air, reds and greens, and the passing ship also started to show different signals with electric fire. The sparks reached the clouds. From every side and corner were torches of fire and the sight of the lightning going out from every ship in the darkness of the night from near and far. This would astonish any seeing eye who did not know where it came from or whether it was born of angels and seraphim from *Hashem* and glittering creatures. The captain of the ship lit his light on the right side on which stood the man who measured the depths of the sea and the boat settled there.

That night the ship did not dock and we did not sleep for almost the entire night because the English passengers who had drunk alcohol were singing and dancing, ignoring the requests from the ship's staff to stop making a noise and being a nuisance. Because of this fact, none of the Jewish passengers were able to rest for one moment. We waited with anticipation for the dawn and I washed my face, my head and my hands as this time we were given hot water in which to wash. I went upon deck to watch what was happening, as for the last three days before our arrival the crew had been busy placing everything in order. They had worked tirelessly to paint the masts red, to wash the walls of the ship inside and out, and had even removed and tied the boards. They were always busy and there was always something for them to do.

Arrival in Cape Town

The morning came, and there in front of us were two [sic] mountains 2,750 feet high,[40] which were called "*Tafelberg*". At evening time both were flat and ascended high into the sky, but in the morning clouds were walking at its feet and from moment to moment, layers of dew would arise. Between the mountains, wide meadows stretched and fortified walls built fantastically. That is the town — Cape Town — that stands between mountains (Fig. 15).

Fig. 15: Cape Town panorama, c. late 19th century. (C. Schrire, coll.)

It is the first city of Africa. Its streets are wide and short. On the seashore to the length of a few English [measurements?] are tall buildings built as well as the structure of the harbour and everything belonging to it. Iron trucks went back and forth. To our heart's gladness we saw light boats and steam boats coming near us with people sitting inside. We also saw Jewish people there. Within half an hour the new guests ascended onto the deck to ask everyone where they wanted to go — they were hotel owners — and what they were able to pay. They were expecting to gather the newcomers to their homes and get some benefit from them. Among the newcomers I found an acquaintance of mine, a native of Neustadt who lived in Cape Town. He too had a guest house and I promised to stay in his house (Fig. 16).

At 1 p.m. on Thursday the boat reached the shore of the town and a poor man came to me and took me on his wagon and he told his servants to bring him my chest and bags and he travelled with me through the Customs House. All the immigrants are brought over there and their items searched to find any item on which duty must be paid or other items that are against the laws of the kingdom.

Fig. 16: Jewish immigrants arriving in Cape Town around the time Yehuda Leib Schrire landed there. See Richard Mendelsohn and Milton Shain, *The Jews in South Africa. An Illustrated History* (Johannesburg and Cape Town: Jonathan Ball Publishers, 2008), pp.28-29.

A half an hour brought us to Mr Heneck's rooms and the three boys also came with me and the people who came with me on the boat.

His black servant, whose physique was strong, handed me water to wash my face and hands and I stayed in his house until the end of the Holy *Shabbat*, two and a half days.

In these two days I went to meet my acquaintances from Neustadt and because many of them are here, some of them came to me on Thursday evening and I promised others to go to them. On Friday morning I went to one of my acquaintances and when I came back to the house I was told that the *shochet*, *bodek* and cantor had asked after me. He was here, and because he did not find me, he asked me to come to him. I went to him and tried to find out about him and I found out that he is learned because he became a rabbi from the Government in the Grodno governorate in one of the towns — the only thing is that he is frivolous. I also enquired about the rabbi. He is an English Reverend, Ornstein.[41] I was presented to him as a Russian native who cannot speak the English language who had been sent for by some people in Johannesburg. I saw that he did not have the spirit of the *Torah* about him and he did not live Judaism. The English ways were his ways and his craft was also like theirs. They would eat non-kosher vermin and were not impressed by the holiness of the *Shabbat*. They built their foundations and have adopted the English laws not knowing that they are the descendants of Judah.

On the same day I sent a telegram to Johannesburg [stating] that I had arrived in Cape Town and that my money had ended. Within half an hour a native whose name was "Vlafik" brought me an advance of £6 because that was what he was told in a telegram.

I also observed in the house of my compatriot that there was no *Shabbat* and no Holy Day and no *Torah* and no G-d. That was why I did not eat anything and he only gave me bread and fish and also strong wine.

After *Shabbat* I paid the best of the money for the hotel and my food and was accompanied to the station by my acquaintances who had travelled together with me to Heneck's house. One took the travelling document and one took my bag inside because the carriages in the train station in Cape Town had a strange structure. The doors are narrow and the compartment rooms can only hold six people, three on one side and three opposite and with seven eyes they watch all the passengers in case they were to bring a big bundle into the compartment that would fill more than the weight assigned to them (Fig. 17).

Fig. 17: Railway Station, Cape Town, c. 1892. (C. Schrire coll.)

The journey to Johannesburg

A very loud *teruah* and my acquaintances and friends stepped back and I called out words of farewell. They waved white cloths and lifted them up and down so that I could see them as long as the light of the candles from the railway station lasted: and the trip started on its way to Johannesburg (see Fig. 4, this volume).

In vain I will try to write and explain the news about the isolated land that I saw on the three days and three nights throughout the trip. Not every tongue and every scribe's pen can describe what I saw and it is unbelievable that almost the whole land of Africa is one stony mountain, marble stones, pebble stones, rocks in field and in rows — it is as if the whole earth were made of white hands from the depths of the earth till the mountain tops with their peaks climbing all the way to the clouds.

The rail tracks went through a very narrow pass carved in the mountain. On both sides were rows of rocks like fortified walls built and carved by man.[42] When the trucks go up, they go round and round before reaching the mountain peaks and then rounding them. From afar the mountains block out the sun that shines as on a wall of iron with an abyss reaching the top of the sky.

Field deer and goats were walking beneath the clouds on the edge of the mountains and forests and herds of sheep, hundreds and thousands of herds of donkeys and mules, were walking back and forth to find grazing from the leaves and thorns growing between the sides of the mountains. Only very rarely did trees grow; they did not look like much and were called ironwood trees because they were so heavy, they sink like lead in water.

We very rarely saw a field or vineyard, which is called a farm.[43] The people who have settled there are Boers. They also acquired sheep and thousands of donkeys and there are stone walls for the sheep. In summer and winter they go into the mountains and valleys to find grazing. The Boers are the inhabitants who have lived in the land of Africa from ancient times and inherited the land from the wild black inhabitants who with their swords and arrows could hit a single hair and not miss. The [Boers also inherited] the whole land of Transvaal to which I was already travelling. The Queen of England fought with them and did not succeed.[44]

I sat in the compartment for two days and three nights travelling between mountains and hills and the train would climb to the top of a rock with the help of a second engine to help it. It also passed through the valleys and bridges with the help of a second. This did not allow the train to progress any faster throughout my trip. I did not turn away from my window for one minute because I wanted to fill my eyes with the wonders and beauties of nature that passed before the travellers. When I arrived at the place which was the station where the passengers going to Johannesburg got off, I also went down.

The people who were responsible for taxes told me to bring my bags because the government of Cape Town was different from the government of Transvaal. The travellers were to pass through Vereeniging and this was also a small piece of land ruled independently. Here in Vereeniging the police men again put their hands in to search my bags.[45]

I hurried to take the document for the coach which was tied to five pairs of long-eared thin-tailed mules. I looked around in case I could find one of my acquaintances from Neustadt who I knew lived there. That is why I was late and missed the chance to get a place inside the covered wagon. Instead I had to go up onto the roof where the passengers placed their bags and clothes. As there were some empty places, they let other people sit up there, so I and another Hebrew who had travelled with me from Europe to Johannesburg had to sit there. They spread a covering over the wagon that turned and rattled from one side to the other upon the sharp slippery stones lying all along the way; hundreds of these stones were scattered all along the way. The wings of the wind carried a very fine dust that covered the wagon and its travellers like smoke from a fire that goes up to the sky like smoke passing through an unsown field. I tried hard to hold my body tightly to the rail of the roof so that I would not fall to the ground. After about 20 Russian *versts* we came to a station where they changed mules for others standing ready, only I could not see the light of day because I had about a finger's depth of dust on my face and on my clothes, my hair and my lips, and I could feel pebbles crushing my teeth. I went down from the wagon on to the land and I asked my acquaintances who were sitting inside to give me a place to sit there. They agreed because they had given me great honour all the days of my travelling with them.

I took off my external clothes and sat inside. Although, of course, the great heat that gathered inside the wagon choked me, I still felt grateful to be alive. I opened the window of the wagon, smoked a pipe and felt a bit better. Inside the wagon I found a traveller from Vereeniging who told me that the person about whom I had inquired had left with his wife and household three days before to attend his son's wedding in Johannesburg. My heart was both afraid and glad at the same time, because when I arrived I would find my acquaintance who knew me well.

We travelled on the mule cart for six hours without a stop and throughout the whole way we saw no forest trees, only dry fields with little hillocks that looked like little bat caves, with holes in the sides of the caves like a half a finger going in and reaching underground. I asked those who knew and they told me that a meerkat lived in them. Afterwards I also saw from afar little animals the size of house cats. They look very beautiful with long bodies and they were the ones that dig in the ground, making tunnels for themselves as well as the field bears [aardvarks] that dig for food underground to eat ants. These will extend their sharp tongues into the ants and the ants climb onto these and they fill their mouths and catch the ants time after time. Field bears also go into these tunnels beneath the ground like animals walking on the ground above.

By three in the afternoon we already could see houses built in the correct way from iron sheets. Everything was built from iron sheets. There were also gardens and trees planted around them.

"Hooray! Johannesburg!" the people called with a great cheer.
"Look! Over there is a great town to G-d," called the others, "this is a town for which our people have looked up to for so long."

Behind them two people could be seen sitting to my right. One of them said: "This is a town whose people will risk their lives in seas and deserts in the hope of the wealth they so much want and this is the goal and purpose of all the people in Europe and I am one of the inhabitants who only intends to make a few hundred pounds and then return home."

Every person expressed their complete feelings. Only I sat silently because my heart told me that in Africa I was not going to do well.

At 3 p.m. we came to town and it was unbelievable that in only eight years the great veld would have beautiful buildings, orderly and organised according to the rules of Europe and thousands of people would be on its streets. Horse coaches, tramway, train tracks, electric fire, rivers of water, shops were not missing there.

Johannesburg

The wagon stood at the stop in Pritchard Street and the passengers started to get down. One fell into the arms of his father and another into that of his acquaintance, this one to his uncle and that one to his saviour who had sent him money for the expenses of the journey. I also heard a voice calling my name. I turned my head and here was my brother-in-law standing and waiting for me, covering me with a crown of kisses and we fell into each other's arms. We travelled in a cart to his house.

Tuesday 15th *Av Menucha* in the Jewish year of 5652,[46] after lunch over there, it was a sleep of pleasure in my brother-in-law's house in South Africa, my destination. In the evening I got up from my bed and there was a loyal messenger sent after me because the man Fettel, the father of the bridegroom, had heard that I had arrived in town. That was why he sent for me to come and take part in the *simchah*, even though I was tired and weary from the labour of a journey of 28 days on the water, two days and three nights on the railways from Cape Town, and six hours on the mule cart and that does not include three days and nights until Vlissingen. I had not even caught my breath!

I washed my face and hands and wore my best clothes. I sat on the two-wheeled horse trap[47] on which most people in Africa travel and I went together with my brother-in-law. Over there I found a house full of men and women, invited guests who had come to celebrate the love. All my friends and acquaintances came to welcome me and received me with great honour. I stayed over there till midnight. I sang and I also gave a *drosha*. I also found the rabbi and the *shatz* of Johannesburg there. I had been brought there to be in competition with the old synagogue. [The congregation] had separated and parted from the synagogue in which he officiated.[48] I saw that he was hostile to me and only because of the obligation of honour was he shaking my hands, but, after that, he did not turn to me again and put his eyes on the plate with the roast chickens that had been placed before me.

He put his hands to give portions to the guests because that was the way of the reverend according to the English law. They always give him everything they prepare and he divides it up for everyone. They divide up the bounty, the meat and the fish for every person. At the end of everything, once I came home, I counted the coins of money which I brought back and behold £11. Aha!

I said in my heart: "In Europe I would only have got 110 [coins] for a wedding. From the days that I became a *shatz* I have never been privileged to bring 100 coins from a wedding. A great future in my eyes. Tomorrow I am going to send to my wife and my dependents the first 100 coins that I was blessed to earn in Africa since the day I arrived."

Fig. 18: Yehuda Leib Schrire, 1897, probably wearing the formal outfit made for him in Johannesburg five years earlier. (Shoshana Shapiro coll.)

Thoughts came into my heart — if your beginning is good, who knows what the end will be? Maybe not so [good], and a very sad idea started to pass into me, only I chased it strongly out of my thoughts.

The next day the head of the community came to talk to me and see my face.[49] They spoke to me in the Ashkenazi language to which they were not accustomed and they were all people of trouble. They were shaven! They had no *payot!* They asked me to cut my beard and my long hair!

"Your Honour," they said, "you are not in Lithuania any more. Over there they will not look at the clothes of the cantor and the reverend. The weightier the clothes and the longer the *payot*, the more honour would be given the person, but in Africa the very honoured ladies will look at the reverend with seven eyes and if they do not like him, even though he continued to amaze the listeners with his singing and sweet words, all of this will come to nothing and to naught."

I heard their words and I was amazed. My heart told me the future. These were not the kind of people with whom I should associate.[50] The eyes of ignorant English types would not like me because their ways were far away from me. I, to their dismay, grew up on the lap of Judaism among the people of Lithuania who do not pay attention to clothes but to talents and advantages. I had already shortened the clothes that I wore up to my knees before they had seen them because I was afraid that they would be a mockery to their eyes. Nevertheless they told me that I could not come to pray in their prayer house in a garment like that. Very quickly they conspired and called a tailor to me, just like one in Lithuania. He stood and measured my height and my length, my width and my breadth, and he went and returned on Wednesday afternoon, the day following the day on which I arrived.

On Thursday the princes of the community came to see me. One of them was very boastful about his wealth and wisdom and he brought me different books of music so that I would learn to pray from them on the following Saturday according to the English manner and style. On Friday morning the tailor brought me the new clothes that he had made for me and they paid the price for it — £9 and 5 shillings that is 95 *roubles*. In my eyes it was worth only 15 *roubles* and it only happens in Africa (Figs 18, 19).

Fig. 19: Yehuda Leib Schrire, 1897, probably wearing the same religious robes he wore in Johannesburg five years earlier. (Shoshana Shapiro coll.)

In the newspaper that came out every day it was written that on *Shabbat* Rabbi Schrire would pray. With a broken heart and a nervous soul I came to their house of prayer where they were praying until the wonderful building that came afterwards would be completed. I saw that they had invited people who were sitting on chairs and the house seemed like a barn with small windows and the ceiling of the house was made of a cloth spread out. The Holy Ark and the table on the *bimah* were also made from the packing cases that had brought goods from England through the sea to Africa.

The end of the matter, I prayed in the evening and also the following day, also on *Shabbat* and the second *Shabbat* and the third *Shabbat*, and during these three weeks the big building [Park Synagogue] on which they had worked so hard was completed.

Big and expensive, I saw it on its inaugural day because the president of the land — the President of Transvaal[51] — came from Pretoria with his ministers, servants and followers. The house was decorated with gold and silver silk, and letters of invitation were sent to all the honoured people to come to the dedication ceremony at 10 a.m. I too received two invitations. One was written and printed in English to present myself in front of the building, and the other one that they honoured me to attend the banquet that they would have at night in honour of the president and his ministers, and the price of the tickets was £3.

I knew in my heart that it was not for a man like me to mix with presidents and ministers and among the English who speak English and Dutch. I would just look a mockery in their eyes. Furthermore I would not be able to put the food and drink into my mouth because they were going to have an abomination of a soup and a non-kosher wine because they liked these kinds of foods.[52] That is why I came to the dedication of the synagogue but I did not go to the banquet, and so passed another two weeks and the terrible days had arrived.

I sat in the house the whole day, and in the evening one of the leaders came to me and told me to write a letter to the committee that would be meeting at 10 p.m. that night about what was needed for the service. I knew that they had already printed an announcement in the synagogue newsletter that I would be leading the High Holy Day services and that anyone who wanted to buy a ticket should come at a certain place and hour. Was it really possible in their eyes that they had already published it and had not asked me first? Why were they doing whatever they wanted to do without asking me as if I were a lowly slave? All those days I only consulted my brother-in-law and Ch.K. for their advice. They told me this was the right way and in my ignorance I believed that this was an order and I did not have the right to question it.

I prepared a letter and I wrote in it the true matter according to me, because I am only writing of those things:

> If you like the style of my praying and it is agreeable in your eyes, then I should get an allowance only for the High Holy Days but if I am to be a regular full time *shatz* then the High Holy Days are included. However if you do not like my praying and only want me to fill the needs to my destruction because the community of Johannesburg would gather to hear someone new and then they would turn their backs on me after the High Holy Days, then, in that case, I only want not less than £50 as a salary for the High Holy Days. But if you want to hear my prayers on the High Holy Days and G-d will make me successful and you will add me to the staff of the synagogue, then I am not going to ask for anything and we shall see how things will fall, and I believe that honest people like you are not going to cheat me.

I wrote these words to them and sent it to them written in the Hebrew language. The next day they came to me and asked me to write it in English because they honoured me to be the cantor for the High Holy Days. I gave their letter to someone to read so that I could understand clearly what their answer was. They said to me that right now there was nothing to talk about and I was to do whatever they asked and the honour would come afterwards.

So I prayed *Slichot* in the Orthodox synagogue instead.[53] They too had hired a little house for prayer.[54] Some people from the big synagogue were also there and that meant they liked me.

The end of the matter was that I prayed the High Holy Days and on the second day I gave a *drosha* on the *bimah* to the community in the Jargon.[55] In the big synagogue the learned gave me their hands in thanks. On *Yom Kippur*, when I ended the *Mussaf* prayers, all the community raised their voices and cheered, "*Yasher Koach*". Also after the *Neilah* service they all cheered loudly, "*Yasher Koach*". After the *Shabbat Ma'ariv* services I returned to my brother-in-law's house and I stayed there.

They gave me £3 for *shechting kaparot*[56] and I was happy that my bread was given and my water was secure and only it was Satan's idea for me whether I should go and pray in the big synagogue in the days of *Sukkot* or to wait until I was called. My brother-in-law as well as Ch.K. told me not to go there before the *shammas* came to get me. On the first day of *Sukkot* I saw that the *shammas* did not come so I prayed in the *beth ha-midrash*.[57] In the evening my acquaintances came to me. They were angry with me because I had not come there to pray. Nevertheless I insisted that I was not going to go before the *shammas* or a loyal messenger came for me.

So passed the period of the Holy Days. I prayed in the *beth ha-midrash* and they did not come for me. From afar I listened very carefully to hear if they were going to send for a different *chazan* who stayed in Kimberley. All of them together were very upset with me because I had not come to them for *Sukkot*. They said that they had already stated in their letter that they had honoured me to be their cantor for the High Holy Days and as the English do not ask cantors to pray every day, the cantor should realise that he has accepted the responsibility. I saw that I had antagonised them, but whatever was done could not be undone and that was why I wrote them a letter to pay me the price of my work.

On *Erev Shabbat* the *shammas* came to me and he had a sealed envelope. I tore the envelope and in it was £25 and a letter of glory that they liked me. I was filled with rage[58] and I cursed them and my advisers and I did not know what to do. If I would have written another letter and asked for the rest of what I asked for, they would only have answered me that I did not come to pray there on *Sukkot*, so they had deducted half my salary. Not only had they sent me £10 for the expenses and £6 for Cape Town, the clothes had cost about £6. That was why I had no justification to ask for the rest or to complain about it. I realised that I had fallen through my own handiwork and I could not get up from this. Who could go to the *beth din* to argue with the person who gave me advice? What is more, to bring it to court would be very expensive and who knows if I would win? That is why I bit the flesh of my tongue and kept quiet.

The *beth ha-midrash* had given me £5 for *Sukkot* and I had already sent £10 home before *Sukkot*. I decided to send her another £15 to pay for my debts and I had £10 left with me. I said, "I am going to try my strength and my craft of baking and candy making."

At the end of four weeks I became a craftsman but I did not see success. I also lost £1 in a bad business. I became a *mohel* in a distant village, a three-hour journey from the town of Johannesburg, and my compatriot gave me £8, so I sat quietly in my brother-in-law's house, jobless. When I learned the ways of the city and its people and its groupings, I had the idea that I should go back to my homeland, having spent six months in Johannesburg without seeing any hope or purpose in staying there.

Then I wrote an article of criticism about the town Johannesburg and the English and this is it. I wrote it in Jargon, only now for my book I have copied it into Hebrew so that it will be forever. The name of the article is "Israel and its Baggage" or "My People and their Goods".

"Israel and its Baggage" or "My People and their Goods".

Everyone will talk about, and a visitor who comes for a minute can also see, the talents and the faults [here]. Allow me — who is sitting in Johannesburg like one of the guests who came to live, but not to settle here, [in order] to make a pound or so and then return to his home [to do so too] — for in a few minutes I learned the spirit of everything.

I worked out the soul of the individual in some things and in different things and will expose to everyone all the mysteries of the young Johannesburg daughter. I kept time and season to myself to explain and describe with a writer's pen the root of everything.

It is unbelievable that within seven years a city could be built in the wild South Africa within rocky mountains and hills of sand. A big city and a fortified metropolis. It is one point that gives light to almost the whole of the land of Africa with its golden sands and houses of bank notes. You would be surprised that in every small town you will find a fellow Jew there stretching his hands and arms and prostrating his whole body wherever there is business to be made. Wherever there is a place to be touched, there he is.

Who is here? I and your fellow Jews. Who is living there outside the city and in the villages, between mountains of stones talking with men in every place you go? There he is. Miracle of miracles, it is he! He has brought his goods, his tools of his craft, his weapons, his bag, his knapsack, as if he were born right here from the womb of his mother, and here it will be better to examine him. His hope to return to pick a straight and good road from Africa to the Holy Land is strong and to pass through the iron bridge[59] without disturbance because from Europe the road is far. It is also hard for him to take out the money. This chase after money delays salvation, and in Africa, if he will only keep two *Shabbatot*, the Messiah would come. Instead he will try to pick up a pound or so and will hurry to his land through Natal.

If my word is not going to weigh hard on the reader and if the printer will not be angry with me because I am increasing the number of words, I will sort through my sack of goods slowly, slowly, so that you will see my fortune. Occasionally it is good to know what is inside the carrier's bag.

I think the sons of Israel need to carry 12 things with him all their days. Without this number 12 he is like a bear without a tail. This number is holy to him from the day he became a nation of 12 tribes. There are 12 months, 12 signs of the Zodiac and 12 *challahs* in the Temple. These are the things in their order:

1. The *Beth Ha-knesset* [the synagogue]
2. The *Beth Ha-midrash* [the house of learning]
3. The *Mikvah* [the ritual bath]
4. *Beth Ha-olam* [the cemetery]
5. *Chevrah Kadisha* [organisation that prepare bodies for burial]
6. *Gemilut Chesed* [charitable organisation]
7. *Chevrah Mishnayot* [*Torah* scholars who study the *Mishnah*]
8. *Shochtim* [kosher slaughterers]
9. *Melamdim* [teachers]
10. *Chazan* [cantor]
11. *Rabbanim* [rabbis]
12. Good for nothings, people who are chasing the wind.

I know you want to know the order and system of every society. New rules like the laws of a New Town [Neustadt?]. In order to find out and follow their ways and deeds I will not spare my toil and I will describe for you everything in its right place.

1. The *Beth Ha-knesset*

We have two synagogues here, one old[60] and one new.[61] Neither of them is decorated with great riches. There is only one advantage to the new one, that is, it is already built on its foundations. The owners of the old synagogue saw and observed that their synagogue was falling apart and with competition with its enemy, the new synagogue, they found a new scheme, a precious stone, to draw the heart of the congregation to come to them. The rabbi[62] who was also the cantor picked for himself a choir of beautiful girls, one after the other, who sang on the High Holy Days and with their pleasant voices gladdened the heart of the people who came to the *Ma'ariv* prayers on *Erev Rosh Hashanah*.[63] With this kind of promotion, they did very well and collected riches, much more than the new synagogue which was stingy and did not spend anything on the necessary things.

The new synagogue saw that the creditors had not been paid for the house that they had built, so they looked for all kinds of stingy schemes, thrift and economy. The first days of *chag ha-Sukkot* they said a blessing of the *etrog* on an *apfelsine* [orange]. The very learned *shammas*, who was like ice to us, bought this fancy fruit in a street that sells cheaply and they could not afford to spend a lot of money to buy a fancy *etrog*. They also found a very ancient *lulav* on the ceiling of the house of the holy and pure rabbi[64] and without spending on anything else, they shook it off. They did not even say the *Shehechiyanu* blessing on the first day and in the *Shema* reading they did not read the readings of *Aser Te'aser* until *Kol ha-Bechol*. They did not want to look like big spenders. They could see their bad situation with open eyes immediately after *Yom Kippur*.

With all their hearts they did not want to say the *Avinu Malkeinu* prayers after *Neilah* because this was also too much and unnecessary. Also to their great disappointment, a *shatz*, a native of Russia, who really knew the laws of the prayers, prayed in their synagogue.[65] He sinned in his soul and with a loud voice said "*Avinu Malkeinu Chatanu Lefanecha*" ("Our G-d, our Father, we have sinned before you"). Indeed they took their revenge on him for doing it in the correct way. They deducted from the reward of his pay and only gave him half the salary; the remainder they held under his hands with the excuse that he did not come on *Shabbat*.

With all this stinginess they stopped dealing with everything that needed to be done. They had not yet paid for the building, so they thought to make a choir of beautiful girls and then they would be saved. The choir was ready and their eyes were looking forward to salvation through the girls, only to their disappointment [they found that] most of the worshippers in the new synagogue had foreign wives. To look for a great salvation to save Israel from its troubles cannot be done from foreign women and from foreign people.

2. The *Beth Ha-midrash*

The *beth ha-midrash* is a fancy building built not long ago[66] when all the *grienes* acted as one and united to come together to pray three times a day and show the people and its leaders — the English people — that there was a special place to say *Kaddish* on the day of *yortzeit* and they would keep it holy and worship every day. The members of the *beth ha-midrash* made sure in advance that a person who did not pay membership fees would not dare to come to say *Kaddish* until he paid 10[?] to the *gabbai*. His rule was an obstacle to many of the Lithuanians because they were left without *Kaddishes* because of the penalty money. Most of them were poor and they could not afford to give penalty money in the days of their poverty. Still they did not complain and were not angry about this rule that took away the rights of the dead, because there was no mercy in the judgement. Also, the poor person who dared to open his mouth about the people in Johannesburg had to give in because he too had *yortzeit* and during the week the synagogue did not have a *minyan*.

In their success they lost the details of their history on their father's side and the date of death and all of their *yichus* and pride of history from their mother's side. A stupid son is protected by his mother.

3. The *Mikvah*

There was a *mikvah* in an honoured house, but few women and one boy came to try to make it work and their husbands did not control it. The talk around Johannesburg was that the women were all walking in the street like *chasidot* with long *payot*[67] and in clothes that exposed them and they were not affected by the purifying *mikvah*. There was a new hope that in the forthcoming days a kosher *mikvah* might be made.

4. *Beth Ha-olam*

We have a cemetery here in a large square but it is for the rich community leaders who make their own rules and regulations. They know the laws and they do not want to take the *grienes* into their company. But my heart tells me that these pretend English cannot always refuse to be in the company of the dead and then the fate of all the dead would be much improved.

5. *Chevrah kadisha*

We have here a *Chevrah kadisha* that is ruling with much strength and this *Chevrah* has more horns than all the other *Chevrah* that are here. It would be nice if they could boast of honest regulations. The members of the *Chevrah* have shown everybody that they know how to appreciate the deeds of the *gabbai*[68] [in order] to increase their honour because they gave him a golden watch as a souvenir and on it was engraved the initials of all the members of the *Chevrah*. He carries this monster on his heart while he is carrying out his work. They spent quite a few pounds on it, but what is the price of gold compared to the honour and glory of the *gabbai*? That is like nothing in their eyes, because when they see the watch on the heart of the *gabbai*, at least they will know what time it is and how much longer they will have to wait until it will fall into their own hands.

They came up with a great rule. Whenever someone gets sick and close to his end, then the *Chevrah* will pay someone else to help with the sick person and support and guard him so that, G-d forbid, he will not take with him any of the Transvaal merchandise on which they have to pay tax. It is an easy thing to find a *griene* to serve as a helper and earn double pay. If someone will, G-d forbid, die, the chosen people will only come then. Everyone will know them and will know that they have been chosen for the holy work because each one will carry a white sash on his shoulders with a red or white rose on his heart to show that he is alive and enjoying the sweetness of a life of luxury. Nobody else is allowed to touch the dead person's goods because any stranger who comes near will die.

The purity, too, is in the pleasure of softness because they moisten the body of the dead so that it will not dry. Because they eat gourmet meals, the worms [too] should not break their teeth on dried flesh. They will wrap the body round properly and put it in a wooden coffin and on it put a cover and iron pegs so that it will not become foul on such a long journey.[69] All kinds of merchandise come by sea from England wrapped in oil cloth and are put into these strengthened coffins with nails. According to my opinion, when it comes time for the resurrection it is going to be very difficult for them to get out. It is very heavy to open a cover fastened with big nails in order to come out of there and maybe they know that a person's strength lies in himself.

6. *Gemilut Chesed*

This *Chevrah* was established according to the laws of England in every detail. For example, Reuven the son of Jacob is temporarily poor and *Hashem* by chance has handed him a good deal on Sunday so that he will be able to earn a few pounds, but the only obstacle to him is the lack of money. He would then go to the *gabbai* and the assigned person in charge to ask for a loan, but G-d forbid he should ask for money on Sunday! Only on Fridays, on the eve of Sabbath, from 1–2 p.m., has he the justification to ask the *gemilut chasadim*. If, G-d forbid, he misses that time, then he must come back on that day and at that hour the following week to ask for his request.

But he cannot just ask the *gemilut chesed*. It must be done in the English language and on a paper printed for this purpose. Also, it is upon the poor person to find three rich people to be guarantors, otherwise he has to pay. This is not such an easy thing because where do you find a rich man who wants to do good to a poor man? If this unhappy man is liked by three people, they would have to wait eagerly for that time in the middle of the day. Then, first of all, the *Chevrah* will take 10 shillings for themselves, because that is the regulation. Inside that regulation there is another: the person whose situation is bad and who asks for *gemilut chesed* has to be one of their members and the 10 shillings is the voucher he has to pay ahead of time. After that the one in charge asks him to bring a voucher every week according to the amount that they decide and they will then give him the rest.

I am not going to deny that before the poor one finds the *gemilut chesed* his road has been blocked by obstacles and the load is too heavy for him to carry. Only it is a thousand times heavier to realise what they have taken from the hands of the lenders and the three guarantors also have to pay against it, so commanders tell their sons after them never again to be guarantors for strangers.

7. *Chevrah Mishnayot*

The *Chevrah mishnayot* also found its way in the Orthodox Synagogue in Africa. Grief and mourning in the *beth ha-midrash* at the planned and regular hour for studying the commandments. Come evening five *grienes* will gather, the darkness of their faces will continue to project the terrible vision on their face in the big house. They are sitting around a table with small candles in their hands, their heads upon their chests, the way the Lithuanians used to sit a long time ago on *Tisha B'av* after *kinnot*. In their hands are small *mishnayot*; they study the chapter together with all their might and with great difficulty until the *parnass* comes to say it is time to say the evening prayers. The *Gemara* people also want to establish their own group. Who knows if they will succeed to learn? Perhaps *Hashem* will forgive them.

The people of the new synagogue saw this and became jealous and they got the idea of starting a *Chevrah mishnayot* also under the leadership of a boy. Only to their disappointment all the *Mishnah* books were printed without vowels. How could they read the name of the *Chevrah* if not one of them can learn? There was a new hope that in the near future that there would be an increase in *Mishnah* books, not in *Mishnah* learners.

Except for these *chevrot* there are also *chevrot* and sub-*chevrot* like the *Chevrah* of the Sabbath Desecrators — the heads of the community, the *Chevrah* of the English *treif*-eaters, the *Chevrah* of those Married to Foreign Women, the *Chevrah* of the Poker Players [most of them] not counting transgressors, the lust masters, the Free Masons, the *Chevrah* of the *ba'al teshuvah*, and in each *Chevrah* there are plenty of *Bnei Israel*, most of them the geniuses of Lithuania and the choice of Zamosk,[70] Polish *Chasidim*, Russian *dayanim*, Prussian rabbis, English reverends, students of Russian high schools — in short nothing is missing there.

8. *Shochtim*

The number of *shochtim* are like the number of synagogues. The new synagogue took to themselves a newly qualified young *shochet* who had just recently come out into the world who has bought and sold on the Holy *Shabbat*. He is not less than any of the chicken *shochtim* to be found in Africa in almost every house because where can you not find a house that does not have there a black *kaffir*[71] who can fulfil the job to kill a chicken and can also fulfil the job of being the *mashgiach* in the kitchen? That is why it is good for them that the boy will feed the meat to the fill and also thin and fat animals and also be appointed as a *mashgiach* for the kosher meat in the butchery, thanks to the old *shochet* who has supported him with his clean hands. The rest of the new community has their situation forced upon them to be stingy and to employ *shochtim* and *chazans* who are naughty boys because they will work for very little salary and they will be satisfied with whatever will be given to them whether it will be a lot or a little, and what can a poor man do in his time of need? According to his ability he will act and suffer.

In the old synagogue they had already taken an old *shochet*, but as our sages have told us "watch out for the old person who has forgotten his study".[72] What is more he had not learned his vocation. The *grienes* of the *beth ha-midrash* employed a Lithuanian *shochet*, a simple man who has followed Lithuanian laws until today. Some women say about him that he never was a *shochet* but it is only their light-headedness speaking from their throats. If he really were never a *shochet* and *bodek*, should they not accept that he does know his craft? Do they believe that Joseph the *tzaddik* could learn the English language in one night? Furthermore he has signed a written contract for three years to slaughter the animals of the non-Jew who sells the kosher meat. If he changes his mind now, he will be on the losing end and will have to pay a penalty. Whatever may be, he took it upon himself to be a *shochet* for that whole period of time. Everyone may say what they will, but the righteous ones will get their just deserts from measure to measure until their sons will become *shochtim* in Johannesburg.

9. *Melamdim*

The teacher had also taken the land of Africa as a milking cow, especially in Johannesburg. One of them came from Lithuania with grand-daughters in Europe who have come to a marriageable age as the law teaches. From the thousands of families that are living here, only eight boys have come to study with him. They can already say complete words with a stammering tongue because he is teaching them with an English accent in his Lithuanian language and that is why they are reciting the words half in Hebrew and half in English. Another teacher came here who also brought with him his set price from Prince Albert. Only this man knows the rules of luxury in its fullest details. He knows that better than he knows how to train and teach the children. That is why they hired him so that he too will toil and tarry.

10. *Chazan*

Chazans have also multiplied here and grow like grass. In the old synagogue there are two. A tailor is the first *chazan* and the second *chazan* too is not a very small ignoramus and not a great musician. With all these many are saying that the time has come to overturn the pot because the last one knows a bit of song while the first one knows nothing.

There are also two in the new synagogue — the first one does not know how to pray and the second one maybe knows nothing. The only difference between the two is that the second one, who is also a *shochet*, looked for tricks and got to be liked by the girls and took one of them to marry and to fulfil the first *mitzvah*.[73] The first one had already filled his stomach to the full. He has hopes that his great day is coming and all the trees of the forest will sing.

The third *beth ha-midrash*, which is called "The Orthodox", wanted to hurt the feelings of the remaining congregation. To annoy them they built the *beth ha-midrash* even though their kind is like an elephant trunk and they are all keeping the laws of Africa and its customs from A to Z. Most of them are *grienes*, sons of Lithuanians who have not yet washed off their greenness. That is why the Lithuanian spirit is written on their faces. They think they are perfect Lithuanians, some from birth.

A Lithuanian man will not turn back from every talent and advantage that is connected in any way to Judaism. Where will you find a Lithuanian man who does not know how to study and how to learn a book and how to sing and how to be a *mohel* and how to be a *shochet* and, when it is needed, also knows how to be a nursemaid and maybe how to be a famous *chasid* whose wife died upon him and a miracle happened to him and he took his son also to be a Lithuanian in every word? We already know that in Lithuania we are short of nothing. We can multiply and increase even without rabbis and cantors and *shochtim*. Wherever they settle down they are only on the side of the opposition because the majority [of Jews] break the laws and have brought in a cantor and a rabbi. That is why the rich can do what they like and in spite of the wish of the heroes, they will strengthen the hands of the receiver to show them that they too are famous people and they will do whatever they want to do.

This opposition also exists in the *beth ha-midrash* and crossed the big sea together with the Lithuanians. That is why we are not surprised that a wagon driver from Lithuania will pray *Shacharit* and the tailor will pray *Mussaf* and the shoemaker will pray on every *Shabbat*. The soldier who found the army work a burden will raise his voice in the *Yom Tov* prayer and they are full with these *chazanim* until it comes out of their noses and they will be fed up with it.

11. *Rabbonim*

The rabbis who are doing the holy work are two, not counting the rabbis who have previously used the crown of the rabbis in Africa. The burden was also upon them to pray aloud once a week.

In the old synagogue there is appointed a famous rabbi[74] from the community of Israel and even though the style of his learning is not sharpness and depth but the opposite, shame and crookedness, and there is no end to his simplicity. He is a simple ignoramus and he is not spoilt to choose [only] from kosher dishes, because he himself likes non-kosher food and is used to desecrate the *Shabbat* in public, like a simple Englishman does from birth. When he first came here he did not let the *shammas* — the cunning fox — stick posters on the walls of the synagogues, saying that all posters must be stuck behind the door on the outside, because in his simplicity he did not know that in the English synagogue a poster like that was not allowed.

If you want to know the time of sunset or candle lighting or to know on which day the *yom tovs* will fall, it is a very simple calculation because they are going to close their businesses according to the laws of the government, and that is when they stop. It is not necessary to know the cycle of the new moon because they do not count those who are born in the old or new moon, so the order of the calendar is unnecessary to them. They only need the simple rabbis and without him they have nothing.

The new synagogue has a rabbi[75] who is praised by the English members because he is capable of talking his people's language, the Jargon, in his old age. There is a hope that a man who can talk like any Lithuanian is made for greatness. With his golden tongue he will take the people's hearts to love him. There is also a very old rabbi who has resigned from his post in Cape Town[76] and became a *ba'al teshuvah* because he returned to his trade [illegible] on Sabbath Day. To his disappointment his mother died and his mourning was heavy upon him so he would come to the *beth ha-midrash* to pray so that the *grienes* would also hear the sweetness of his voice and his English accent coming out of him with great purity.

End of the matter. In Johannesburg there is more hunger than plenty and this time it will stay and not be destroyed forever because they are not going to set their words on the laws of the *Torah*.

12. No goodniks

You can also find no goodniks in every place you turn, not 10, not 20, hundreds are going round doing nothing, counting the pebbles on the road or on the fortified walls. In the first year that the government stopped giving certificates of [illegible] for the court house, all of them were walking all day up to midnight and waiting. Maybe a chance would come that they might get little jobs like saying psalms for the sick. To their disappointment every inhabitant of this praised city chooses to die without a confession or the saying of psalms and only a special one got very rich and grew a double chin and lots of money from psalm singing.

There is a *meshulach* from Jerusalem who came here to collect the impure funds to fill the stomachs of the people in Jerusalem who had sent him here. This man has already changed his holy garment that was made according to the law because his fat stomach could not contain his clothes. He bought with full money, and more, a garment of silk from a Malay cleric — there are plenty of them here — who used to wear it in his mosque. This garment the *meshulach* wore on *Yom Kippur* when he came to the old synagogue to listen to the sound of the girls who sang a new song and only his love for the songs of the psalms which the girls sang impressed him to love and to stick to their songs.

Dear reader, knowledgeable and wise inhabitants of Johannesburg know very well that I have not yet finished explaining everything that went on around there. I am giving my words only to those who were not there and who do not know anything about the Johannesburg community. I am writing this little bit to them so that they will see how my fellow Jews and Jewesses have brought their baggage here. Their old clothes have already lost their freshness and the wise ones have not been successful in taking out the lice and leprosy since they became a nation.

If the reader will find enough pleasure in this article I will give you more in the coming days only with the double condition that if every person goes through it with a critical eye, let me know. It might help some of the individuals and the public. With the merit that we pass onto the public, we shall enjoy the meal in the times of the *Mashiach* and we shall all live to participate in the meal of the Leviathan and Jacob will rejoice and Israel will be glad.

****

I wrote this article a few days before *Purim* because I saw and looked and observed the corrupt ways and customs and my soul was disgusted. When I saw that my hope to put down a strong anchor in Johannesburg and build a house there was lost, I started to plan to go back to the land of my birth in Russia and I decided to write for a memory everything that I went through from the days that I came.

I looked at the new rabbi who came from Kimberley to be a rabbi and cantor in a place where the English had led me astray.[77] This man is praised by the Englishman. His height is average, he is stout, and on his fat neck he has a white collar which the English priests wear in their houses of worship. I also spoke with the man[78] who is lifted up above all others many times. I heard the good sermon that he gave at the dedication of the new synagogue, about a shoemaker, who was boasting in his *Torah* that he had heard it from the rabbi of the shoemakers, but he is a real ignoramus, like all the English *rabbonim* that came to Africa.

When I talk about him, I still remember the introduction that I gave on the night of the dedication of the synagogue. The rabbi from the old synagogue went up and gave a speech in the English language and after him came Rabbi Isaacs, the rabbi of the new synagogue and he also spoke in the English language and after that I went up.[79] When I saw that a large crowd of Russian origin were standing in front of me and that they had not understood the first speaker, I raised my voice and I said that our rabbi said [....] and I spoke not in English or in French but in our language and I connected the dedication with the dedication of King Solomon and I gave a good short speech and when I had finished the introduction I saw that Korach and his followers[80] were separated from their congregation and only the people that had not yet lost their spirit came close to me.

After we came here to South Africa in the young town of Johannesburg that was founded seven years ago, we gathered together every G-d-fearing person and every man whose heart had led him to it, and established a *Chevrah Mishnah* to learn the six books of the *Mishnah*, one chapter every day in the evening and to set regular times for *Torah* learning just like their brothers were doing in Europe and as we had also done wherever we were on our soil. In the year 1891, they started to learn in a small group but now in 1894, when more members had joined, they listened and added orders and rules to the *Mishnah* learners' group. G-d would strengthen their hearts to learn and teach and fulfil.[81]

May we live to see them inherit goodness and blessing till the days of the Messiah to see the Righteous Saviour that will gather us from the four corners of the world to light up our lives.

****

The Customs of the Inhabitants[82]

Now I said I was going to describe to the readers the customs of the inhabitants of Africa. There are different people here whom I saw and I looked into and investigated their ways and customs during the months as well as from knowledgeable and loyal people who saw and examined every family and tribe and put it into their hearts and decided to examine them. The Blacks or *Kaffirs* have many tribes — you cannot number them because every tribe and family was called by the name of the place or the land in which their ancestors lived. Some of them are also called by the name of their king or leader and their leaders come and go and can do whatever their hearts desire. The rulers in this land or country are Zulu, Mosotho, and the name is Zululand or Sotholand in the colony called Kaffraria. The ones who were born in the region of Cape Town have more names as well, like the Hottentots, Malay, Sheshwana, AmaXhosa, Zulu, Matabele, Bushmen, Sotho, Tsonga.[83]

Each tribe had a ruler and a king and their names were worshipped as though they were holy men. In their homelands, many families live on a piece of land surrounded by walls that they build with stones and clay, not of bricks, like a fortified town, and it was called a "kraal". Over there they build houses for each family, and fences for the sheep and goats. Each man had many wives according to his wealth and how much he could afford. The men rest and the women do all the work and shepherd the flock. Most of them go naked like the day they were born and only put a little piece of material or goatskin on their private parts. They have among them a tribe where the men put a piece of carved wood on their heads like the crown covering the *Torah* and this is what they wear when they appear before the women and their king. This tribe was circumcised and they look dark. When the boys of the kraal grow up and reach the specific year for their circumcision, they all gather and go out of the camp and make a temporary hut. In the morning when the sun comes up, a special man from the village comes and cuts off a piece of their foreskin with a piece of glass. After that he smears the house and their faces with a white plaster and they only come back to their houses after seven days. The circumcised boys sit outside the camp as they are impure and little children are sent by their parents to carry their meals to them and place it outside the hut of the circumcised so that they will not be in contact with them. According to knowledgeable people, many of them die there. Only those who heal and regain their strength will be considered as men and able to state their opinions along with the members.

Most of the time the tribes fight between each other, and to beat or kill the son of another tribe is not considered a sin, and when they come to their leader or chief they will boast about it in order to find grace in their eyes. In addition, the hatred between the tribes can be as great as the love between one another within their tribe as if of one soul. Everything he has, he will give to his brothers and he will be called by the name brother. When one returns, they take a sheep from its master to eat and then in the blink of an eye that eater will let his brother eat from his share and then they drink. When drunk they are like wild animals and wild desert creatures and are willing to do crazy things to hundreds and thousands of people.

The mines

All these things will be found in the city of Johannesburg. From a few will come the business life, and the *kaffirs'* work in the mines. These are the caves that are under the soil and they bring the gold out from there. I was in the mines twice with one of my acquaintances to know and to see how they extract the gold and how they do it and I shall write what I saw.

A well of gold of great length and depth is running in the womb of the earth that they call a "gold reef". This is [like] the vein full of the blood of human bodies going down and sending from it little veins like branches from a fresh tree. This gold vein was running in rocks in the depths of the earth that is hard like a stone. It is a big vein almost opposite the sun on the face of the globe. When the prospectors — the learned and knowledgeable in this science — find a piece of earth where there will be a reef, then they let the government or the owner of the company know and they send different machines over there and build structures on that piece of land. The engineers plan to start showing where to dig the tunnels and they call the *kaffirs* to come to work.

Before they start digging into the depths of the earth, sometimes even hundreds of feet according to the depth of the reef, they bore a deep and wide shaft and upon that they build a structure on tall posts and upon them a machine with two wheels turning on axles of iron, one going up and one going down. The wheels turn from the strength of a second engine standing in a big shed not far from that tower. Chains of iron are attached to the machine and on the wheels and the axles. This machine brings up the soil from the depths of the shaft and the stones will be blasted by the blacks with dynamite. Then they bring the stones and the crushed soil to the mill where it will be ground very finely with iron hammers which are going up and down in a steam machine, so that the whole thing will be ground fine. The stones will be ground to dust and sand. They bring the sand to a big trough, on one side of which they put a hose pipe that washes it strongly. There is a chute from the other end that goes down a slope and on it are attached pieces of wood with nails just the way builders construct a ladder to go up a wall. On the wood they spread quicksilver which in its nature gathers gold and attracts it to it. Then they open the end of the trough from the side opposite the flow of water and the water washes away the sand together with the gold down the chute. When the water passes carrying the gold with it and it comes to the mercury, the gold sticks to it and the sand flows on. If there is still any gold left in the remaining sand, they bring the sand to the first trough and do it all over again. When the diggers in the earth find a reef, they will follow it under the ground. That is why they have made wooden poles with thick wooden beams upon them so that the soil will not fall over them. Most of the time they will find water there bubbling from the womb of the earth. That is why there are machines to pump out the water day and night, always with the help of a machine. This is the method of the mines and [how] the gold tunnels work.

These *kaffirs* almost all come to the Transvaal and they work in the mines. Their salary is high but they waste their money, especially the ones who take to drink, and also to bring presents to take to their houses, and they will be left with nothing for all their toil. From them will come the life and the businesses for all the inhabitants of Johannesburg, Kimberley and other towns with mines.

****

What happened to me

I know myself that I am not a very quick scribe or a critic to explain every nation, religion and custom properly, even if I have seen a lot and I have tried to enquire to find out what it was and what I saw. This is my nature — to observe everything with open eyes and for all of this, I said, look in this memory book which I wrote for myself and my sons, may they live to learn the knowledge of geography.[84] That is why I am going to stop writing about what is not concerning me and I will return to write what happened to me.

Man's salvation will come to nothing and cursed will be the one who trusts human strength. The end of the matter was when I saw that I had no reason to settle in Johannesburg, I spoke to Rabbi Isaacs and another English person whether they knew of a good place where I could get money for my return expenses.[85] They promised me that they would give me £50. I saw that Rev. Isaacs was not much better than his pal Harris and the two of them together choose the way of darkness. Harris was angry with me because I did not include him when I gave a *chalitzah* to a desperate woman. Isaacs had a complaint against me because I made a *chupah* for Mrs Lipshitz, my sister-in-law's sister, as she was a member and a worshipper in their synagogue.

That is why after Passover and *Shavuot*, nobody came to me to find out if I had even earned enough money to send £5 each month to my wife. Only then I realised that what would it do for me, to continue sitting in my brother-in-law's house eating the bread of charity, being a wanderer parted from my beloved wife and children? They must be so miserable living in a foreign land without me. I was moving like a shadow and the sadness was tormenting me like rot in my bones. When I saw a man sitting in his house with his wife by his side and his children around him, envy would eat my flesh and I could not console my soul.

That is why I said, "Come what may, I am going to return to my house and home and I shall return even before the High Holy Days even though it is so upsetting that I have to come without anything."

Even though I hid my grief, I asked Lipshitz and Lapin to support me with only £20 for the expenses of the journey because I had slowly managed to collect another £25 during those days. When the people of the *beth ha-midrash* heard that I was ready to go back to Europe they started to tempt me to stay on for the High Holy Days and they promised me £25 so I hesitated whether to travel or to stay. My hope was that Lipshitz and Lapin would give me £25 so that I could be in my house by the High Holy Days.

End of the matter. These people delayed me from day to day until seven days into *Elul*. After that they came and said they had only collected £12 from the community and most of the people said my brother-in-law Globus still asked me to pay him for expenses. While I was still complaining about my bitter fate because I could not return to my house and arrive at my destination, at least not before *Sukkot*, an argument [broke out] between the leader of the *beth ha-midrash* committee and the *parnass* who said he was not going to give £25 for the High Holy Days because he had to pay for the building and wanted to ask people to volunteer to say prayers without payment.

I saw that I fell between two stools, not to stay in Johannesburg and not to travel. I rented for myself a kind of a big room for £10. There I made benches very orderly and organised many. That cost another £8. A book and a *shofar* I borrowed from my acquaintances. I wrote a poster [announcing] that I was making a *minyan* for the High Holy Days. Either that way or this way a big fight broke out with the *beth ha-midrash* until they fired the *parnass* from his position and another one came into his position and he was one of my acquaintances. Then they saw that even if they also gave me £25, I would still not profit because I had already paid the price for the room and the wood. So the people agreed to give me £15 to be for a *shatz* from the first day of *Rosh Hashanah* and one service for *Yom Kippur*. I realised it was better for me to accept £15 in cash than money that has not been born yet, and I promised them to fulfil their wishes.

After the High Holy Days I was left with £35—£12 that Lipshitz and Lapin gave me and £5 from the sale of the books I had brought with me. The money remaining that I still had in my hands totalled £70. I stayed another month in Johannesburg with my brother-in-law and when the sickness spread I looked after him devotedly.[86] Then I left Johannesburg to travel to my house and to my home. I said to myself that the expenses would cost about £30 and I would bring home £40 with me.

Return to Cape Town

Sunday 22 *Cheshvan*[87] I took the travelling document for the iron trucks and I paid its price £6[88] — two days and three nights. I travelled to Cape Town and [reached there] on Wednesday in the morning. I left my luggage and bags for safekeeping in the station and hurried to go to one of my acquaintances so that he would come with me to buy the boat ticket because it leaves on Wednesday evening every week for Europe. 1 November. This man listened to my words and after a few moments he said to me:

"Listen to me, my friend. Why are you in such a hurry to return to Russia? Why do you not stay here? Every week a boat leaves from here. There is plenty of time.

Wait here until I go and see some people who have already enquired about you and want to hold onto you. The day is still young. I am going to meet these people and afterwards we shall go there and see how things fall."

The man told me that a society had been formed in Cape Town called *Agudat Achim*[89] and they had employed a *shochet* and *bodek*. Now the *shochet* and *bodek* had gone and they were forced against their will to take the meat from the English *shochet* and *bodek* to their great disappointment. Furthermore, now that I was here I could be a cantor, a *shochet* and a *bodek* for them. The society would be built and the community established around me.

End of story. Midday the *parnass* of the society came to me. They also brought the butcher who was not Jewish. This man promised to give me £7 a month. They promised me £3 so that would be £10.

I said to myself: "These are the winter days in Europe. Not the time for hiring cantors. Let me try to sit out the winter days in Cape Town and later let us see what the time would tell."

Great and majestic deeds from *Hashem*.
In a desolate desert seeded with salt
Riding in open fields
Brought his people to Africa.[90]

FOOTNOTES

1 Italics denote a foreign language and underlining denotes a biblical or religious expression. Inserts for ease of comprehension are bracketed, as are illegible or unusual words.

2 For mention of 1894, see Yehuda Leib Schrire, Diary, p. 85.

3 21 April 1892.

4 Oshmanya (Ashmyany, Yiddish *Oshmany*, Lithuanian Ašmena, Ašmiany) is now a town in Belarus 25 km (15½ miles) from Vilnius. In 1880 there were 5,050 citizens of whom 2,501 were Jews. The May 1858 census lists 85 Schrires — or variants of the name — as living in Oshmanye. The writer was born there in 1851, and he and his parents are included in the list.

5 Zizmory, near Vilna.

6 Yehuda Leib Schrire never actually mentions his wife, Gela (Gelia) Globus, by name in the accounts contained in this volume. According to the 1864 census for Dieveniškės in the Oshmanya District, she was the daughter of David and Tsipa Globus/Karchmer, who was 10 years old at that time (Paul Cheifitz, 2015, pers. comm.). Although Yehuda Leib lists an H. Globus of Johannesburg in his address book (see Appendix II.3, this volume), South African naturalisation records for 23 August 1907 specify only a "Solomon" Globus from "Devenishki", Russia, aged 57, a speculator living in Aberdeen, Eastern Cape, who arrived in Cape Town on October 1899 and moved to Aberdeen in December 1900 (Paul Cheifitz, 2015, pers.comm.). Family legend has it that he was a six-footer of great physical strength, who injured a workman when he drove his cart into a Johannesburg ditch and was subsequently advised to flee. He moved to Palestine and returned to South Africa some years later (Harry Schrire, Memoir, this volume p.158). An elderly patient confirmed this story to Samuel Schrire's son, Louis, making it likely that Solomon, not "H" Globus was the brother-in-law of Yehuda Leib. If so, this would have made Globus 42 years old in 1892 and Schrire, 41.

7 The name given to Gideon after he tore down the altar of Baal (Judges 6:32).

8 Moshe Mordechai (Max) (1881-1953).

9 Samuel (1889-1949).

10 Annie (1891-1918).

11 Known in Yiddish as "Raseyn", it was part of the Vilna Governorate until 1843 when it fell under the Kovno Governorate. It was one of the first Jewish communities established in Lithuania, and became known as the "Jerusalem of Zamut Rasenaiun".

12 A Russian measurement of length: a *versta* or turn of the plough is 1.0668 km (3,500 ft). We translate it here into its English usage of *verst* (pl. *versts*).

13 They were Yitzchak ben Shmuel (1821–1911) and Batya (Basia) Malka (c. 1828– ?). See Yehuda Leib Schrire, *Tolada*, this volume, footnote 5; and Appendix I, this volume.

14 He actually lists five brothers, making a total of six including himself.

15 Second largest city in Ukraine.

16 Smargon, like Oshmanya, is located north-east of Grodno.

17 This is the first of several mentions of a possible reader, suggesting that this account was intended to be read by others, specifically his two sons as mentioned at the end of the text.

18 The evening of the Sabbath on which they are due to read the weekly portion of the Pentateuch called *Parshat Shalach*.

19 Memel, now Klaipeda, is a town in East Prussia, now part of Lithuania, 53 km (33 miles) from Neustadt Sugind.

20 Insterborg was located in East Prussia near Koeningsberg, now Kaliningrad.

21 Vlissingen, now Flushing, is located in south-western Netherlands on the former island of Walcheren. It is strategically situated between the Scheldt estuary and the North Sea. After 1870, parts of the old town were demolished to build new docks. The breakwater is constructed in such a way that nowhere else in the world do large ships pass so close to the shore.

22 He is describing the breakwater here.

23 Idiomatic expression meaning that they are keeping a close watch. From "God has seven eyes" (Zachariah 4:10).

24 Yiddish.

25 One does not carry on the Sabbath.

26 Breakwater.

27 He is mistaken; it is the North Sea.

28 He calls the doorpost the "*mezuzah*" due to its location, which is where such an object would be placed in a Jewish house.

29 Jews are prohibited from lighting pipes or carrying even an umbrella on the Sabbath, and rules of modesty would prevent them from holding hands in public.

30 "I have put the Lord before me at all times" (Psalms 16:8). Thanks for this reference to Yaniv Nachmias.

31 He apparently always walked with a stick, possibly due to having had polio as a child (see Schrire, Memoir, this volume, p.157).

32 SS *Dunbar Castle* was built in 1883 by Barclay, Curle and Co. of Glasgow, Scotland, for the Union-Castle Line. In 1895, it was sold to Fairfield Ship Building and Engineering Co. and renamed the SS *Olympia* which ran aground on Bligh Reef, Alaska, on 10 December 1910.

33 A fathom is 1.829 m or six feet. The actual measurements of the steamship were a length of 102 m (335 ft), a beam of 12 m (38 ft), and a tonnage of 2,837.

34 A *parasa* (pl. *passoat*) was a unit of measurement equal to 3.84-4.608 km (2⅓ — 2¾ miles).

35 These are Russian measurements — a *versta,* or turn of the plough, is 1.0668 km (3,500ft) and an *arshin* is 71.12 cm (28in).

36 9 July 1892.

37 The settlement was founded in 1478.

38 Presumably the ship's bridge.

39 *Amah* is a cubit = between 48 and 57 cm, suggesting that the ship lay anchored around a mere 15 m from the town. This might be wrong.

40 It is actually 1,086 m (3,563 ft) high.

41 London-born Rev. A. F. Ornstein was the rabbi from 1882-1895. Previously he had been the headmaster of the Birmingham Hebrew National Schools and had trained to be a rabbi at Aria College, Portsmouth (Louis Herrman. *The Cape Town Hebrew Congregation 1841-1941: A Centenary History* [Cape Town: Mercantile-Atlas Co Pty Ltd, 1941], p.55). It is not surprising that the writer would not have approved of an English rabbi, who, in turn, did not like the "foreigners".

42 He is describing the Hex River Pass, built in 1876 to carry the main railway from Cape Town north to the diamond fields of Kimberley. It snaked up 735 m (2,353 ft) from Worcester to the top of the Karoo mountains east of the Hex River Valley, and was constructed with the maximum possible gradient and tightest curves in order to avoid extra work and expense. He is also describing the portals of southern Africa's first railway tunnel, which were of dressed stone masonry. Despite its rapid and cheap construction, the pass served for over 100 years and was the starting point of the country's first railway line to the Rand.

43 In 1886, seven years after the opening of the Hex River Pass, the first tentative export of table grapes was made to Britain using the empty train trucks on their return journey to carry the grapes.

44 This was the First Anglo-Boer War (1880-1881), a rebellion against the British annexation of the Transvaal by the Boers, that re-established their independence under nominal British suzerainty.

45 President Kruger erected a Customs House in Vereeniging to which all wagons had to go for clearance. Inside the wood and iron building, and on both sides running parallel with its length, were platforms between which the wagons passed. An exasperating clearance procedure was adopted, with each wagon compelled to off-load its freight completely for a meticulous examination conducted at the leisure of the officials.

46 8 August 1892.

47 Cape cart (Peter Hall, James Hall Museum of Transport, Johannesburg, pers. comm.).

48 This was Rev. Mark Harris of the first congregation, the Witwatersrand Hebrew Congregation and its President Street Synagogue. He performed circumcisions and funerals without the committee's permission, pocketing the unauthorised fees he charged, and also pocketing some of the donations and subscriptions he collected for the synagogue. The entire committee resigned in protest, forming a new congregation when Harris outmanoeuvred them at a meeting to discuss terminating his employment by bringing in supporters who were not congregation members to vote for his re-employment. Schrire was brought out to work for the new congregation, the Johannesburg Hebrew Congregation. Harris's congregation was renamed the Witwatersrand Old Hebrew Congregation.

49 Probably Emanuel Mendelssohn, founder of both the congregations, and Hyman Morris, president, and ex-president of the old one, himself the son of a cantor.

50 For Schrire's *bêtes noires* see Gustav Saron, *The Jews of South Africa: An Illustrated History to 1953 With an Epilogue to 1975*, Naomi Musiker (ed.) (Johannesburg: Scarecrow Books, in association with the South African Jewish Board Of Deputies, 2001), pp.7–28; Marian Robertson and Mendel Kaplan, "The Chevra kadisha — Jewish Helping Hand and Burial Society: Johannesburg's first organized social welfare work", in Mendel Kaplan and Marian Robertson (eds.), *Founders and Followers: Johannesburg Jewry 1887–1915* (Cape Town: Vlaeberg Publishers, 1991), pp. 92-114; Richard Mendelsohn, "Oom Paul's Publicist: Emanuel Mendelssohn, founder of the first congregation", in Kaplan and Robertson, *Founders and Followers*), pp.72-91. Mendelssohn and the English Jews who had established both synagogues wanted their congregants to be like themselves: modern, anglicised and middle class. The East European Jews were initially horrified, but after a while they also acculturated, and these practices were retained and adopted in all the congregations until the establishment of Orthodox congregations there in recent times.

51 President Paul Kruger opened the Park Synagogue on 15 September 1892.

52 Mendelssohn and his congregation, although nominally Orthodox, had abandoned many of the Orthodox practices, including observance of the Sabbath and dietary laws, although they kept the High Holy Days and the rites of passage.

53 In 1890 the more traditional East European Jews, unhappy with the English practices in the other synagogues, had formed what became the Johannesburg Orthodox Hebrew Congregation, following Lithuanian practices. In 1893 they established their own house of worship in a small converted house in Ferreirastown. It was known as the *Griene beth ha-midrash*.

54 It was a large room with whitewashed walls, an ark and wooden benches, and could seat about 300 people.

55 Schrire, being a strong proponent of the use of Hebrew, uses "Jargon" as a derogatory word for "Yiddish".

56 Slaughtering a chicken for *kaparot* (atonement).

57 The Orthodox synagogue.

58 His son, Harry, said of him: "What a memory! What a temper!" (Schrire, Memoir, this volume, p.168).

59 "Iron bridge" as used here, possibly refers to a popular Jewish folk tale that on the Day of Resurrection all humans will gather on the Mount of Olives opposite the Judgement Seat on Mount Moriah. Two bridges will span the intervening Valley of Jehosephat, one of iron and stone and the other of paper. The heathens will cross the iron bridge which will collapse sending them to their deaths, whereas all the Jews will cross the paper one and enjoy eternal life. See Zev Vilnay, *Legends of Jerusalem* (Philadelphia: The Jewish Publication Society of America, 1973), p. 264. A similar Arab legend is also recorded there (ibid., p. 266).

60 President Street Synagogue of the Witwatersrand Hebrew Congregation.

61 Park Synagogue of the Johannesburg Hebrew Congregation.

62 Rev. Mark Harris.

63 The use of a mixed choir was controversial, but Mrs Mendelssohn, the wife of the founder, was a soprano trained at the Berlin Conservatory of Music, and encouraged this practice.

64 Rev. Harris Isaacs, who arrived early in 1893.

65 He is referring to himself here.

66 This was the most orthodox of the synagogues and attracted the very religious *grienes* (see below) like Schrire. They opened their own synagogue six months after he arrived.

67 Their hair was not covered so that their locks hung exposed like the *payot* of *Chassidic* men, and their clothes were immodest.

68 The treasurer was Max Raphaely.

69 Traditionally, wooden dowels, not iron pegs, are used on coffin lids. Metal is regarded as a contaminant and a weapon and is not used on Jewish coffins, which are lightly sealed and closed with wooden pegs (Rabbi Reuben Suiza, 18 October 2012, pers. comm.).

70 A town in south-east Poland.

71 The now-derogatory term *kaffir* was commonly used to denote a black person at that time.

72 From September 1892 to October 1894 the *shochet* and second minister was Rev. B. Ginzburg.

73 The commandment "to be fruitful and multiply" (Genesis 1 - 28).

74 Rev. Mark Harris.

75 Rev. Harris Isaacs.

76 Rev. Joel Rabinowitz had left Johannesburg before Schrire arrived. He was the Cape Town Hebrew Congregation's rabbi from 1859 to 1882 when he resigned and, although he was nearly 60, enrolled at the South African College to study metallurgy. He qualified as an assayer, went to the goldfields, and was invited by Mendelssohn to conduct the first High Holy Day services for what was to become the first Hebrew Congregation. He also was Kimberley's first temporary minister. He later returned to Cape Town.

77 Rev. Isaacs moved to Kimberley in 1898. Samuel Goldreich, president of the other congregation, said at his farewell function that he was glad that Rev. Isaacs was going and that Rev. Isaacs ought to be glad to get away from a congregation with so much dissension. See Stephen Cohen, "The South African Zionist Federation and the South African Jewish Board of Deputies: Samuel Goldreich and Max Langermann", in Kaplan and Robertson, *Founders and Followers*, p.200.

78 Rev. Philip Wolfers.

79 He might be wrong here because the officiating rabbi was Rev. Wolfers. Rev. Isaacs came the following year (Morris Abrahams, *The Jews of Johannesburg 1886-1901.* [Johannesburg: Scarecrow Books, in association with the Jewish Board of Deputies, 2001]. p.17).

80 Korach rebelled against Moses. His name is synonymous with disharmony and conflict.

81 This paragraph, written after the completion of the diary, has been inserted here from the end of the book.

82 Meyer Dovid Hersch described the circumcision practices of the local indigenous tribes in 1896 in *Hatzefirah*, Warsaw. Schrire's friend, N. D. Hoffmann, was also concerned with this matter, though his report was published only 23 years later, four years after Schrire's death (Nechemiah Dov Hoffmann, *Book of Memoirs: Reminiscences of South African Jewry,* trans. from the Yiddish by Lilian Dubb and Sheila Barkusky [Cape Town: Jewish Publications-South Africa, Isaac and Jessie Kaplan Centre for Jewish Studies and Research, University of Cape Town, 1996], pp. 9–11).

83 The multiplicity of tribal names reflects the accelerated movement of native peoples to the Cape, which began when a European settlement was founded there in 1652 and accelerated after the establishment of the British colony in the nineteenth century.

84 Max and Samuel (footnotes 8, 9). The Diary might have been written before the birth of his youngest son, Harry, in 1895, but the omission here of his daughter, Annie (footnote 10), is probably deliberate and in keeping with the exclusion of women from serious and religious matters.

85 Many immigrants wanted to return to Europe, and the Jewish welfare organisations were inundated with requests for passage money. The London Jewish Board of Guardians and the local organisations granted some money towards the ticket but would expect the immigrants to raise the balance themselves (Gwynne Schrire, "Adapting to a New Land: The Greener in Cape Town 1900", *Jewish Affairs*, 1990, 45:5, pp. 42–46; "Litvaks who Returned to Europe and Why", *Jewish Affairs*, 2008, 61:1, pp. 7–14).

86 A smallpox epidemic raged in Johannesburg from 1893 to 1895, and thousands became ill.

87 1 November 1893.

88 The first train reached Johannesburg on 5 November 1892, after which no more dusty trips needed to be made from Vereeniging.

89 This was the Roeland Street *Shul*, *Agudat Achim* (Association of Brothers), which opened in opposition to the Gardens *Shul*, which was regarded by the East European Jews as the *Englisher Shul*.

90 This poem is written in *gematria* (a system in which letters of the Hebrew alphabet are assigned numerical values) so that the combined value of all the letters add up to the Hebrew year 5653, or the Gregorian year 1893. It is accompanied by numerical calculations with which the author had added up and changed words until he could get a concluding poem that would express the correct total. Thanks to Rabbi Dr Lionel Mirvish for working out the *gematria*.

3. *TOLADA*[1]

History and occurrences, causes and adventures, from birth to my death, with short critique in a clear and explicit language, in song and epigram for eternal memory

Yehuda Leib Schrire
Translated by Devis Iosifzon; edited and annotated by Devis Iosifson, Gwynne Schrire and Carmel Schrire[2]

Editors' Note: *Tolada* (Appendix II.1) is a poem written in a hardback notebook that measures 19 x 14.5 cm (7½ x 5¾ in). It appears to have been handmade, with some unevenly sized pages that were bound with strong stitching between heavy black boards. It has reinforced corners, and the spine is decorated with gold embossed lines. A hand-cut, ogival-bordered label is pasted on the front, inscribed in cursive Hebrew, *Tolada*.

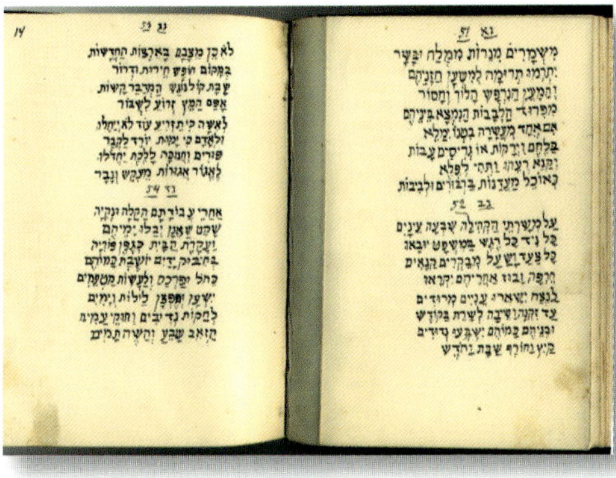

Fig. 20: Pages from the *Tolada*, by Yehuda Leib Schrire, showing his handwritten script. (C. Schrire coll.)

The text itself was handwritten in block Hebrew letters using black ink (Fig. 20). There are marginal annotations generally written in smaller block letters but also, occasionally, in cursive Hebrew. The main text consists of 150 stanzas, 8 lines each, numbered in Arabic numerals and Hebrew from 1-131, and thereafter, except for stanza 147, in Hebrew *gematria*. The text is generally written on both sides of the page and together with the title page totals 74 written pages. Seventeen alternate, left-sided pages are numbered 1-17, but the rest are not. There are several blank pages at the end, one of which contains a line written upside down, reading: "The history of well-known people [will be] inscribed in a record" (Job 19:23).

Tolada was composed by Yehuda Leib Schrire at one or more times around 1910. The neatness and uniformity of the main text, together with the rarity of corrections (as in stanza 105), suggests that this is a fair copy transcribed from earlier texts. The use of several different nibs suggests that it might have been transcribed at different times and likewise the label on the front cover may be a later embellishment.

****

1. The history of famous people
Might be an eternal souvenir for the next generation.
Wealthy heroes would feast and enjoy abundance,
Lost travellers on perfumed mountains,
Kings and ministers, governors and leaders,
Their bravery and wisdom written in stone
By many nations and individuals,
Fiery mountains, terror and wind.

2. The complete history would be beneficial,
Like seeds in the ground.
There would be hope and expectancy over the years
Of being satisfied with its goodness from its offerings in the field.
The history of individuals might also be fruitful
A valuable lesson to those who are talented
And a rod of correction to those who rebel
And competition would make them study and become better educated.

3 All the more so, a long chain of history
Is an inheritance for sons and daughters.
It is the cure and medicine which brings relief
It would make pleasant links with one's love for one's family.
Reading it would bring them an understanding and education
About past mishaps, occurrences, and adventures
An evidence of clear warnings for them to hear, so that they may fear and learn
And choose good and refuse evil.

4. They might also know how to judge honestly
For their parents' journey was not an easy one.
They were not brought up in scarlet[3] nor used to pleasures
And have known only trouble and misfortune.
They worked hard and experienced hardship, poverty, and shortages.
Before they had aged in years
Their teeth had become blunt from eating unripe fruit
And they did not experience fortune in this world

5. Nevertheless their childhood strength was not forgotten.
They maintained their faith with all their might and soul.
They never rested in maintaining their religion.
As long as they lived they encountered goodness
And a magnificent reputation remained after their departure.
They had a long life, with respect and wealth
And this history was a souvenir
Documented forever and ever.

6. I was born[4] in the year 1851[5] in Chaled [?][6] **In the vicinity of Vilna**
To parents known for being honest and educated.
Like many others I was a naughty and wild child
Their first-born[7] and a delightful child to my parents.
Fortune, wealth, fields, and orchards
They never obtained nor did very well[8]
And many times even food
Was lacking day and night.

7. Satisfied[9] and confident
Both of them content
With a belief in G-d's mercy
This was their hope in their whole lives.
Loyal[10] Jews, gentle souls, and generous
Satisfied with little yet with serene[11] spirits
They fostered and raised me for ten years
And nurtured me like a young cedar
This was their hope in their whole lives.

8. I left my home in the town of Oshmanya.
I left my father's house to study in a *yeshiva*, **Zufran-Vilna-Valazin-**
Torah and religious studies from a rabbi,[12] **Valchenik-Alsan-Lida?**
Living on charity in quietness and confidence.
I went back to visit my family only seldom
Those who provided me with all the best as their firstborn
Fed me with what they saved from themselves
For the desire of their eyes, while their own feet were clad in old shoes.

9. Depression and pressure encouraged my talents
To pave a route in the battles of this life
And despite my youth I became a teacher,
A *shochet*, a *bodek*, a cantor[13]
A violinist and a baker, **Kovno-Lodz**
A poet and a cobbler,
Making carvings and drawing[14] pictures,
With many wonderful and magnificent talents.

10. Writing and speaking in seventy[15] languages
Like Bezalel Ben Uri[16] a thinker, **Bialystok-Bialispedok** (?)
Translator, scribe, critic and author
With no sense nor purpose, with weighty mistakes **Siraz-Warsaw**
In the way young people express themselves
As though knowing everything while there was nothing[17]
Their talents would dissolve like foam from the sea
Carried by the wind which scatters it everywhere.

11. At the age of twenty I was a successful man.
Many people thought highly of me,
Pretty girls with dowries and a bride price **Suwalki-Brisk**[18]
Were promised to me in marriage.
At this time I was shaken badly
And several years passed
As I saw my goals becoming idle
I myself dug the grave that ended my youth.

12. I was married in the year 1879.[19] **Devinistock District of Vilnius**
This started the period of the battle of life.
I was happy during the first year,
I had not yet felt the burden of a beheaded heifer.[20]
I decided to live in a little town **Zizmar** [21]
As a cantor, preacher, *shochet*, and *bodek*
I gave away my privileges as a first born for very little in return
To rebuild that which was destroyed and strengthen all the breaches.

13. I brought happiness to the people of Zizmar with my singing.
Like people, like priest[22] they loved me as much as they loved themselves.
I delighted them at *Shabbat* and at festivals
Both young and old sought my attention,[23]
Elders rose up[24] and youngsters hid
I was carried by them in the air like a favourite child.
Then I saw that they became poorer and started to emigrate.[25]
Charitable donations and wealthy people became fewer and fewer.

14. I was envious of the liberation movement[26]
Although I had all I needed and more
I was tired of my ministry
To be like them building and destroying.
I had enough of the life as I had known it and decided hastily
To serve as the lowest of the low.
I rebelled against my accolades and against my burden
I travelled to Warsaw like a nomadic wind.[27]

15. For five years I had found peace
But overnight I was tempted by a spirit to escape.
I was fooled by a letter
Received from my friend and uncle to try my luck. **A. Zuckerman Warsaw**
In a big city so that when the time was right
My fortune might succeed
In becoming rich
And transforming a dry cane into a flourishing almond tree.

16. To my sorrow I had not managed
To settle down in a sure place[28]
And I accepted my uncle's advice [29]
To go to Poland, which was a prosperous vineyard[30]
Where one might find peace, respect, and wealth,
Where one might build one's house like "high society"
The source of influence, success, and happiness,
Where one might live in serenity forever and ever.

17. For a whole year I had been travelling
In towns and countries with groups and choirs
And after wandering and hard physical labour
I was lost in exile and toiled in vain and trouble[31]
The choir singers were rebellious and went hungry.[32]
Their voices were like an open grave to ruin:
They were my enemy like a bone in the throat,
Instead of bringing honour they shamed and disgraced me.

18. I disconnected myself and left, like a bowshot[33]
I escaped from them to a bustling town.
I escaped from one danger and fell into another.
I chose an occupation of expertise:
As a young man I was trained to make sweet delicacies[34]
From sugar as a carved and sculptured work[35]
And my work kept me warm[36]
I found pleasure and entertainment in my work and labour.

19. Two years had passed and gone.
I was content in this new period,
An end to being the taskmaster to voices
I earned a living from hard labour **Brisk**[37] **deLita**[38]
Towards the end of the day before evening
I would rest in the garden in tranquility
I was happy from the bottom of my heart
Walking for my pleasure in the nearby avenues.

20. Two years passed as quickly as the blink of an eye.
My soul and spirit were desperate for a change.
I worked very hard
Cooking and baking from dawn to dusk
And my share was only dry bread.
I wanted to know for how much longer
Would my share in this world be hard work,
My pay a bag with holes.[39]

21. My heart tempted me like a gullible dove.
My dream returned to find a well-established place.[40]
Unfortunately I reverted
To the previous position of being a *shochet* and a cantor.
A new town on the Prussian border **Neustadt Sugind**[41]
Invited me to live there with respect.
It took me two *Shabbats* to conquer the town
While they listened carefully to my prayers.

22. For eight years they tormented me.
I became famous and had a wonderful reputation,
I also had a good reputation worldwide
Paid with money and goodly vine[42]
In South Africa where there were gold mines **Johannesburg**
A magnificent Synagogue had been built.[43]
I received a message from acquaintances
That many people wanted me in their community.

23. Letters, messages were exchanged back and forth
Promises, offers, and the means to travel.
I left to go to them
With excitement and confidence and without fear.
When the money arrived that I had asked for
A large sum in cash
A new period started
To minister to English Jews.

24. Ho! Rough seas carried me on your wings
Because in the storm and turmoil you are like me.
My heart too was troubled[44] and I was taken to the place
From wave to wave and from trouble to trouble.
Indeed this wind was like a man's spirit
With aspirations for alternatives and changes[45]
Until he ceased dying[46]
Desperately seeking adventures.

25. A bad temper since his youth,
No limits to his desires.
Climbs mountains and walks through valleys
His biggest love was seeking wealth.
But success was like a spider's web
In his hands it was still like melting snow
Human strength weakens a son that causes shame[47]
Held in his hand until the sun was hot.[48]

26. I was never obsessed with getting rich
Only to fulfil a missing desire for life.
My wife and my sons were my fortune and my honour.
To provide enough for their needs
I had wandered to a faraway land for their sakes
To provide the best for them and to rescue them from trouble,
Desperately seeking with a torch in every crack and hole[49]
To find a decent income.

27. One of a thousand would be chosen by G-d
For him, on a safe road and with confidence
To reach peace, happiness, and blessings.
I was invited to go there as a guest.
I was also tempted myself and was feeling lust
To pick fruit from the tree of knowledge.
With a handicapped leg[50] and with the foot of pride[51]
I went and travelled to try and to experience.

28. In the year 1892 I arrived in Cape Town[52]
A bustling city in South Africa.
Like in a small city my fellow Jews there were
Walking as if lost in the wilderness of a desert,
Farther and forward to the big city
Of gold metal and good people,
Where the sun shines in the black of darkness
And there are palatial houses and courts fit for kings.

29. The railway had not yet been laid
To Johannesburg, my destination.
On a very slow wagon I made my way,
My wagon was constructed as a double decker.[53]
The heat of the sun was like an oven,
All the crops were dried out for there were no water resources,
Desolate desert and destructive wind,
High hunchbacked mountains[54] reaching to the skies.

30. Black people as black as a raven,
Buttocks uncovered[55] they would dance like kings.
Their teeth were white like evening wolves.[56]
They stared with astonishment,[57] young and old
Stretched their hands in madness and commotion
And they spoke to us in a foreign ridiculous language,[58]
Chased us and asked nothing
The eyes of all wait upon us[59] to give them food.

31. We ascended mountains, we descended into valleys
A whole day long, from morning till evening
Until we came to the tumultuous city[60]
Dirty with mud and wearing stained clothes,
Hungry and thirsty from the torturous journey,
These six weeks felt like years.
Helpless and with trepidation
I fell into the arms of my faithful acquaintances.

32. But there too was no dawn yet,
The sun of success was still in thick darkness[61]
As though in the whiteness of snow[62] like white wool[63]
Some dark spots shade its splendour.
In this "cruising generation" was a rabble mob,
The lust for gold was the only reason for them to gather there,
An endless craving and egotism
They were the leaders of the people[64] wanting the limelight.

33. Those who embraced the bosom of a stranger[65]
Stood before him committing breaches.[66]
Those who forget G-d[67] are violent people[68]
Eaters of abomination, and the mouse,[69] everything that creepeth upon the earth,[70]
Every raven mingling after his kind.[71]
Those who are violating covenants and profanity
With shaven beards[72] from a razor that was hired,[73]
Were the vast majority in the capital city.[74]

34. They despised their own language and would only speak English.
Carpenters and belt makers from the small towns,
Polish and Lithuanian refugees rule in judgement[75]
Ladies and young women that are at ease[76]
Slaves[77] and birthing mothers
With stretched forth necks and wanton eyes[78]
"Eyeing out" the rabbis and cantors[79]
To choose and to select who was a good match and who was pleasant.[80]

35. They found my long beard to be a deficiency,
They viewed my Hebrew language as a defect,
They thought I was too orthodox.
Against an older generation[81] which disregarded aesthetics[82]
The other side[83] started the dispute.
They quarrelled strongly with strife and complaints
Party against party they came close together to judgement[84]
The cry of distress and calamity accompanied[85] many meetings.[86]

36. I stayed there for a year and a half.
I had left my sons and wife in Europe
As I had believed that I would return to them,
I had chosen my country of origin.
I also realised that a man like myself
whose wings were cut[87] was not strong enough
To deal in commerce,
Slavery and hard labour.

37. In this country the demand was only to
Lose the sense of shame and leave disgrace behind.
Restraint was abolished so they could spread the net
To hunt as much as they cared to try.
I said to myself that as a *shochet* and cantor
I was born to make a living,
Happy with gifts and presents
And I should return to the place where I was intended to be.

38. The train service started to go.[88]
Evening and morning carriages were transported
Dragging its way through storms and tempests
With different passengers in <u>humble spirits</u>[89]
Black men and black women <u>gnashing their teeth,</u>[90]
Digging and building with hammers[91] and axes.
Amongst the passengers we were the only two Jews.
A lost father who was returning with a grudge in his heart,

39. His son and daughter-in-law who was a reincarnation of Jezebel[92]
Had invited him to come with prayers and pleadings
And when he arrived he found ideas of bad intention and destruction:
<u>He is in the gourds</u>[93] and his wife is in the baby marrows!
They had turned their backs on Judaism
And chosen to follow other people's laws[94]
And the old man had refused to eat[95] since their food was impure[96]
And he returned to his country like a tree in autumn.

40. For two days we were locked and enclosed
Amongst drunkards — we could smell it in our noses.
With our shoes on our feet and belts on our waist,
Holding in our hand our little packages.
At dawn on the third day
We were glad to arrive in Cape Town,
Hoping and sure that on the following day
I would find peace and quiet in the Mail Ship.

41. Ho! The man whose eye is open[97] feels his way like the blind!
Although every trap and every snare is against him
He passes through without fear or weakness
And he will not be scared in case they come close and touch him
And if talents of gold, precious stones,
Roses and flowers, would be offered to him,
He would refuse calmly and step on them
And his sore feet would wander and move on.

42. With closed eyes like a blind man
I was born into this world with a false hope
Pursuing it without restraint[98] and with many faults,
To many payments for disdained desire,
To many devices[99] for despicable lust.
Do you know in the morning what the day might bring?
You follow something which has no foundation
With desire and passion up to the grave and abyss.

43. As long as his heart beats and he is alive
Man will aim for success in great agitation and noise
Until all his years have perished.[100]
Before getting desperate and losing hope
Scouting his way to the north and the south[101]
Perhaps he will rebuild and may succeed
And would bear and suffer in true spirit
Till the sun came and the darkness of night.

44. For wife and sons he was sold as a slave,
His soul and body were theirs.
As a donkey used for transport or a bull with a heavy load
Descending to valleys and ascending high hills.[102]
And when he becomes old and loses his freshness and his vitality
He becomes a disgrace to his sons and daughters
Who would detest him like a snail that melts away:[103]
Those kind of things were my experience.

45. Respected old women and honest old men
When the curse of G-d was upon them[104]
Asked for food from their dear sons,[105]
Started worshipping Baal[106] and the monster Asherah.[107]
Their eyes stopped seeing the light and there was no one to talk to.
They would starve from hunger, grief, and sighing
Like a poisoned arrow at all times and seasons
Shot at a target in the family's vicinity.

46. I was also guilty of loving my family
My eyes were watching the docks for the ships
The masts of the Mail Ship shone and glowed
Like unfurled wings in the existing winds.
Tomorrow at noon I should be flying away and be at rest [108]
To hug my sweetheart with my right hand.
I would soon find myself a refuge[109] on the wings of the dove[110]
There to my wife and sons, there to my mother and father.

47. I put down my luggage in the railway station
And went to town to see my acquaintances.
I did not have a ticket for the ship with me
I was looking for a reference to get the price.
On my return home I got a cheering welcome:
"You have truly fallen on us from heaven."
A letter had been sent to me the day before announcing
That they were willing to offer me a position. **Cape Town**

48. As *shochet* and cantor in the other congregation, ***Agudat Achim***
A new synagogue in opposition to the English one [111]
Was striking roots like a fruitful vine.
It did very well and was prosperous
And the meat dealer would pay seven-fold
If everyone as one would only buy from him.
They would also pay double
Because they had faith in me.

49. I got frightened when I heard this because Thy ways were perverse before me
And the hopes I had for Africa had not yet been lost.
Other than that, they kneeled,[112]
They promised that even to the half of the kingdom it shall be performed.[113]
A house, meat,[114] double fee,
If I would agree to stay with them[115]
While on the other side of the ocean
My soul was aching for the love of my family.

50. In my imagination I created a vision of life in Lithuania,
The life of cantors and their terrible state.
Their goals and hopes were in my heart
My hair stood on end out of fear and anxiety.
Little towns like fields of graves,
Streets filled with mud and swamps[116]
With shoes torn into pieces,
People moved around as though dead.

51. From yeast, candles, salt, and meat[117]
They would make a donation for the upkeep of their cantors.
And the troubled fountain[118] diminished more and more
The separation of hearts[119] which was amongst them.[120]
If one of them managed to fill his belly
With bread and vegetables or thick groats,[121]
People would become jealous and it would become a wonder
As though one were eating delicacies, swans, or *latkes*.

52. The ones who served the community were under a magnifying glass.
Every movement, every sentiment in a sentence,
Every step would be criticised radically.
Disgrace and scorn would be shouted at them,
They would remain very poor for ever
In their ministry until old age
And their sons also would have had enough of wandering
Summer and winter, on *Shabbat* and during the month.

53. Their situation was completely different in the new countries.
There was freedom, liberty, independence!
The harsh voice of the oppressor has stopped
The spoiler ceaseth[122] from breaking arms.
If a woman has conceived seed[123] they had not hoped for yet,
When a man died and descended into a grave
They would stop going at *Purim* and *Chanukah*
To gather pennies from both the perverse[124] and the pure.[125]

54. After their labour, which was easy and clean,
They would spend their days in peace and tranquility
And the housewives like a fertile grapevine
Would sit like them doing nothing
As on unholy days[126] and decorate and make delicacies
As they wished[127] day and night
To imitate philanthropists and the laws of other people.
The wolf was full [of food][128] and the unblemished kid.[129]

55. These kinds of thoughts and terrible ideas
Filled my heart and my blood was boiling.
There was still time[130] to see and to be seen
My wife and sons would still protect me.
All my life regret[131] has tormented me:
If I left Africa this time
I would never be free of need.
I was being stubborn for no reason.

56. Everyone told me
That there were ships all the year round
And if I found any shortcomings I could
Get back to Russia if that were the right thing to do.
I was convinced by their arguments and I signed a contract
To stay there for three years.
I became known as cantor and as *shochet;*
Although my spirit revived, my soul was sad.

57. Early in the morning I would get up
To slaughter the poultry and purge the meat.
I would arrive early at the abattoir
To make all the preparations
And after fulfilling my duties
I would return to my home happy and content.
Everything was in order
I was satisfied and happy.

58. I had already prepared a house and utensils **Russell Street**
I had also sent money to bring them here,
My wife, my younger and older sons;
For four souls I did moan as a dove.[132]
It had been five months
Since I had last seen my beloved.
People and women gathered
To welcome them and bring them to my home.

59. The week passed with happiness and joy
My wife observed their manners and customs
My little sons[133] were in every nook and corner
Dancing like deer on top of mountains.
And then onto my sun at midday climbed
A little cloud no bigger than a man's palm.
Meanwhile terrible things
Punctured my liver and gave me wormwood to drink.[134]

60. The butcher who employed me **Bayers Etkampf**
Went bankrupt and fled.
My source of support failed
My heart was filled with fear of death.
I arrived in the morning as <u>I was accustomed</u>[135]
To come every day to his business,
But the door was locked; and then I understood
That the merchant has <u>eaten his own meat</u>.[136]

61. Embarrassed and astonished with trepidation
I brought the message to the leaders of the community. **?..tzky and Berman**
Like lightning and thunder from clouds in the sky
The whole party <u>trembled and were in anguish</u>[137]
Looking for solutions at urgent meetings[138]
To keep the trade with the support of the community.
From house to court and from street to outdoors
They gathered for support and to make arrangements.

62. I was told by them that from the next day on
I must come and go at the slaughter house
And fulfil my duty as I had done so far,
But must prepare the meat to be slaughtered for two days in advance.
I realised that I had fallen in a deep ditch
And I could not upset my wife's heart
To tell her that as for the <u>food convenient for</u>[139] us
There was no hope. Ha! Because I was fooled!

63. I had built a house <u>on a sharp rock</u>[140]
That a light wind could overturn.
The flowers in my paradise had become <u>briars and thorns</u>[141]
And the grapes I had planted in the vineyard turned unripe.
Desperately I said to myself that the end had come
<u>From whence cometh my help</u>[142] and <u>my daily bread</u>?[143]
I was a <u>target</u>,[144] like a target for an arrow
Africa would not allow me to <u>swallow my [own] saliva</u>.[145]

64. It was very foolish of me to bring my family
Before I was aware of my unstable situation
I was wandering around like a shadow of a man, my spirit was down
Because my home was destroyed, battered down, crying out.[146]
Despite my spirit I remained a *shochet* and a salesman,
Sitting in the store, waiting for customers
To earn money from the profit of the business
The keystone which was abandoned by the diligent *Torah* scholars.[147]

65. I kept my post for a whole month.
In the same way my wife also stood in the shop.
I was assigned[148] to give the day's takings to the manager[149]
And to weigh every cow and sheep.[150]
And for my hard work
The remaining profit was reserved,[151] which was a blessing for me
Because if there were to be a financial loss
It would be up to them to cover the loss and manage the operation.[152]

66. That is how we followed the secure road.
From the early hours of the morning until late at night.
My wife started working like me
She rose early like a woman of valour.[153]
Three months passed,
Business was better,
The supervision of the official manager was removed
And we were busy with business and stock.

67. I was summoned to be a cantor, for a whole year[154]
I fulfilled my duty in prayer happily.
Business at the shop was doing very well.
Weddings and births were also added.
First thing I told myself
Was that I should establish a *shtiblach*
And into my little house in the lounge
I would invite people from the street to pray.[155]

68. Instead of only during *Shabbat* and Jewish Holy Days
The visitors would gather and make plans.
There was no support or help in the rented hall,[156]
It was closed and locked and they would not open it.
So I made my flock become accustomed to listen
And come day after day, both evenings and mornings.[157]
When I realised the place was not adequate
I rented a hall for prayer at a high cost.

69. At a later time and when the crowd grew
I bought a big house
Where they prayed for a number of years.
Studies were held in a special room and people were becoming more learned.
Until a synagogue[158] was built on the Jews' street
In the style of synagogues of the Old Country
Also a study group was formed to attend lessons[159]
And our life became like that in a European town.

70. To found a school crossed my mind
A *Talmud Torah* school for youth.[160]
I told my friends about my idea
To give me a hand and to clear obstacles.[161]
I dealt with fraud and deviousness:[162] but I prevailed
With work and labour with fathers and sons.
I suffered a lot from deceits[163] and from teasing:
I was like a target for witty sharp arrows.[164]

71. The indolent English, like Ammonites and Moabites,
Made obstacles everywhere
About teaching knowledge and religion to mischievous[165] sons,
And teaching them ways to strengthen their belief.
With voices of lightning, noises and thunder,
They put up a fight and made objections.[166]
They only withdrew backwards from time to time
And could not do harm or anything.

72. G-d has not forgotten me.
I expressed my honest thoughts
And young boys in naughty Africa
Started learning *Talmud, Tefillah*, and *Torah*
I assigned two teachers **Schulman[167] 1, Morrison 2**
Who were paid for teaching
And went collecting with might, [168]
Collecting contributions month after month.

73 I dedicated space in my house for prayer
I would greet everyone when they came and when they left.
In the basement of my house I made a *mikvah*
Because in this way I fulfilled my duty.
A year and a half passed:
We had not yet found the appropriate kosher place
And then we made a kosher and beautiful *mikvah,*[169]
Marble floored and painted *vermilion*.[170]

74. In the meat business work I also picked up
Many friends and loyal customers
And G-d's kindness blessed me.
I bought and sold for a few years
I bought houses, big houses,[171]
And made an income from renting out the houses
Until the terrifying year of difficulties
Greeted me with an outstretched arm.[172]

75. In the year 1901 during the Boer War[173]
Cape Town was full of people like locusts.[174]
Rich and poor, exiles and wanderers,[175]
They took part in all the trades
And property prices doubled
Golden coins were easily obtained
As buyers and merchants and middlemen
Were gathered from all over the country.

76. And since there were so many homeless people crowded together
The disease started to cut the people short.[176]
There were rats from under the earth
And some also came in with ships from across the sea.
Mud and neglect and lack of hygiene
Black and white people were casualties,
Both the faint-hearted[177] and men with vision[178]
Fearing death they walked like shadows.

77. My wife who was working at the meat shop
Watched the bustling town from a distance
And the wagon passing by painted vermilion[179]
With the Plague [Board's] Sanitary Workers like harbingers[180] of death.
And boys running alongside making noises
Following the cart carrying the victims.
She fell and fainted without saying anything,
Her skin full with bruises and wounds.

78. Sorrowfully she lay on her deathbed[181]
For ten days in a critical condition.
And when she was just feeling better and gaining back her strength,
She saw the wagon spread out with a number of the souls.[182]
The pallor of death covered her face
And her disease returned stronger than before.
Her face swelled until one could not see her eyes
She lay disappearing into her bed in despair,[183] like a dead person.

79. It was clear to me that her disease was incurable
And the quack doctors were no good.
Spying on my business, looking for flaws[184]
Careless women made a commotion
And their reproaches fell on me:
I was cruel, I had no mercy!
My young sons also suffered a lot.
Then in my deep sorrow I took an oath

80. To leave Africa without returning,
To go to my beloved homeland
Seeking rest in a good pasture,
Returning the heart of the children to their fathers[185]
Or choosing a good town in Israel[186]
Among clever writers and loyal doctors
Resting from my labours, saved from slavery
After being a total slave for fifty years.[187]

81. I sold my business to strangers
And my household appliances from basement to ceiling.
Only pillows and down duvets and a box with books
I kept as minimal souvenirs.
With money, I said to myself,
I could buy new things anytime.
I accumulated provisions for the journey like an ant,
Without being fussy from bread and wine.

82. As for the big houses which I left behind,
I made arrangements with households:
Neighbours of the houses which I had rented out
Would collect the money and make payments
Towards the mortgage bonds and for the requirements of the town,
And the balance would be sent to us.
With farewell greetings, thanks, and singing,
We said goodbye to our friends and those who came to see us off.

83. Our knees were shaking with fear while passing through the check-up
Because the town doctors were examining every passenger.
Aware of the plague, they had closed the access by sea.
And "tickets as bricks",[188] like the image of an amulet,
Were a good omen and a sign of life.
Only the possessions were held up and we remained naked.
In vain we tried to bribe officials
And to our anguish we also sold those.

84. Pillows and duvets were humped like mountains,
Bed sheets and pillow cases, cotton and towels,
Rolls of fabric, new and old,
Silk clothes and nice bedding,
Shas and *Poskim*[189] and all kinds of books,
Books of *Midrash* and knowledge and wisdom,
I gave away without saying anything
I abandoned desperately, I made a complete end.[190]

85. Once I saw that all the obstacles were removed
And the ship was about to leave,
Belongings were spread all over.
And I could not sit and do nothing.
Without delay I quickly hurried
To sell against my will.
I also left the money with him
So that he could send it over to me in the future.

86. For three days we were happy
Watching waves reaching to the sky.
Our children danced around like sheep,
Up and down, in and out.
Suddenly we were surrounded by shouting,
"A child has fallen!" A scared crowd[191] in chaos,
My daughter[192] screaming bitterly raising her hand
To signal us to come down there.

87. Like deafening thunder and lightning
We were alarmed by what we saw when we arrived there.
Our child[193] was not amongst the crowd,
Only his little hat rolled in blood.[194]
He was taken into the doctor's room!
We heard voices calling us,
"He will live! No damage, nothing happened!" [195]
We saw him falling past our heads. [196]

88. From the sudden panic and from depression
The illness attacked my shocked wife.
Within one night she swelled like dough.
She lay down limp moaning like a dove,
And I dared not call the doctor
In case they said the plague had started.
I worked hard to hide her from their eyes
And my heart was in pain that she was dying.

89. With her words she harpooned my kidneys [197]
Because she believed they would throw her dead body into the sea.
My hair bristled as I listened to her desperate talk.
In misery I was taking care of her trouble and she could not be comforted.[198]
I tipped the ships' staff
So that they would pretend it was the manner of women. [199]
I changed her bed and cleaned the cabin,
Changed her clothes from used to fresh.

90. In sadness, sighing, and impatience
The days passed, as though each day was a year.[200]
A voice was heard:[201] that in two days [202]
We would be in Europe. We would come to London!
She was feeling better and her skin grew back
With white spots,[203] scars and blisters.
We suffered a lot in those ten days,
Imprisoned as in a closed Noah's Ark.

91. In terror and fear we went ashore
Wearing a mask[204] on her face and gloves on her hands.
Then began a new era.
European life was expensive,
The money ran out very fast
We had not yet found a place to settle
All the hotel owners were greedy,
Ripped us off[205] while we were resting and healing.[206]

92. In London the capital was busy with people.
We rested for five days
In tumult,[207] noise, with no absolute silence,
At double prices[208] and with generosity. [209]
We heard about Frankfurt on the River Main
Which was full of righteous and observant people,
And at the hotel where we were staying
Were told wonderful stories that it was placed in heaven. [210]

93. From the railway to the steam carriage
The journey started and we hurried to get off.
In the middle of the night and in heavy rain
We tracked our way in the dark and our feet stumbled
On sackcloth and bundles, baskets and chests
As obstacles at the ship's entrance.
Wild boys and naughty girls,
Cheering and singing in excited voices.

94. The morning shone in the rich country of Holland —
That was where the ship anchored —
And the railway
Was all ready to go.
Inspection of our luggage started,
Royal Customs duties on some of the items,
Voyage tickets, answers, and questions
About the children's ages.

95. We travelled for an entire day.
The carriage carried us as on eagles' wings [211]
Mountains and hills dancing in front of us
Further and further on,[212]
Ruins and castles centuries old
Displayed for eternal memory,
Streams and rivers and seeded fields,
Wheat and barley, cumin and nigella.[213]

96. The spectacle instilled us with vigour
Looking at the Main[214] plain[215] and the Rhine
Fortified towns in the midst of heaven[216]
Opulent houses filled with fortunes.
There were wonders at every footstep,[217]
Crowds of people like locusts swarming,[218]
Vineyards and gardens on mountains and hills
And on the hilltop herds turned red. [219]

97. In jolly Frankfurt, the perfect beauty,
We entered through its gates at sunset.
In a perfect hotel
We chose to live amongst those who came.
For two weeks we were walking on hot coals
Until we found a house to live in. [220]
Furniture and all the household utensils
To be arranged in an exemplary order one could be proud of.

98. We lived like this for two years
Amongst the absolutely righteous[221] and wise men.
A big metropolis[222] under heaven[223]
Was Frankfurt, the eternal miracle.
Sublime charity and organisations of goodness
With extensive caution and strictness [224]
Were divided into two divisions[225]
Because the other side was plotting hastily. [226]

99. Crimes and sins in a high hand,[227]
Covenant breakers and those who scorned the *Torah*.[228]
There also was a house and a farm[229]
And a death courtyard[230] for sinners.[231]
Blessing and curse,[232] death and life[233]
Every man would turn to his goal,
Either a devil for devils, or an angel from heaven,
For charm and beauty, would be his direction.

100. Their charitable allocations were unbelievable
To support the poor generously
In sublime projects which cannot be praised enough
Golden treasures given as charity,
Free hospitals
Free for everybody,
Collecting tithes
For the local poor and for distant emigrants.[234]

101. In 1901 my parents came to stay with me.[235]
It made me happy for five months.
My children[236] met my elderly parents
With respect for the elderly and the frail.
The night we said goodbye
When they returned to their homeland,
We remained standing petrified
And I felt like a nomadic bird away from its nest.

102. My heart was full of sad thoughts:
Would I ever see them alive again?
Where? Where to? Only the Lord knoweth the thoughts.[237]
We would reunite there in heaven.
I was crying a lot,
I was in shock for a whole day.
Ideas and imagination made me restless,
I was walking around like a lunatic for a whole month.

103. Days and months passed
And I found peace in Frankfurt.
My reputation amongst people grew and they would gather in my house
With generous[238] expressions of affection.[239]
My sons went to school,
I became a member of a prominent synagogue.[240]
Kobez al Jad[241] had not forgotten me:
The congregation called me "The African".

104. And suddenly the hand of G-d was sent to me
His burden forced[242] me to suffer.
Suddenly sadness and sighs
Broke my back and hurt me:
My only daughter[243] became dangerously ill
The doctors said there was no cure
And she spread her arms begging
That they save her body and soul from death.

105. Three well known doctors were called
To consult and give wise advice.[244]
They all agreed "Surgery! Surgery!
Quickly to save the poor creature.
If you delay for a day or two
You will kill a pure soul with your own hands."
A known disease rules in life
And can be healed by surgery from the silence to come.[245]

106. We called an ambulance on the phone
And the hospital attendants like angels of horror
Arrived at the house very quickly.
They carried her in her bed, her eyes dark.
My wife also climbed into the ambulance with her
And went off with her to escort her.
I kissed my poor daughter while I was crying
On her cold cheeks — she was almost dead.

107. I shall never forget that night
Tears as water washed like a stream.
I preferred to be poor, to rob, and to kill
Or in bodily torments with a lion,
Or in fire and water, with burning tar
I would suffer these with a calm and peaceful mind
Just to see my only daughter among my children
Remain alive and invigorated.

108. I was a foreigner in a gentile country
Without relatives or rescuers at a time of trouble.
A noisy storm of
Bitter weeping in the dark of night.
My two sons in a bitter eulogy
Noisily in a corner of the house.
<u>My eyes failed</u>[246] to pay attention to it
I wanted to know if the surgery was successful.

109. Early next day before dawn
The sound of my wife knocking on the door,
Her face pale like <u>white wool</u>[247]
She walked across the threshold, walking and tripping:
"Go and see your daughter who twitches."
She was dying. Oh! Despair!
The doctors have found gurgling in the intestine[248]
A putrid infection was coming out.

110. And as the clinic was for a foreign congregation
Which was not for observant Jews,
What if the pure soul died
And they still kept her body?
Maybe we could still succeed
In transferring her body to a Jewish hospital
So if our daughter were to die there
We would be able to see her with our own eyes.

111. When I arrived there the doctor told me
Not to touch her for a day or two
Unless I wanted to speed up her death
By moving and transferring her while she still was alive.
If she were not moved,
There was still hope:
Her post-operative temperature would go down
And gaining her strength back would be useful.

112. Three bitter days passed,
Passed and gone in grief,
In sorrow and in moaning. We were tired of wanderings
With a continuous expectancy for goodness.
With lots of mercy and divine grace
Our daughter's condition improved.
The prayers said by many people had reached high above
There was liveliness in our spirits and our hearts.

113. This illness brought expenses
The doctor's bills were a heavy burden
Seven times more expensive openly and secretly[249]
These sucked and ate our money.
Bitter letters arrived:
The rent on the houses had gone down[250]
The properties needed maintenance for windows and walls
Mould and lime and painting red.[251]

114. Also our eldest son[252] who remained
In Cape Town, urged us strongly
That if we stayed any longer at the place we had chosen,
There would be no hope in the future
To see any prospect of riches from the houses,
Since without us there, there was chaos.
"If you wait for too long where you are staying
You will find your houses as the tents of Kedar." [253]

115. To the sorrow of our soul[254] and to our dissatisfaction,
We left Frankfurt, the city which was the bestower of crowns. [255]
We left our son[256] there at school
To finish his studies at the temple [257]
Where they taught *Torah* and education.
Furniture from the house and an expensive pipe organ
We sent ahead in haste and in panic,
By a direct ship to Hamburg.

116. We left Frankfurt in 1904
On the day of next day of *Shabbat*[258] of the Passover.
With kisses and tears our son, our dearest,
We left in a foreign land to fulfil
And carry on in peace the achievement of his goal
Of finishing his high school,[259]
With the price of money to be educated in the art of teaching
And to fulfil his needs with G-d's help.

117. We spent two days in London
At the house of my acquaintances who knew us.[260]
When we saw his daughter[261] we thought in our hearts
To have her as a wife for our eldest son [262]
Who for two years had been in commercial ties
Together with them in South Africa.[263]
They had heard about him for some time now
That he was an educated man and a man of charity.[264]

118. We crossed the sea[265] and came to Cape Town
At the end of the Boer War. The despondency,
The silence, were like in a small village,
The crowd faded more and more, people hurried and hastened.
With every passing month its citizens felt
The situation deteriorated.
Hundreds of homes had been built in its streets[266]
While the number of people had decreased.

119. We had been idle for two years,
Surviving by renting out our properties.
Although we had watched their condition deteriorating before our eyes
We worked hard to maintain them.[267]
But when the day came to pay
Rates to the city council and interest to the creditors,
As in a nightmare, as in a hallucination or sleep,
We were left stressed and oppressed under taskmasters.[268]

120. Those very wealthy and rich in gold
Had melted, disappeared like snow in the heat.
Great lords,[269] owners of treasures,
Had collapsed and become impoverished from one day to the next.[270]
The bond owners had taken their property
Which they had acquired through hard work.
They had disappeared and their estate had been cancelled:
In grief and sighs they wrung their hands.

121. And the disaster got worse and caused chaos.[271]
Artisans had no work,
Work at the docks became scarce.
The new immigrants fled like refugees from the violence.
Houses and shops, built for splendour,
Stood empty and smitten with destruction.[272]
In old rags and torn clothes[273] and long hair[274]
Old and young[275] wandered in the streets.

122. G-d's grace never ended:
We received a favour from a moneylender,
A loan of money with interest
Which lifted and improved our situation.
Then we saw there was no hope
To cover our needs from the houses we rented out
Because their prices had gone down and it was not possible
To fill our bellies from the tenants.

123. We returned to the meat trade[276]
Like a drowning man holding on a sharp sword.
Maybe it could help all of us to escape the worst:
There was no hope of being saved without it.
We knew that unlike in early days
When we were successful,
There were now many more
Butchers, cooks, and artisans.

124. Our hands were empty
To deal in commerce and property
It was a bad time, ready for calamities
To construct a building on a rocky crag.[277]
The price of everything had gone rock-bottom
Since the money was gone, confidence was gone
Since there were few left to stand in the breach[278]
Plenty of bills for meat accounts piled up.

125. We did not sell the properties when we returned
When we had saved three thousand for ourselves.
Only a false faith had tricked us
That the buyers would add improvements.
And now our money was gone and we were lost
And how could we take care of our shortage?
There was no cure or remedy to fix our disaster
We were facing a terrible situation.

126. Our oldest son had got married
To his wife,[279] an educated girl
It was the girl whom he had not yet seen
Whom we had chosen in London in hope and in expectation
That she would be a woman of virtue,
A seamstress, author, who would look well to the ways of her household,[280]
Her hands busy day and night
May they live long and blossom as an olive!

127. From their trading business with its good reputation and honour
They found their livelihood, a bread of angels.[281]
Mingling in the centre of town[282]
Their pure behaviour would be praised by people.
Only my second son who was tall
Although he was young,
To whom until now we had been like a supportive wall for him,
Was safely in Frankfurt,

128. Where he finished his school in exact sciences
And went to London to attend college.
He did well in his exams and succeeded and went forward
To become a doctor or a rabbi and advocate.
Now in our situation the way was perverse[283]
And we could not afford to achieve that goal.[284]
Aha! How the pain in our hearts had grown
Since there was no help in times of trouble.

129. We worked in vain and spent gold.
To sacrifice his best years in public
We despaired of having high hopes.
Although his future goals had been his parents' goals,
Despite our wishes he begged for bread[285]
Contaminated by a desecration of all sanctity[286]
He would eat bread[287] like anyone else[288]
On holidays, *Shabbat*, *Yom Tov*, and *Rosh Chodesh*.[289]

130. If the country were going to suffer from a havoc from *Shaddai*[290]
There would be no advice and wisdom and there was no remedy
To improve the situation when it was bad.
Who could judge or find fault?[291]
Blessed was He forever, the one who was good towards all
His mercy has not ended and after two days he would revive us.[292]
In the year 1907 hope in G-d
Would bring with its wings cure and life.[293]

131. The order of the wealthy and famous had come to an end
They were expelled from their houses and property with a firm hand
Naked and hungry without clothing or home.
The outcry was everywhere
Yet we praised the Lord and had trust in him.
We were still standing on our feet
Then as now we were alive
He would be good to us and renew our good fortune.

132. From day to day and from week to week,
From month to month and from year to year
It deteriorated drastically and yet it kept going on.[294]
Jolly Cape Town, faithful city.[295]
Hundreds fled wherever they could
To a place where there would be a hope of finding food.[296]
Like war refugees they escaped in a hurry
In pain and depressed,[297] nonstop.

133. Shops and houses were locked[298]
Luxurious houses and palaces
Windows shattered in small pieces
And in desolation[299] discoloured like bereaved widows
On every step, poverty[300] conquers.
There were no buyers, there was no construction,[301] silence prevailed.
No hope, forever and ever
And Cape Town the city remained like a *Sukkah*.[302]

134. A new year according to the Christian calendar
Month of *Tevet* year *Taf Reish Samech Chet*[303] according to Jewish calendar
Time for the joy of the harvest ingathering,[304]
But those who had invested their money have sunk along with our properties.
Time for payment time has come, with interest and compound interest[305]
And in our possessions there was nothing.
Then the sun sank and darkness came
And disasters started coming in with a commotion.

135. The ones who lived in the houses were depressed and poor[306]
If we could only drive them out completely[307]
The corruptions,[308] discolouration, speckled and grizzled[309]
Damages to the houses like a heap of ruins.[310]
There was a broken roof and here it was the windows,
The plaster was removed from the walls of the room.
To fix the ruins, a broken reed,[311]
To repair the contraventions of the houses[312] for door and locks.

136. The tenants stopped paying
The rent which was fixed for the house.
Lacking money they had no shame,
They asked for bread to break their hunger.
And to take them to different levels of court
Would not do any good, just add work and hot air.
We would be burdened with paying the expenses
For a police officer and a clerk, paper and fees.

137. Letters and certificates came one after the other
From urgent creditors, demanding possession,
From tax and customs, insistent and hurried,
Pressuring, demanding, causing distress.
We could view with our eyes wide open,
As if fearfully at the top of the mast,
A ship weakened on all its sides,
Drowning us at sea.

138. We received a series of letters and documents
As a solution at a time of trouble.
Experienced people with influence
Ordered us with warnings of punishment,
Without making us pay anything of ours
To the bond holders who are suing for possession,
That claiming "we don't have" would protect us
Until the cry went throughout.[313] Then the problem would cease.[314]

139. Household utensils from top to bottom
We cleared out, kindled,[315] as a man takes away dung.[316]
Old, worn, and patched shoes[317] and broken tablets.[318]
We left them to find plunder
Before the official came to inspect the house.
Everything in its place went in deadly silence,
Like after a fire from an orchard to a single olive,
Like a lodge in a garden,[319] like Sodom overthrown.[320]

140. Three months have passed and gone
The court case about the houses has not yet ended.
Deeds and certificates have piled up
And our unstable ship passed through the passage.[321]
The walls and the houses were left to the creditors
And we were left without assets
And on the pyre were cedars and cypresses
And all our hard work with them.

141. For thirteen years we had worked and laboured
To accomplish something in the battle of life
And in a twitch of an eye we had lost it all.
Like a flood washed away by the chimneys of the sky
The universe was erased with no memory of the forefathers.
Like a night's dream it has passed and like a disappearing shadow
Three thousand gold sovereigns in cash
Burned, melted, from the high heat.

142. A whole year had passed
Then as now we were still alive.
Although our spirit was broken
We would not despair and in G-d we trusted.
He would also not abandon us in the future,
He would open his hand and feed us to saturation
And on Him we would rely and project our hopes
Since He was our father from the womb.

143. I was fifty-eight years old in the year 1909
And my gentle wife was fifty-four.
Our days and years were bad and few.
We were not born to wealth, but for labour and hardship,
We were not accustomed to indulgent pleasures
To follow great things[322] or carnal lust.
We did not aspire to soar to the skies
And fill our desire with expensive things.

144. While the sun was clear in the sky
And the success illuminated our windows,
We acted decently to be law-abiding
In an orderly fashion, in the lifestyle of our home.
Our hearts <u>were not raised</u>[323] to go in arrogant ways
To compete with the rich who had lots of treasures
With silk clothes, <u>fine cotton and blue</u>,[324]
Horses for a carriage and electricity[325] <u>for lights</u>.[326]

145. That was why when the sun sets
And evening shadows cover the skies
Now, like before today, like last night,
We are content to be amongst the living
With food to eat and clothes to wear.
G-d would also give us in the future
And if it were tight now, we would <u>wait till it was later</u>,[327]
Since the sun would bring a cure to the wretched.

146. Expectancy from the government also failed
Already today it would have cheered up our spirit
Since it was <u>too early</u>[328] and from curses to blessings
Time would bring to our wretched brothers.
Although the regime's new laws
From the Union of South Africa[329]
Declare <u>the beginning of the end to</u>[330] the <u>grievous visions</u>[331]
That blind the eyes like <u>salt from Sodom</u>.[332]

147. To uproot the government from Cape Town
And to relocate it in Pretoria on a <u>fruitful hill</u>[333] **1909**
Leaving only the Parliament as a memory.
Instead of wheat, barley, nigella,[334] and cumin,
Ministers, judges, and their loyal workers
Moved their homes to live there
And erected houses, became dens of vipers
And the <u>tumultuous city</u>[335] became a <u>land utterly desolated</u>.[336]

148. And yet her nobles[337] would boast[338]
Since the Union brought blessings
Trade and real estate flourished in its cities and towns.
The port also brought employment
For hundreds of the wretched who were suffering from hunger
A vivid spirit returned as it used to be in the past,
Sparks of success were flying like clouds
And people had money.

149. If the will of G-d would be upon us as well
To make our way successfully and make rules,[339]
Then towards this purpose we aim:
To make *aliyah*[340] and be shown[341] the best of lands.[342]
It is the land of our ancestors' lovely land.[343]
To live there in tranquil peace,
To return to the nest like a wandering bird
From the Valley of Hinnom[344] and from the desert of Mattana.[345]

150. Since in all the time we spent
In South Africa which we had chosen
This was the only aim we had in mind
And these were the things we discussed:
We wish we could be in the land of our forefathers,
In the Holy City which was reunited.
To the despair of our minds we have not succeeded
And to this day it remains the only objective.

FOOTNOTES

1 According to the comprehensive five-volume Hebrew–Hebrew dictionary (Abraham Evan-Shushan) which Devis Iosifzon used extensively in this translation, the word *Tolada* might denote all or some of the following: result, consequence, corollary, outcome, effect, illation, sequel. It is also an old-fashioned style/word for "history". We use it as such here.

2 This is a literal translation that follows the original text as closely as possible. The original contains almost no punctuation other than an occasional exclamation mark, and consequently we have inserted punctuation for ease of reading. Other protocols used here include italics for foreign language, underlining for biblical, religious words and phrases, and bold type to denote an insert in the original.

3 Proverbs 31:2. A woman not scared of the snow because her children were clothed in scarlet. G. R. Driver, *Canaanite Myths and Legends, Old Testament Studies*, vol. 3 (Edinburgh: T&T Clark, 1956); and Mark S. Smith, *The Ugaritic Baal Cycle: Introduction with Text, Translation and Commentary of KTU 1.1–1.2* (Leiden: E. J. Brill, 1994), p. 443, explain that in Ugaritic the word, translated as "scarlet" is a special form of the number 2, meaning that the children are covered in double layers of clothing.

4 Came into this world (lit.).

5 His birthdate of 1851 is derived from the Lithuanian census of 14 May 1858 where he is listed as being seven years old. His death notice also notes that his parents were Isaac Schrire and Bertha Kimolevski (Western Cape Archives and Records Service, MOOC 6/9/701 2880). See also Nechemiah Dov Hoffmann, *Book of Memoirs: Reminiscences of South African Jewry*, trans. from the Yiddish by Lilian Dubb and Sheila Barkusky (Cape Town: Jewish Publications-South Africa, Isaac and Jessie Kaplan Centre for Jewish Studies and Research, University of Cape Town, 1996), p. 39; Carmel Schrire, *Digging through Darkness: Chronicles of an Archaeologist* (Charlottesville and London: University Press of Virginia 1995), pp. 12–20.

6 Ushmina/Oshmanya county of Vilnius, now Belarus. Before the World Wars, it was located in the Vilna Guberniya (Gail Flesch, 2011, pers. comm.).

7 Fruit of the womb.

8 Financially, materially speaking.

9 With what they had.

10 Faithful, perhaps practising.

11 Complacent (lit.).

12 Reb Mayles's *Kloyz* in Vilna was supervised by Rabbi Yitzchak (Hoffmann, *Book of Memoirs*, p. 39).

13 He studied as cantor under Reb Pesach Karliner and also under the Warsaw cantor Gritzhendler (Hoffmann, *Book of Memoirs*, p. 39).

14 See Appendix III, this volume.

15 An undoubted exaggeration to denote many.

16 The architect and decorator of the Tabernacle.

17 Ecclesiastes 9:5-6, meaning that though young people think they know everything, actually, they don't.

18 Yiddish. Refers to Brest Belarus today, origin of the influential Soloveitchik family of rabbis.

19 He was married on 14 October 1879, out of community of property, to Gertrude (Gela) Globus, daughter of David Globus (c. 1855 - 30 March 1934) (Western Cape Archives and Records Service, MOOC 6/9/701 2880; Gail Flesch, 2011, pers. comm.). For clarification of Schrire's marginal notation that reads "Devinistock", see Yehuda Leib Schrire, Diary, this volume, footnote 6.

20 Deuteronomy 21:1 - 9.

21 Žiežmariai, Lithuania.

22 Hosea 4:9-11.

23 In the original, the line begins with a citation from Deuteronomy 1:17 "... low and high alike ..." to denote all sections of society, rich and poor. It is usually used in reference to the meting out of justice, but here the rest of the line refers to seeking his company, or being close to him socially.

24 In respect and astonishment.

25 After the assassination of Tsar Alexander II in 1881, there was a wave of pogroms in Russia and discriminatory laws made it increasingly difficult for Jews to make a living. Allowed to leave, two million Jews left Russia between 1881 and 1914. Shmuel Ettinger, "Emigration during the Nineteenth Century", in Hayim Ben Sasson, *A History of the Jewish People* (Dvir, 1985). See www.myjewishlearning.com/history/ modern-History?1700-1914/Emigration, accessed 15 November 2011.

26 He uses the word "*herut*" here, which means "freedom". It was a period of interest in Jewish nationalism, part of which was the interest in developing Hebrew as a living language. Schrire, like his Uncle Zuckerman, was part of the *Maskilim* or enlightened people of the Emancipation movement (see footnote 29). *Kobez al Jad*, the journal to which he contributed, was the journal of the Hebrew publishing house *M'kize Nirdamim* founded in Lyck, East Prussia in 1862, and was a vital tool of the Jewish Enlightenment movement that specialised in scientific reprints of ancient Hebrew manuscripts. It was also active in Berlin and Frankfurt and still exists today under the auspices of the Hebrew University (see stanza 103, footnote 241).

27 Dry, warm, east wind.

28 A firm place (Isaiah 22:23); reliable and well-established.

29 His uncle, Reb Avraham Zuckerman, was a scholar of the Enlightenment movement and an author of Hebrew books (Hoffmann, *Book of Memoirs*, p. 39). He was also a publisher, listed according to a stamp on the title page of Schrire's novel, *Shoshanah Novelet* as a bookseller at Warsaw, Nelerki 15 (Yehuda Leib Schrire, *Shoshanah Novelet* [Warsaw: Warsaw Typography Alexander Ginz, 1879]; See Appendix II. 6, this volume).

30 A corner patch, difficult to cultivate but once taken well care of, can be very fruitful. Jerusalem *Talmud* on Isaiah 27.

31 Isaiah 65:23.

32 Proverbs 17:25.

33 Genesis 21:16.

34 Confectioner.

35 Chronicles 2, 3:10. His youngest son said he could make sweets and once built a sugar replica of the Neustadt *shul* where he was *chazan*, as a gift for the visiting provincial governor (see Harry Schrire, Memoir, this volume, p.158).

36 Provided my needs like Abishag the Shunammite who kept King David warm in his old age (1 Kings 1:3).

37 See footnote 18.

38 Lithuania.

39 Haggai 1:6. Very little money.

40 Isaiah 22:23.

41 Neustadt (now Žemaičių Naumiestis), was the birthplace of Samuel Marks, a South African industrialist and financier (Leibl Feldman, *The Jews of Johannesburg (Until Union – 31 May 1910)*, trans. from the Yiddish by Veronica Belling [South Africa: Jewish Publications, Isaac and Jessie Kaplan Centre for Jewish Studies and Research, University of Cape Town, 2007], pp. 101–02; Hoffmann, *Book of Memoirs*, p. 39; Richard Mendelsohn, *Sammy Marks: The Uncrowned King of the Transvaal* [Athens: Ohio University Press, 1991], p. 1).

42 Ezekiel 17:8.

43 This was the Park Synagogue opened by Paul Kruger in September 1892. Designed in the Italian Renaissance style to seat 800, it featured ornate entrances and pillars as well as a dome painted in blue and gold, with gold stars and multi-coloured moulded wreaths (Richard Mendelsohn, "Oom Paul's Publicist: Emanuel Mendelssohn, founder of the first congregation", in Mendel Kaplan and Marian Robertson [eds.], *Founders and Followers. Johannesburg Jewry 1887–1915* [Cape Town: Vlaeberg Publishers, 1991] p. 81). Meyer Dovid Hersch said that " ... the new congregation has built itself a veritable palace" ("Our Jewish Brethren in South Africa", in Joshua I. Levy (ed.), *The Writings of Meyer Dovid Hersch (1858–1933): Rand Pioneer and Historian of Jewish Life in Early Johannesburg* [Johannesburg: Ammatt Press, 2005], p. 90).

44 Isaiah 57:20. "Troubled sea".

45 *Ha lifot u'tmuro* ("alternatives and changes") is the title of a book by Abraham Shalom Friedberg (*"Har Shalom"*) (1838-1902). It is also used in *Nietzsche and Zion* by Jacob Golomb (Ithaca, NY: Cornell University Press, 2004), p. 236, mentioning *"Havu li halifot u'tmurot mamash"* ("bring me real alternatives and changes").

46 "Until he ceased dying and descended into the grave" is the exact form used in a book by Rabbi Eliezer Shmuel Ranin from Neustadt, printed in Kovno in 1910; it is also found in a book by Rabbi Chaim Yehuda (Lipot) Schlesinger from the Serbian village of Padej, p. 46, and in the book *Horev*, by Rabbi Shimon son of Rabbi Raphael Hirsh, p. 11.

47 Proverbs 10:5: "a son that causes shame" falls asleep during harvest unlike the wise son who prepares for a rainy day during summer. Yehuda Leib blames himself here for being weak like the son that causes shame.

48 Nehemiah 7:3: "Until the sun is hot".

49 Searching/checking in holes and cracks by using a torch. On the night preceding Passover, the 14th of Nissan, a formal search of the house for unsanctified food, known as *bedikat chametz*, is conducted by candlelight because a torch will not penetrate every crack and hole.

50 He limped and he walked with a stick, possibly due to a childhood bout with polio (see Schrire, Memoir, this volume, p.157).

51 Psalms 36:11.

52 The Hebrew year given here covers 22 September 1892–10 September 1893. His date of arrival in 1892 accords with his naturalisation certificate of February 1898 that states that he had been in the colony for six years. Hoffmann, *Book of Memoirs*, p. 39, claims incorrectly that he arrived in South Africa in 1891.

53 Genesis 6:16. Refers to the construction of Noah's Ark.

54 Psalms 68:16. Jagged mountains, high mountains, reaching to the sky.

55 Isaiah 20:4.

56 Zephaniah 3:3.

57 Ezekiel 4:16.

58 Isaiah 28:11: "Stammering lips and another tongue".

59 Psalms 145:15: "The eyes of all wait upon thee".

60 Isaiah 22:2.

61 Job 38:9.

62 The term "snowy white" is used as a metaphor — a similar use is found in Mendele Mokher Seforim (Shalom Ya'akov Abramowitz).

63 Ezekiel 27:18.

64 Deuteronomy 33:5. Leaders.

65 Proverbs 5:20.

66 Psalms 106:23.

67 Psalms 50:2.3.

68 Bullies.

69 Isaiah 66:17.

70 Genesis 1:24.

71 Leviticus 11:15. Different animals associate with their own kind.

72 Non-believers.

73 Isaiah 7:20. Hired mercenaries or soldiers used by God, in this case, a barber. Religious Jews do not shave and those who do are not permitted to use a razor (*Talmud Makkot* 20a). In modern times certain kinds of electric shavers as opposed to razors are permitted.

74 Isaiah 23:8.

75 Isaiah 32:1. Honesty, following good conduct.

76 Isaiah 32:9. Careless daughters, surrounded by the comforts of affluence.

77 Female slave, in biblical usage.

78 Isaiah 3:16. Deceiving with the eyes, as an indication of pride and haughtiness.

79 Women eyeing them for potential match-making.

80 Psalms 133:1. For a good life.

81 Old fashioned.

82 From the early 1890s the earlier Anglo-German pioneers were increasingly joined by arrivals like Schrire, who came from the more traditional Jewish communities in Eastern Europe. This created tensions within the Jewish community (Mendelsohn, "Oom Paul's Publicist", in Kaplan and Robertson, *Founders and Followers*, p. 77).

83 Other party.

84 Isaiah 41:1. To solve the dispute.

85 Isaiah 15:8.

86 Richard Mendelsohn describes the dissension that took place in the synagogues (Mendelsohn, "Oom Paul's Publicist", in Kaplan and Robertson, *Founders and Followers*, pp. 76–79).

87 Possibly a reference to his lame leg.

88 When he arrived (stanza 29) there was no railway, yet now he states that the railway "has started to go." By this he actually means that construction of the rail link has begun, noting as he does that black men and women were engaged in the heavy labour. The first train reached Johannesburg on 15 September 1892. G. A. Leyds, *A History of Johannesburg: The Early Years* (Johannesburg: Nasionale Boekhandel, 1964), p. 62.

89 Proverbs 16:19.

90 Lamenlations, 2:16.

91 Chisel point rock hammer.

92 A seducer, like the biblical Isabel (Jezebel).

93 A family of plants, *Cucurbitaceae*, that includes gourds and zucchini. Aramaic expression from the *BT Megilah* (scroll 12), If the man is after lust, then his wife is also a harlot, to imply that the man and his wife are alike (http://benyehuda.org/tavyov/meshalim.html, accessed 9 December 2011).

94 Usually refers to assimilation and leading a non-orthodox life.

95 He refused to eat non-kosher meat. It echoes a 19th-century story by Abraham Shalom Fried, called *Lock of Hair*, about old Rabbi Elazar Ben Harsam who refused the orders of Philippus the Greek (aka Philip II of Macedon, 382–336 BCE) to eat non-kosher (*treif*) meat in public.

96 Non-kosher.

97 Numbers 24:3: "… the man whose eye is true", whose eye is open, meaning uncertain.

98 Isaiah 14:6.

99 Ecclesiastes 7:29.

100 Job 6:18.

101 *Yemen* (Heb.) usually refers to south as direction.

102 Psalms 68:15.

103 Psalms 58:8: "like a snail that melts away" [as it moves] …" refers in some interpretations to an unfaithful married woman who becomes pregnant and walks in a certain way to disguise her sin.

104 Misfortune.

105 Support from their children.

106 Canaanite god.

107 Ugarit goddess.

108 Psalms 55:6.

109 Psalms 55:9.

110 Wings of the dove are mentioned for the first time in the Babylonian *Talmud* in the story of "Winged Elisha" who fooled a Roman soldier who caught Elisha with forbidden *tefillin*. When asked what they were, Elisha replied "wings of dove" (Babylonian *Talmud*, Tractate Shabbat).

111 This was the Roeland Street *Shul*, *Agudat Achim* (Association of Brothers) which opened in opposition to the Gardens *Shul*, that was regarded by the East European Jews as the *Englisher Shul*.

112 Begged.

113 Esther 5:6.

114 Salary.

115 To take the job.

116 Bog, mire.

117 The religious institutions in poorer communities were supported by being granted monopolies for staples like salt, yeast, candles and wine that were often held by the wife of the rabbi or cantor.

118 Proverbs 25:26. A muddy spring of water.

119 Jewish expression, referring to arguments and disputes which cause rivalry.

120 Rivalry between members of different congregations.

121 The hulled grains of various cereals that can be the basis of *kasha*, a porridge-like staple meal of Eastern Europe and Eurasia.

122 Isaiah 16:4. The one who ruins and destroys.

123 Leviticus 12:2. Refers to an unplanned or unwanted pregnancy, premature, consequence of a forbidden or sinful act or lifestyle.

124 Micah 3:9. Anyone who distorts or is dishonest.

125 2 Samuel 22:27.

126 Weekdays.

127 Only found in 19th-century writing in Hebrew.

128 Part of an expression for someone who does a good deed without any cost to himself.

129 Exodus 12:5.

130 Habakkuk 2:3: "For the vision is yet for an appointed time ...."

131 Hosea 13:14.

132 Isaiah 38:14.

133 Moshe Mordechai (Max) (1881-1953) and Samuel (1889-1949).

134 Bitter plant, *Artemisia absinthium*, used for making absinthe.

135 Numbers 22:30.

136 Ecclesiastes 4:5: "... and *eateth* his own flesh".

137 Deuteronomy 2:25.

138 Language used mainly in the ultra-orthodox society on their Yiddish announcements (*pashkvilim)* that were posted on a public place in Orthodox Jewish communities. *Pashkvilim* were sometimes distributed anonymously but often carried rabbinic or activist group endorsements (Wikipedia). The poem describes an urgent meeting called for people to discuss important and urgent issues that literally reads "necessary/required meetings".

139 Proverbs 30:8. Daily amount of food necessary for one's existence. An expression still used today.

140 1 Samuel 14. A rocky crag.

141 Isaiah 5:6. A combination used by the prophet Isaiah to symbolise the destruction of the Temple.

142 Psalms 121:1.

143 Proverbs 30:8.

144 Job 7:20. As a target to be attacked.

145 Job 7:20: "Will you not look away from me for a while, Let me be, till I swallow my spittle?" He felt that he was not given enough time even to gulp.

146 Job 30:24.

147 Psalms 118:22.

148 A form found in R36 *Baba Metzia*, which is the second of the first three Talmudic tractates in the order of *Nezikin* ("Damages").

149 2 Kings 25:19.

150 Leviticus 7:23 mentions this combination.

151 Genesis 27:36.

152 It was the manager's responsibility to cover the loss and deal with the business.

153 Proverbs 31:10.

154 To read from the *Torah* on Saturdays.

155 A room in a private home would often be used for communal Jewish prayers and community gatherings.

156 Around 1896, before the Roeland Street Synagogue, *Agudat Achim* (Association of Brothers) was built (footnote 111). The congregation used a hired hall for Sabbath services which served a small *minyan* (Hoffmann, *Book of Memoirs*, p. 24).

157 Jews congregate in a *minyan* to pray every morning and evening.

158 Roeland Street Synagogue. Around 1900, sterling floated free, and the Second Boer War (1899-1902) stimulated the local economy. Businesses flourished and £10,000 was raised by donations (Hoffmann, *Book of Memoirs*, p.24).

159 Hoffmann, writing in 1916 about a group that met around 1904, specifically lists Reb Y. L. Schrire as a member as follows: "A group of old-time students of the *Talmud*, worthy citizens, meet every evening in the Roeland Street *Shul* to study a *blat Gemara*. About twelve years ago the group met once a week; later they met twice a week. This group has grown to fifty members ..." (*Book of Memoirs*, p.29).

160 Ibid., p.27.

161 Isaiah 45:20: "... crooked places straight ..."

162 Proverbs 8:8.

163 Isaiah 30:10.

164 Isaiah 5:28.

165 Also refers to the first six *parshiyot* (portions) of the *Torah*. The Hebrew word here is *Shovatim*. In addition, this is mentioned in the Babylonian *Talmud* regarding the "*ba'al teshuvah*".

166 Although money was donated specifically to build a *Talmud Torah*, only a "small rather dingy house" was added at the back of the *shul* for this purpose. "The many protests by those donors against this folly of the committee were of no avail" (Hoffmann, *Book of Memoirs*, p.24).

167 Yehuda Leib Schrire (mistakenly listed as M. L. Schrire) is acknowledged as a founder of the first *Talmud Torah* in Cape Town in 1899. See Gustav Saron, *The Jews of South Africa: An Illustrated History to 1953 With an Epilogue to 1975*, Naomi Musiker (ed.) (Johannesburg: Scarecrow Books, in association with the South African Jewish Board of Deputies, 2001), p.72.

168 Exodus 14:8.

169 Hoffmann said there were five ritual baths or *mikva'ot* in Cape Town in 1916, (*Book of Memoirs*, p. 23).

170 Mentioned in Jeremiah 22:14 as *sarsaru*, biblical word for "red" from Akkadian.

171 He and his wife Gela bought the following houses: nos 37, 39, 41 and 41B Constitution Street; nos 96, 98, 100 Harrington Street; nos 78 and 80 Commercial Street and nos 1 and 3 Bryant Street (Western Cape Archives and Records Service, mortgage bonds DOC 4/1/460 556; DOC 4/1/524 1536; DO 4/1/620 4932; DOC 4/1/708 1149; DOC 4/1/708 1150; DOC 4/1/1011 508; Insolvent Liquidation and Distribution Account MOIB 2/3186 337; MOIB 2/3251 991; MOIB 2/225 4 96; MOIB 2/3376 355; MOIB 2/3501 434.) The 1899 *Juta's Cape Town and Suburban Directory* lists Scheire L [sic] as a butcher at 38 Harrington Street with Scheira [sic] Mrs having a boarding house in Leicester House, 56 Boom Street. In 1904, on their return from Europe, the *1904 Juta's Cape Town and Suburban Directory* lists Louis Schira [sic] living at 62 Harrington Street. He died in his residence at 80 Commercial Street. Most of these properties fall within the Sixth Municipal District of Cape Town, or District Six, defined in 1867 as shown on the 1909 map in Vivian Bickford-Smith, *Ethnic Pride and Racial Prejudice in Victorian Cape Town* (Johannesburg: Wits University Press, 1995), pp. xxii–xxiii. Bryant Street lies on the other side of the city in the area known as "Bo Kaap". The ethnically diverse community who lived here were brutally evicted under the apartheid regime in the 1960s (Bickford-Smith, pp. 176, 214); Ciraj Rassool and Sandra Proselendis (eds.), *Recalling Community in Cape Town: Creating and Curating the District Six Museum* (Cape Town: District Six Museum, 2001).

172 Exodus 6:6.

173 The Boer War of 1899 and 1902 was fought between Britain and the South African Republics of the Transvaal and the Orange Free State.

174 Joel 1:4. *Cankerworm* — biblical word for "locust". At this time over 25,000 refugees flooded into the city and the Jewish population there doubled (Gwynne Schrire, "Immigration Restriction, Plague and the Jews in Cape Town, 1901", *Jewish Affairs*, 2008, 63:3, pp. 3, 16; Elizabeth van Heyningen, "Cape Town and the Plague of 1901", *Studies in the History of Cape Town*, 1981, pp. 66–107).

175 Isaiah 49:21.

176 2 Kings 10:32. Victims of the disease (Gwynne Schrire, "Immigration", p.16).

177 Deuteronomy 20:8.

178 Joel 2:28.

179 This was the ambulance sent to fetch plague victims to take them to the Uitvlugt Plague Camp, near Ndabeni (Gwynne Schrire, "Immigration", p. 19).

180 Billy Goat which also means "male". The last word in line denotes grave or pit (Psalms 30:9).

181 It is not clear exactly what illness Gela had, but it is possible that it was the bubonic plague that was epidemic in Cape Town at that time (see footnote 174).

182 Exodus 12:4.

183 Job 9:23.

184 The Bombay Plague Research Committee in 1898 defined the plague as a "... disease which is essentially associated with insanitary conditions in human habitations" (Van Heyningen, "Cape Town and the Plague", p. 69). This is why the butchery was targeted and spied upon for evidence of unsanitary conditions and malpractice.

185 Malachi 3:24. Return to traditional birthplace, or to the hometown of the older generation.

186 Good Jewish community.

187 He was 50 years old in 1901, suggesting that he meant for his whole life. His decision to leave is discomforting; he knew that the plague was contagious and that it could be deadly, and he was certain that his wife had the disease, yet he apparently had no qualms about taking her on board ship where she might well have infected other passengers and other ports of call.

188 Unknown term.

189 *Talmud* and rulings of law. He must have saved his *Shas* (another name for the *Talmud*) which was present in his grandson Theodore (Toddy) Schrire's library.

190 Jeremiah 30:11.

191 Psalms 75:4.

192 Annie (1891–1918).

193 His youngest child, Harry (1895–1980).

194 Isaiah 9:4.

195 In his memoir, Harry said that he fell from one deck to a lower one but all he remembered of the accident was being given a banana when the stitches were removed. He arrived in London with a bandage around his head (Schrire, Memoir, this volume, p.162).

196 He apparently fell over the railing from a higher to a lower deck.

197 Expression for emotional pain. He had good reason to be anxious having defied the quarantine regulations (see footnote 187).

198 Isaiah 54:11.

199 Genesis 18:11 uses this expression to refers to Sarah's advanced age, but here it is clear that Gela was pretending to be menstruating.

200 Ezekiel 4:6.

201 Genesis 45:16: "The news reached Pharaoh's palace ...." The literal meaning is "the voice was heard."

202 2 Chronicles 21:19.

203 Leviticus 13:2. Discoloration. Rashi gives an example of this usage to denote a white or a light/pale/bright/clear spot.

204 1 Kings 20:41.

205 Literally, "undressed our skin off" — meaning overcharged.

206 Exodus 21:19. Time spent healing without being able to work.

207 Isaiah 33:4.

208 Double fees.

209 Psalms 145:16. Mentioned in the grace after meals.

210 Psalms 148:1. Talking about the place of God.

211 Exodus 19:4.

212 Isaiah 3:16: "daughters of Zion are so vain / And walk ... with mincing gait."

213 A spice also called fennel flower, nutmeg flower, Roman coriander, or black caraway.

214 German valley of Main.

215 Genesis 13:10. Wide valley surrounded by mountains.

216 Deuteronomy 4:11. On top of mountains and hills.

217 Deuteronomy 2:5.

218 Isaiah 33:4.

219 Zechariah 1:8. Red colour, probably caused by the setting sun.

220 They lived on Bergerstrasse in Frankfurt for two years.

221 Used in a different order in Genesis 22:14.

222 2 Samuel 20:19. A big Jewish community in a metropolis.

223 Genesis 6:17. On this earth.

224 Expression still used today in Orthodox society.

225 2 Chronicles 35:12. Possibly referring to the Orthodox and the developing Reform movement.

226 He implies that the "other side" was cunning and suspicious as opposed to being cautious and strict (footnote 228). There is no biblical reference here for the combination, though both "plotting" and "hastily" appear in the Book of Job.

227 Boldly, brazenly.

228 The same expression appears in several books and as a whole line in a book about the history of Chassidism 1740–1840 (Rabbi Yekuthiel Aryeh Kamelhar [1871–1937], *Dor Deah*). It refers to those who "break the covenant and have contempt for the *Torah*", namely, Jews who have moved away from their roots and tradition and who, by breaking fundamental laws, create contempt for the *Torah*.

229 Written in Hebrew transliteration of the English word "farm".

230 Poetic name for cemetery or graveyard, used in Genesis 10:26 ("*hazarmaveth*") and in *Berachot*, *Seder Zeraim*, p. 18.

231 *Talmud Masechet Sota*, no. 3. The spelling in the poem is "*OVREI AVORA*," which, because of the hand printed block Hebrew letters, is very similar in appearance to "*OVDEI AVODA*," which refers to Jews who worship non-Jewish idols, a deadly sin in the *Torah*.

232 Deuteronomy 11:26.

233 The whole line refers to the choices we make in life and their ramifications, as in Deuteronomy 30:15.

234 At a time of peak emigration from Eastern Europe, German Jewry collected money to help refugees in transit through Germany to America.

235 His parents were Yitzchak ben Shmuel (1821-1911) and Batya Malka (1928-), to whom he dedicated his novel *Shoshanah Novelet* (see footnote 29). He annotated the reverse side of a photograph of his father as "My father teacher Yitzchak son of Rabbi Shmuel Schrire may his candle be lit. Born in the year 1820/1821." Sylvia Schrire, the wife of his grandson Theodore (Toddy) said he was known as "*der alte*". The Lithuanian census lists Itzsko son of Shmuila as aged 38 in 1858, meaning that he was born c. 1820, and lists his wife as Basia, then aged 30. What is confusing is that their son, Yehuda Leib, born in 1851, was called MORDUKH LEIB here, possibly indicating that somewhere along the line he changed his name. They also had a one-year-old daughter named Slava. Yehuda Leib notes that he was one of five sons, but lists five other than himself (Schrire, Diary, this volume, p.93, footnote 14).

236 Samuel (footnote 133), Annie (footnote 192) and Harry (footnote 193).

237 Psalms 94:11.

238 Psalms 145:16.

239 Psalms 7:18. Also means "making love" (physical).

240 Mentioned in a *midrash* about the Book of Exodus, same word used for "church" in modern Hebrew.

241 *Kobez al Jad*, the journal of the Hebrew publishing house (footnote 26).

242 Proverbs 16:21.

243 Annie (footnote 192).

244 Proverbs 24:6.

245 It seems that she was suffering from appendicitis, and that the infection was possibly sufficiently advanced to have caused peritonitis. Surgical intervention became common after the 1890s, yet she was probably lucky to have been in Germany at this time because medical practice there was more advanced than in Cape Town or Lithuania.

246 Psalms 119:123.

247 Ezekiel 27:18. A pure white wool.

248 Borborygmus, or stomach growling, rumbling, gurgling, grumbling or wambling (*Wikipedia*). Given the high mortality rates in hospitals, the writer was justifiably afraid of surgical intervention.

249 "Openly and secretly" normally appears in the reverse order, "secretly and openly", as in the *Shacharit* (dawn) Jewish prayer. The form used in the poem appears (with the same meaning) in the book *Migdal Oz* (A Tower of Strength) published in Koeningsberg 1860, p. vii, by Rabbi Moshe Chaim Luzzatto (1707–1746).

250 When the Boer War ended in 1902, there was a glut of rental properties in Cape Town when thousands of refugees who had previously crowded there returned to the Witwatersrand.

251 Deterioration of properties increased, and later court records show builders' and plumbers' accounts and sanitary inspectors' demands for repairs of his properties filed in the Insolvent Liquidation and Distribution Account MOIB 2/3186 337; MOIB 2/3251 991; MOIB 2/225 4 96; MOIB 2/3376 355; MOIB 2/3501 434.

252 Moshe Mordechai (Max) (see footnote 133).

253 Psalms 120:5. The tents of Kedar, Ishmaelites, were black.

254 Deuteronomy 28:65.

255 Isaiah 23:8.

256 Samuel (footnote 133) was studying under Dr Ganz (Schrire, Memoir, this volume, p.163).

257 An expression used as a honorary name.

258 Leviticus 23:11. Often regarded as the next day after the first *Yom Tov* of Passover.

259 Advanced studies in a college or university.

260 The home of Joseph ben Tuvia Mauerberger (1859–1916), b. Lazdjaj, Lithuania, m. Sarah ?Kalvarisky (Kramer), father of five children, including Rebecca, Bertha, Rochel, Israel, and Morris (Gail Flesch, pers. comm. 2011; Alfred Lipsey, Arizona, c. 1998, pers. comm.; Mendel Kaplan assisted by Marian Robertson, *Jewish Roots in the South African Economy* [Cape Town: C. Struik Publishers, 1986], p. 308; Carmel Schrire, *Digging through Darkness*, p. 17; Carmel Schrire and Gwynne Schrire, Context, this volume, Fig. 10 and Schrire, Memoir, this volume, pp.161-162; Appendix III. 1, this volume).

261 Rebecca (Becky) Mauerberger (1882–1963).

262 Harry wrote that his mother decided she would be an ideal wife for Max. His father was impressed that she knew Hebrew and Yiddish and was involved in organising Zionist activities (Yehuda Leib Schrire, *Tolada*, this volume, p.131, stanza 126; Schrire, Memoir, this volume, p.163; Schrire, *Digging through Darkness*, p. 17).

263 In their absence, Max had gone into partnership with Israel Mauerberger, as Mauerberger & Schrire, a wholesale soft goods shop based at 72 and 76 Darling Street, Cape Town. Here they were supplied with job-lines from London by Israel's father, Joseph, who had a shop on Commercial Road in the East End of London (footnote 260; see also Kaplan, *Jewish Roots*, pp. 308–309; Schrire and Schrire, Context, this volume, p. 17; Schrire, Memoir, this volume, p.162).

264 A man of high quality.

265 They left on the *Avondale Castle* from Southampton on 25 April 1903.

266 R. W. Murray confirmed this impression when he complained that in District Six "... houses of all shapes and sizes were built, without any drainage being thought of, much less provided. The population grew and had to be provided for in the way of house room. People built where they liked and how they liked, with no object but that of rent" (Nigel Worden, Elizabeth van Heyningen, and Vivian Bickford-Smith, *Cape Town: The Making of a City. An Illustrated Social History* [Cape Town: David Philip Publishers, 1998], p. 170).

267 As a result of the plague being blamed on dirt, a reluctant city council employed sanitary inspectors to examine houses and issue warrants demanding that repairs be conducted and areas cleaned. Where a case of plague occurred, the house was evacuated, hosed down with disinfectant, thoroughly cleaned and white-washed, and clothing and household effects were disinfected or destroyed. Over 2,000 houses were demolished and rebuilt. See R. McKenzie, ed., *The Cape Journal, Album 3* (Cape Town, 1998), p. 29. Among their court papers were summonses to the Schrires for cleaning their yard, attending to sanitation and carrying out repairs on the houses that they rented out (see Schrire and Schrire, Context, this volume, p.19).

268 Exodus 5:6.

269 Genesis 27:29.

270 By 1903 South Africa was passing into an economic depression which lasted until 1909, one of the severest and most prolonged in the previous century. (Robin Hallett, "The Hooligan Riots, Cape Town: August 1906", *Studies in the History of Cape Town*, 1979, vol. 1, p.44).

271 The unemployment led to social unrest, political meetings, and public violence, as in the Hooligan Riots in August 1906. Shops in District Six were looted. One of the leaders, J. H. Howard, in a speech to the crowd, condemned stealing goods, breaking windows and Jew-baiting. David Goldblatt, a Yiddish printer, advised Jewish dealers and auctioneers to stay away from the Wednesday Parade sales. Barney Levinson, a Russian cigarette-maker, who, like Howard, was a member of the Social Democratic Federation, was arrested and later acquitted of an inflammatory speech (Hallett, "Hooligan Riots", pp. 45, 62, 65, 73).

272 Isaiah 24:12.

273 Jeremiah 38:12.

274 Leviticus 13:45: "... his clothes shall be rent, and the hair of his head shall grow long ...."

275 Jeremiah 51:22.

276 Harry said his father went back to *chazones* (being a cantor), journalism and *shechita*, while his mother, being the business head of the family, decided to open a kosher butchery to cater to those who were averse to buying from a mixed shop where both kosher and *treif* (non-kosher) food was sold (Schrire, Memoir, this volume, p.163).

277 Job 39:28. I Samuel 14:4. A precarious cliff.

278 Psalms 106:23.

279 Malachi 2:14.

280 Proverbs 31:27.

281 Psalms 78:25. *Manna* from heaven.

282 Proverbs 9:3. High society.

283 Numbers 22:32.

284 Samuel (footnote 133) had to abandon his law studies at Jews' College in London because his parents could no longer afford to support him.

285 Psalms 37:25.

286 Combination found in an essay from 1918 by Zvi Chatz, http://benyehuda.org/shats/threshold.html.

287 Proverbs 23:6.

288 Ordinary people, non-observant Jews.

289 The usage here denotes ignoring the markers of the Jewish calendar.

290 Isaiah 13:6. Havoc from the Almighty, suggesting a big, inevitable disaster.

291 Job 4:18: "And cast reproach on His angels."

292 Hosea 6:2. Shortly.

293 Expression found in a interpretation of *Mishnah Avot*, 4:36.

294 Isaiah 24:20. "The earth is swaying like a drunkard." The commentary for the biblical verse is the same as in the context of the poem: a description of deterioration.

295 Isaiah 1:21.

296 Proverbs 30:8. "Never during my lifetime has depression been so acute. People with nice houses have had to sell all their furniture and are now living in one room" (Hallett, "Hooligan Riots", p. 45).

297 Babylonian *Talmud, Yebamot* 47.

298 Form found in a *midrash* about Genesis 1-14.

299 Isaiah 24:12.

300 "Suffering", in biblical language.

301 The government stopped construction on public works and the number of large buildings being built dropped from nine in January to six in May 1906. "Not for many years had the number of hands in the building trade been so reduced ... and in almost all branches of industry the same condition appears to have obtained" (Hallett, "Hooligan Riots", p. 46).

302 From a line in a poem, "Prayer for the Dew", by Rabbi Elazar Biribi Kilir, one of the greatest sixth- to seventh-century poets, some of whose poems can be found in Ashkenazi *machzorim* (High Holy Day prayer books). One commentary is a city being empty, deserted by its inhabitants, like a ghost town, which fits the rest of the verse of the poem.

303 1908.

304 *Sukkot* celebration of harvesting the crops.

305 Written twice in modern and also in biblical form which refers to a forbidden kind of interest.

306 Isaiah 48:7.

307 Exodus 11:1.

308 Jeremiah 5:30.

309 Genesis 11:10.

310 Isaiah 17:1.

311 2 Kings 18:21.

312 2 Kings 11:6.

313 1 Kings 22:36.

314 They were advised to declare insolvency in April 1909 (Western Cape Archives and Records Service, MOIB 2/3385 337).

315 Exodus 22:5.

316 1 Kings 14:10.

317 Joshua 9:5.

318 Deuteronomy 10:2. Refers to Moses who placed the broken tablets next to the whole ones in the Ark of the Covenant, and is an expression that implies that one should not denigrate someone who has lost his intellect or his possessions.

319 Isaiah 1:8.

320 Lamentations 4:6.

321 They were declared insolvent. Gela, his wife, declared in court on 4 April 1909 that she had done fairly well until 1906 when the shortfall occasioned by the loss of rent due to non-occupation of premises by defaulting tenants forced her to disburse £200 over and above the revenue she received from these properties. Finding it impossible to pay the interest on her bonds, she tried to negotiate with the bondholders, but they refused to do so. One of her creditors took action against her, and her estate was placed under compulsory sequestration (Western Cape Archives and Records Service, MOIB 2/3251 991).

322 Jeremiah 45:5.

323 Ezekiel 28:17.

324 Esther 1:6.

325 Electric street lights arrived in Cape Town in 1895, and the Dock Road Electric Station which opened in 1904 made electricity more widely available. Although at first there were only 20 customers, by 1904 usage had grown to 1,300 subscribers. Schrire seems to have regarded electricity as a luxury on which he chose not to squander his money (Jane Carruthers, "G. H. Swingler and the Supply of Electricity to Cape Town", *Studies in the History of Cape Town*, 1984, vol. 5, pp. 212, 214.)

326 Job 3:4.

327 Judges 3:25.

328 Habakkuk 2:3.

329 Declared in 1910.

330 Isaiah 46:10.

331 Isaiah 21:2.

332 *Chazal* said that special salt from the mountain of Sodom should be used for all the sacrifices in the Temple. It was regarded as the most pure kind of salt and there was a special salt chamber at the Temple dedicated to the ritual. http://www.jewishencyclopedia.com/articles/13043-salt#anchor4.

333 Isaiah 5:1.

334 See footnote 220.

335 Isaiah 22:2.

336 Isaiah 6:11.

337 Psalms 94:4.

338 1 Kings 21:8.

339 Ecclesiastes 10:5.

340 *Aliyah*: to go up (lit.); to emigrate to Palestine/Israel.

341 Part of the *Mussaf* prayers reminiscent of the custom of sacrifice at the Temple.

342 Genesis 47:6.

343 Popular line from a poem written by the Lithuanian-born poet Kadish Silman, later set to music.

344 Joshua 15:8. Gehenna.

345 Numbers 21:18.

346 "Despondent spirit", Deuteronomy 28:65.

4. REMINISCENCES, PARTLY BIOGRAPHY AND PARTLY PEOPLE I HAVE MET, BEING THE MEMOIR OF HARRY SCHRIRE

Harry Schrire[1]
Annotated and edited by Gwynne Schrire and Carmel Schrire[2]

Editors' Note: These reminiscences (henceforth the Memoir) were handwritten by Yehuda Leib's youngest son, Harry Nathan (1895–1980), and then transcribed by his daughter, Vivienne Stein, around 1978. The manuscript was typed onto a computer by his son Arthur. It consists of Harry's reminiscences of his early childhood and school days, growing up in District Six, and includes notes on his ancestry in the "Schrire clan" as well as his parents and neighbours. It ends when he left Cape Town to study medicine in Edinburgh, a period that he censored.[3] We have deliberately retained its occasional idiosyncrasies to impart the richness and flavour of his actual speech.

****

My Family

Before I become decrepit and while my memory still functions, with gentle urgings from my family and friends, I willingly submit these efforts. These mainly concern the history of the Jewish community of Cape Town from the beginning of this century, and are mostly of course about the Schrire clan. I happen to be the oldest surviving member, besides Sarah,[4] who is a Schrire by marriage.

My late father, Reverend Yehuda Arieh (Judah Lion), arrived in South Africa in 1891.[5] Born in Oshmanya, Lithuania, near Vilna in 1851, he studied at Tels Yeshiva (Tilsit College) and at Vilna in Lithuania as a young man,[6] and must have gained a vast amount of Talmudic knowledge. Besides his mastery of Hebrew and Yiddish literature, he was a good musician.[7] He became a *chazan* at a young age. He travelled from *shtetl* to *shtetl*, giving of his best, till he became well known. He had a fine tenor voice.[8] He composed and wrote his own notes for a full choir. Before coming to South Africa, he was the *chazan* for 19 years in Neustadt Sugind, on the Russian side of the German border. My father's right leg was crippled, most likely due to polio as a child. He was never seen without a walking stick.[9] He regularly contributed articles to an American Jewish periodical *Americaner,* in Yiddish, and to a London paper *Hayehudi*, in Hebrew, for both of which he was paid, though not very much. And he published a novel (love story) in Hebrew, which is in Toddy's library.[10] A proper hard-cover book. The name is *Shoshana Novelet*.[11]

I was told that he was brought to South Africa by Sammy Marks, of Lewis and Marks. Sammy, hailing originally from Neustadt, had a great respect for his old *chazan*.[12] Lewis was Sammy's brother-in-law, both having most likely arrived in the Transvaal via London. They started the first liquor factory and became good friends with Paul Kruger and his staunch supporters, against the British. They soon acquired land and mineral rights. Lewis visited Neustadt and used his riches to erect buildings for the Jewish folk and disbursed plenty of charity. It is said that he spent 20,000 *roubles*, which was a large sum in those days.[13] The news spread all over Lithuania "GOLD IN THE STREETS OF AFRICA" — bedlam! A rush of immigrants ensued.

While in Neustadt, the Governor of the Province was about to pay a visit. It was customary to honour him with a special gift from the Jewish community. This job fell to the Jack-of-all-trades, Reb Schrire.[14] He built a lovely replica of the *shul* where he was *chazan*, in SUGAR — iced, coloured and perfect.

My grandfather's brother in Oshmanya, in the last century, was friendly with the local *Graf*, who would ask my great uncle to play a game of billiards. The genes of this uncle were passed on to me. I became a bit of a champion at the game in Edinburgh. My winnings at snooker and billiards helped to pay for my lodging. My mother's maiden name was Gertie Globus and she was related somehow to the famous Rabbi Zuckerman. They had four children who survived (after three others died of measles) viz. Max, Sam, myself and sister Annie.[15] My mother's brother, Globus, was a character. He was a big man and mighty tough. In the very early days in Johannesburg, they were busy digging ditches in the streets for pipe laying etc., when Globus drove his horse and cart into one of these. I'm not sure whether he killed or hurt a workman. The court case got too involved for him. He was next heard of in Palestine, where after a time he was in trouble again. Some of the Jewish settlers had an argument with some Arabs, who drew knives and became nasty. Globus nearly killed some of them. Back in Johannesburg he settled down without further incidents — as far as I know.

My father came to the Wolmarans *Shul*[16] in Johannesburg, as *chazan, shochet, mohel* and preacher. He was not happy in Johannesburg and longed to get back to his family in Russia. On his way back, he was induced to stay in Cape Town, on the condition that his family was brought out. The family duly arrived on a Saturday, in 1894, and had to walk the whole way from the docks to the town. They settled in Barrack Street, where I was born on *Tisha b'Av* on 15 Sept 1895. This house, from what I recollect, after the Boer War, faced an open space with broken-down buildings, which in earlier days were military barracks. As children we used these as playgrounds. I remember these spaces where Fillis's and later Pagel's circuses performed. This area is now occupied by police courts and government buildings around Caledon Square.

My father was a good violinist and in Johannesburg he supplemented his income by giving lessons. In his later years he stopped playing the violin, because his left small and adjacent fingers were damaged while opening a bottle of beer, which burst and cut a tendon in his wrist. Old Mr Karnovsky (of Sive and Karnovsky) who was somehow related to the Globus clan, told my son Len all about my dad's performances. Mr Karnovsky's family left Johannesburg during the Boer War and stayed with us in Cape Town for a while.

My dad's compositions were written in two large black ledger-like tomes which have both disappeared, together with most of his library — in Hebrew, Yiddish and German. There were two *Gemorahs* (Jerusalem and Babylonian), treatises and other allied writings. The walls of his study were covered with books. Toddy Schrire, the oldest, most erudite third-generation Schrire, a fine Hebrew scholar (on top of his other well-known professional accomplishments), rescued a few tattered books here and there.[17]

Father was not enamoured of the English language, because it was not pronounced as written. His knowledge of English literature was gained through the medium of German and Yiddish publications.

He had a wonderful pair of hands — he could build and mend anything in his little workshop upstairs in our house on the corner of Harrington Street and Boom (now Commercial) Street. It was a tiny room, out of bounds to all, littered with nails, screws, springs, chisels, screwdrivers and diverse tools, string, wood, cardboard, wire, etc. If there were no visitor on a Sunday morning for a game of chess, the door of the workshop was closed and all you could hear were noises issuing sporadically. At times Max would arrive from the Parade with more springs, etc., and rusty tools, which were later polished and sharpened to look like new. Father would beam with joy.

After a while something would emerge. On *Chanukah* the leaden *draidlech* and metal candle holders. *Purim* — then he produced his masterpiece. This was a contraption on which, after he wound up springs from the Parade, a figure would jerk forward a few steps, raise some sort of chopper, and off came Haman's head to the accompaniment of a musical box — also made by him. Any broken toy, pot, instrument in the home was sent upstairs and most times, became as good as new — some Sunday in the future. For the holidays, he took over the kitchen and proceeded to make most tasty sweets — all kinds and shapes. For wedding and *bar mitzvah* presents, the request from the celebrant was often for a poem. This took the form of a book or a *siddur* with an appropriate poem in Hebrew or Yiddish. The Oudtshoorn[18] congregation commissioned my dad to make an *Oren Kodesh*[19] for their *shul*. From specially selected wood he carved with the tools at hand, straight and round chisels, penknife and fretwork saws, for a long time. It was a fine piece of work.[20]

My mother used to brag that his brilliance was partly due to the genes he inherited from the famous *Gaon* (saint, or "super-rabbi") Sherira, mentioned in Graetz history and the *Encyclopaedia Britannica*.[21] I cannot prove this claim, but when I approached him he said that in his youth he had a hazy recollection of a family tree verifying this assumption. In answer to my query as to how our name originated, he jokingly replied "*Shrirus Libom*", the wildness or naughtiness of their hearts, as it appears in some prayer or saying. This seemingly meant to demonstrate what a naughty boy I was.

All I can say is that any Schrire I met or heard about came from Oshmanya.[22] My father had two brothers who immigrated to America to escape military service. One of them changed his name to Levin. Years ago Toddy met some of the members of the second and third generation.[23] When I was in Tokyo some time ago I met a big financier whose father and uncle ran away via Harbin and China and landed somewhere in the East, ultimately reaching America. When we tried to trace some sort of relationship, I casually mentioned the magic name "Oshmanya". The name rang a bell. He remembered the name being associated with his father's birthplace.

When in Israel I encountered Shriros, Schrires, and Shriras, with the same password. These came through Odessa. There was the oil millionaire Shrirow from Baku in the early part of the century and who helped President Chaim Weizmann with his education in Switzerland. This can be verified in his biography *Trial and Error*.[24] When the Bolshies came to power, he was deprived of all his possessions. His two daughters and son, highly cultured folk, were stranded in Paris between the two Great Wars, where they were discovered by Max and his wife Rebecca (parents of Toddy and his two brothers Isch and Dave). Max helped them financially a bit till they landed in Israel. The two sisters both lectured in French at the Tel Aviv University. We still keep in touch with them.[25]

They put us on to another set of Schriros, on a kibbutz near the Lebanon border. These were charming people, cultured and sophisticated. They had come from

Odessa many years ago and had a son and grandchildren, all living on the kibbutz.[26] At this kibbutz we met a visitor, a lady Dr Shriro, also from Odessa, whose husband was liquidated by the Nazis while they were students at the Sorbonne. Seemingly he was a member of the French underground. She worked at a Haifa hospital as a child specialist. We also contacted a handsome, tall, Shriro, who is an engineer with the Haifa municipality. We visited his modern flat on Mount Carmel.

There was an outbreak of bubonic plague in Cape Town at the end of the Anglo-Boer war, and my parents, who were considered fairly well off with an income of fifty pounds per month from rentals from the property in Harrington Street, decided to take a trip to Europe.[27] They had been offered five thousand pounds for the property by a man called "Kaiser", but refused to sell because there was a boom at the time.

My parents and three children, Sam, Annie and myself, departed, leaving my eldest brother Max, then about 19 or 20 years old, behind. We stopped over in London for some time. Max, who had been apprenticed to a photographer in Cape Town, opened up as a photographer in De Aar and followed the British army all over the country during the war (see Fig. 9).[28] He managed to accumulate TWO THOUSAND GOLDEN SOVEREIGNS by the end of the war. He met Israel Mauerberger, who was then in partnership with Smollan in Johannesburg. The two of them started M&S (Mauerberger and Schrire), a wholesale soft goods store on 72 & 76 Darling Street, Cape Town, about 1902 or '03. They were supplied with job-lines from London by Israel's father, who had a buying office *cum* store on Commercial Road in the East End.[29]

The Mauerbergers took our family in hand while in London. Their family consisted of a father (no mean Talmudist), the oldest daughter Rebecca (Becky), Bertha (mother of Lord Goodman), Rachel, and the youngest Morris. My mother, a champion *shadchente*, decided that Becky would be an ideal wife for Max.[30] My father was greatly impressed by her knowledge of Hebrew and Yiddish, and her organising ability in Zionist activities. In fact, she was one of the London representatives at the Basel Zionist Congress, where she rubbed shoulders with Herzl, Zangwill, Ushisskin and many of the leaders of Zionism. Toddy has a framed photograph of that meeting.[31]

Israel brought out his brother Morris, known as "Morrie", in about 1905, to work for M&S.[32] Morrie must have been about 15 at the time, and was full of ideas, young and ambitious. His main reading consisted of American booklets describing the rise of the self-made tycoons and he was determined to do the same here, and he succeeded. When his father died in London and left him a small sum of money, Morrie opened a tiny shop at the lower end of Hanover Street, and sold a few reels of cotton for a while. Sometime later, he and Joe Ochberg, brother of Ochberg senior, opened a shop in Wynberg called "Castle Drapers". Morrie, being headstrong, broke with Joe, established Stanhope Drapery and brought his American ideas to fruition. He took in a young man, Gus Ackerman, who was a commercial traveller, to manage his Wynberg branch.[33] Morrie acted as buyer, financier, shipper, etc., and added 10% to goods put into the shops. Whatever profit was shown was booked to Gus — not drawn. Drawings were fixed, and the balance ploughed into the business, to be used to finance the concern. An older man, Sam Kirsch, who was working for M&S as a pen-pusher and traveller, was brought in to manage the main shop in Claremont, on the same terms.[34] The war was on and things were booming. Next to join, in 1919, was Leon Segal, also a traveller for M&S.[35] He got Segal's Smart Store in Lower Main Road, Salt River.[36] It became Ackermans Ltd (not public), in order to sound more Afrikaans.[37] Stellenbosch, Paarl, and so on followed.

Morrie, having seen my father slaughter a fowl, and being averse to the sight of blood, avoided eating flesh or fowl. He existed mostly on fish, eggs and tinned sardines. A non-drinker and non-smoker, he saved a lot of money.[38] I nevertheless remember him driving up Harrington Street on a second-hand Harley-Davidson motor bike, one of the few about at that time. He was a godsend to M&S later on, when wholesalers were not doing too well, by absorbing their rather out-dated stock into a new venture called "Bergers". The *Potash and Perlmutter* business of M&S was now well away.[39] They managed, by a friendly process of clever nagging, to break away on their own and let Morrie concentrate on his factories.[40] I must admit that Morrie was a great psychologist who saw more with his one good eye than many of us did with two good ones.[41]

We stayed in a boarding-house in London for a while, and it was decided that the family move to Frankfurt-am-Main, the then most orthodox city in Europe. I had arrived in London off the boat with a bandage round my head. I had fallen from one deck to a lower one. All that I can remember is that I was given a banana when the stitches were removed.[42]

We lived in Bergerstrasse in Frankfurt for two years. I was at kindergarten and gradually forgot my English. One of the lads called me "*ein verdampter Boer*" [sic *verdamde*: a damned Boer], and automatically received a punch from me. The next day my mother got a red *warnung tzetl*. I think I was threatened with expulsion.

It transpired that fighting was not encouraged at this high-class school, especially since this lad was a Rothschild.

Meanwhile the situation in South Africa was deteriorating. The property market had dropped to rock bottom and the house had been vacated — very little rent coming in. We said goodbye to Frankfurt, leaving Sam behind to study under Dr Ganz.[43] He was to become a "*Rabiner*". After 12 or 18 months, Sam was sent to London to continue his studies at Jews' College. He lived in an upstairs room in a boarding house, and below his window was a glass roof, well blackened by London grime and soot. Absentmindedly he jumped onto this so-called roof and fell right through, on to a waiter carrying plates of food. Poor innocent Sam, a dedicated *yeshiva bocher* was in a mess ... so was the waiter.

After a while Sam was brought back to Cape Town. He took his Matric first class, then read Law, in which he came first in the Cape Colony. In those days each colony conducted its own exams. His Teutonic ways, which he had imbibed in Frankfurt, remained with him. He would go to bed with a revolver on his bedside table, and three books. Starting on his German book, he timed himself exactly to half an hour — next the French book, a half hour — and lastly his English book, a half hour. The candle was blown out and he was asleep within minutes. A few pals helped me to drag him out one night, still blissfully asleep — bed and all — on to the landing (minus revolver). We left him there till the morning. He had an ice cold bath every morning — summer and winter. This was as much a ritual with him as laying his *tefillin*. He was genial, methodical, punctilious and honest. Round-faced with a very fair skin, he was a first class *chup* for any *shadchan*. In addition to all his *ma'ales,* he was a very good pianist, his favourites being Beethoven and Wagner. We used to play music together at home. Father on the violin, Sam at the piano, and Max and the rest of us singing. Then there was the time that they decided to have revolver practice in the back yard. Dad took a shot and scored an unexpected bull's eye. He sent a bullet through the water tank on the low roof. A flood ensued!

Back in Cape Town again, the property had to be surrendered, as they could not get even two thousand pounds for it. The bond could not be covered, or something to that effect. Father went back to *chazones*, journalism, *shechita*, etc. My mother, being the business head of the family, decided to open a kosher butchery to cater to those who were averse to buying from a mixed shop — kosher and *treif*. Of course this was a come-down from the Schrire *yichus*. Father had very little to do with this venture. Luckily, the capable blockman/manager, Shapiro, carried the whole show, including the delivery of baskets of meat on his shoulders. He subsequently took over the business.

I must mention here that my brothers and sister, having been born in Russia, were children of a Reverend, as stated on their birth certificates. Mine states "son of a butcher", because at the time of my birth my father was a *shochet*. My *yichus* is not as hot as theirs, which I proved by becoming the black sheep of the family.

Our own home, which later became Mrs Behr's boarding house, was a home for strays off the boats. The poor folk arrived at the docks penniless. They had to show five pounds (to land) which some of them did not possess. This is where the trio of champion *shnorrers* came into the picture. These three musketeers — Mother, Mrs Bloch, and tiny Mrs Zuckerman[44] — visited the Jewish commercial houses for donations, and were never refused, nor were questions asked. Gradner, who kept the books for the little shopkeepers, was given the necessary amounts and smoothed the way for the aforementioned unfortunates to land. Quite a few (now high up and well away) were palmed off onto us, where they were fed and lodged. Ultimately they were put on a train to relations in Johannesburg or Oudtshoorn. The rest were given handcarts and sold herrings and cucumbers. When they amassed enough money (not forgetting a small pittance sent home), they bought a horse and cart and started *smousing* in the small country *dorps*, and further afield. These people founded many great commercial enterprises in this country.

Shul

At the beginning of the century there was only one recognised *Rav* in Cape Town to my knowledge. This was Rabbi Bender of the Gardens Synagogue. Reverend A. P. Bender came from London in 1895, the year I was born. M. A. Cambridge — very anglicised — Hebrew lecturer at the South African College[45] at the top of the Gardens. Most popular with gentiles, bachelor to the end of his life, he was fond of lecturing to the young, especially girls, who liked him very much. Rather pompous, he was disliked and belittled by the old orthodox crowd (unjustly). A fine English-Jewish gentleman.

The *frumme* Jews from Districts 5 and 6[46] had little love for the Gardens *Shul* — the "*Englisher Shul*" — seen in a milder form today between the Reform and older (Orthodox) *shuls*. There was the *Beth Midrash* on Constitution Street and the Ponevitzer *Beth Midrash* not far away. I don't remember if there was an established, old style *heimisher Rav* until Rabbi Mirvish came to Constitution Street *Beth Midrash*.[47] Before his arrival, and even during his earlier days, my father acted as unofficial judge and adjudicator in many disputes between Jews, so as to avoid the shame of going to court. People accepted his findings as legal and binding.

Now the Roeland Street Synagogue appeared on the scene, mainly launched by Morris Alexander,[48] supported by the orthodox element somewhere between Constitution Street and the Gardens *Shul*. This congregation was on its way up. The Schrires were associated with the founders. At that time our President was Morris Alexander. He was a prominent advocate, able and respected, devoted to Jewish communal affairs and a staunch defender of the Indians. At Cambridge University he met a young student, the daughter of the famous American, Prof. Schechter.[49] They married and settled in Cape Town. There was an affair in the Dutch Reformed Church Hall in Church Square, in honour of his return from (or departure to?) America. A public reception and presentation was given and I had to read an illuminated address, written in Hebrew and English in gold embroidered lettering by my dad. There was I, on the stage, in my brand-new knickerbocker suit specially made by that grand old staunch Gardens *Shul* veteran, the popular military tailor of Plein Street, pointing to my jacket which was twisted and needed straightening.[50]

A year or two later Prof. Schechter (a name to conjure with among Jews and gentiles alike) arrived on a visit to his daughter and son-in-law.[51] Prof. Schechter was an authority on ancient Semitic languages, also head of the Jewish Seminary of America (Liberal). After the *Shabbat* service, my dad was introduced to him by Alexander. An argument soon developed. The Prof. pulled some papers from his pocket to prove his point. His hand with the papers was politely pushed aside and he was gently told that the synagogue, on a Sabbath was not the place for bundles of paper. Seemingly the Prof. belonged to a more modern school. He actually arrived at our house the next morning. He and my dad corresponded with each other later. A section of our *Yidden* disliked Alexander because of his second marriage and other family affairs. I do not wish to discuss this matter. His wife left him.[52]

Our congregation had its own *Chevrah Gemora,* where my father read the *Blat* and was head of the *Amobge*.[53] The company were Witten, Rubin (*buch hendlers*),[54] the huge Papert, Fine (produce), Halperin, Ben Jaffe (meat?) — a collector of art — and others who escape my memory. There were many more who, with their descendants, left great names behind them. Schach (property), the actor Leonard's[55] father and grandfather, Zuckerman (wholesalers) — one son became Sir Solly Zuckerman.[56] The Schrire clan did pretty well too.

Kadish Brothers, the jewellers, stood at the doors of our *shul* on *Yom Tovim* to keep the kids from running in and out. One of the brothers became a Christian Scientist in his old age. Another jeweller was that tiny man Goldberg, Ariel's father, an argumentative, *frumme* supporter of our *shul*. Dr Ariel Goldberg was born in Palestine. The very learned Papa Goldberg, very learned, also had a scrap with Schechter, because Schechter, being Liberal, rode on *Shabbat*. The wealthiest *frumme* Jew in Cape Town in those early days was the "*Reicher* Harris", who was a smallish man with a large beard. He founded the blanket mill, named after him.[57] Greatly respected and generous, he would arrive on *Rosh Hashanah* in our *shul*, accompanied by his sons and son-in-law (Gesundheid),[58] and together they would *shnodder* a few hundred pounds. This was a terrific amount of money in those days. This was repeated in the other *shuls*.[59] They had a large house at the top of Schoonder St.[60]

I have memories of *Rosh Hashanah* services when *chazan* and choir started singing "*Mi Yichye Mi Yomus*" (in the coming year "Who will live and who will die?; Who will choke; drown?" etc). The women would watch my mother, who at that moment would burst out crying. This was the signal for the old ladies to start weeping. Round about *Rosh Hashanah* we used to go to Woodstock beach to practice the custom of *Tashlich* — casting sins into the water. We also practised *Shlogen shaines*, smacking away with leaves at 5 am in *shul*. At *Havdalah* on Saturday evenings, I remember smelling the herbs and looking at our fingernails under candlelight. Being sent to friend's houses with goodies at *Chanukah* — *Shalaga Mones* — and receiving pennies for my trouble. Before *Pesach* everybody would get busy, plucking grapes into a barrel for wine and later, for *bedek chometz*, Father with a brush and pan would sweep up crumbs purposely left in the corner. There were also nut games after *Seder*.

There were three *cheder* rooms at the back, in which I was taught for a few years under the able supervision of our principal, Mr Geffen, a capable and modern teacher assisted by our likeable jolly *shammes*, Morrison, a learned and fine person.[61] His daughter Deborah, a fellow student of mine, became a Doctor of Medicine and a very prominent Zionist leader.[62] If I missed a lesson, my father would write a note in Hebrew explaining the reason for my absence. This note acted as our *dikduk* — grammar lesson — for the session.

When a *bocher* arrived from Namaqualand or South West Africa, for the *Rosh Hashanah* service, he was taken in hand by our popular *shammes*, given a *tallis*, a *siddur*, a good seat, and made welcome. These lads could be recognised a mile off. A large brimmed hat, yellow boots, very shy and raw, these men made it their business to visit Cape Town every few years, to meet with their own folk, after being stuck in the *bundu* amongst natives. He got an *aliyah*, and with Morrison prompting him, would *shnorrer* so many sovereigns for the *shul*, *chazan*, and not forgetting the *shammes*. He was invited to meals at various homes, especially those with marriageable daughters. He returned the compliment by taking them to a (live) show (no "bioscope" to be had). The *shadchanim* got busy. Sometimes it was discovered that he had a wife in *der heim*, and had accidentally fathered a few *shochere* back in the *bundu*. I have since heard that a few characters, who are big noises today, fitted the latter category. "Mum's the word."

Our first *chazan* in Roeland Street was Glushik, an excellent cantor with a wide repertoire. He was highly trained both in sacred and operatic music.[63] His son Leopold conducted our choir, in which I was leading alto. His younger son, Adolph, was also in the choir. Ariel Goldberg was a good soprano, he joined our choir from the Gardens Synagogue. I was rather hot stuff, and was honoured with most of the important solos, until another alto, Halperin, stole some of my glory by alternating with me. This did not suit me. During one festival, when he was doing my part (pretty well, I admit) I stuck a pin into his soft parts. He jumped and yelled. Leopold caught hold of my ear and that was the end of me. Besides the buffeting from him, I received another dose at home. I had my revenge the following Sunday. With the help of our Harrington Street gang, *matzah* bakers Cohen and Bloch's sons, and others, we hid in the narrow lane, opposite the coloured church, waiting for Leopold to come riding down our street on his bicycle, as usual. This lane was stacked with boxes of bad eggs, placed there by Mr Fagan the egg dealer, to be collected by the dirt cart on Monday morning. We let him have it. We did not stop to see the mess, but quickly disappeared. He lodged a complaint with my father but nothing was proven. Our gang and I had a rough time in the choir afterwards.

When Glushik and family left for America via Glasgow and Leopold became a surgeon, he was succeeded by another *chazan*, Strod, of similar calibre.[64] Our new cantor and choir were the talk of South Africa.

There was one incident that I must relate here. We were singing a lovely new *Hallel* or something else which was out of the ordinary. You could hear a pin drop after the end, except for the tapping of a stick. The congregation turned to the source of the noise. There was my father, livid with rage, tapping away. He quieted down and the service continued to the end. Strod, our *gabba*, and a few of the leading members demanded an explanation for his unseemly behaviour. He apologised, and asked Strod to call on us the next morning.

When he arrived he was accused point blank of being a *goniff*. The fat was in the fire:
"Did you compose that tune?"
"No," was the answer. "I found it amongst my father's compositions."
"Did your father compose it?"
"I don't know. I suppose so."
"Then your father was a *goniff!*"

WOW! My dad then brought out his two large black *Gemora*-like books and showed him the identical work, written in his own manuscript, completely set down for *chazan* and choir.

"I knew your father in Russia. He sometimes visited me. How he got hold of my work beats me. This must have been more than 20 years before, if not longer."

What a memory. What a temper. They remained good friends until Strod took over in the Gardens *Shul*.

School

Normal College, part of which is now the Rust en Vreugd Museum, was the school for most of the Jewish boys and girls in our district. It later became Central High — I think — and most of our playground is now a large garage.[65] Our school was a post-Matric Teachers Training College. I went through this institution from kindergarten to Matric. My memory goes back to Miss Wilson in Standard Three, Burton in Four, Von Bonde (Bokkie) in Five, Devlin and Hart in Six, and then on to Smith, and last but not least our popular and brilliant principal, Whitten. Half of the teaching staff were Scotsmen, hard-headed and competent. Hart was our Latin master and was also in charge of our sporting activities. SACS (South African College School), which considered itself a superior school, containing many Jewish boys, was our greatest rival.

I remember Zion Getz and Maurice Glickman. Maurice, newly arrived in those days, would help me in maths and I would do the same for him in English. A few of the boys were of doubtful coloured parentage, but this did not worry us. There were also remittance men, from Britain, well-educated and refined, who had gone to seed through drink. Some of these would help us with our homework, right up to Matric, for a drink. There were lots of country boarders who towered above us physically — hence my broken arm in a vital soccer match. Harold Hosking, in later years a big shot in soccer, was centre forward and I was inside right. Dr Kark and his brother set the fracture. A short while after, I was leaning on a fence, watching our team play, when my arm snapped again. This was reset again by a bone specialist, Dr Simon (from Germany *aus*) at a different angle.

Fig. 21: Mellish Farm, Vredehoek, c.1900. http://www.flickr.com/photos/capelight/7211877242/. See also Hans Fransen, *A Cape Camera. The Architectural Beauty of the Old Cape. Photographs from the Arthur Elliott collection in the Cape Archives*, (Johannesburg: AD.Donker and Jonathan Ball Publishers, 1993), p.61.

On Sunday mornings we sometimes bunked *cheder* in order to play football or cricket on the brickfields, which were just behind Mill Street. These were open areas leading to Mellish's farm, where fruit and *dennebals* grew in abundance (Fig. 21). The fences were guarded by big dogs, but we made friends with them. Being fine Jewish gentlemen of good families, a deputation would knock on the door and ask permission to collect apricots and peaches that were ripe and ready to drop off the trees. There was plenty of fruit on the ground as well. If refused, these were nevertheless commandeered with the connivance of the hounds, our pals. Any new resident who wished to join the gang had to pick one of us, equalling his size and weight, and fight it out. Only then was he accepted. You soon learned the finer points of self-defence and how to avoid and mete out punishment. The other street gangs had great respect for us. No dirty play permitted, only fists.

Where Canterbury Street and Commercial Street meet there was a hotel and on the opposite side there were raised houses in which the Cohens and Blochs (*matzah* bakers) lived. The factory was higher up the road. Next to their homes there was a small Indian shop. The gang would gather near the shop and call for two volunteers. They entered and asked for one penny's worth of sweets. They would point to the top shelf. The poor owner, sensing a trick, but not willing to lose a sale, would grab a chunk of firewood in one hand and open the jar with the other. At that critical moment one of the heroes grabbed a watermelon and ran. The other chap got the wood against his body. Being a one-man shop, the gang got away. The melon was slaughtered, the man with a sore back getting a double helping, the peel thrown at the shop, and everybody was happy.

That is one of the reasons that we were called the "Harrington Street Loafers". We were no exceptions. Most youngsters of our age were cruel and irresponsible.

M. J. Cohen the *shochet,* the "Krakenover Cohen", a good family friend, arrived in the early 1900s and soon settled in Porterville Road (now called "Gouda"). He was a great admirer of my father. His wife ran a general dealer shop whilst he acted as *shochet* for the Imperial Cold Storage situated at the slaughterhouse near Porterville village, which was a good distance away. The mule cart arrived early on certain mornings to take him to the slaughterhouse. I spent the school holidays with them and became friendly with the eldest son, Joe. His brother Solly became a well-known surgeon in England. Another brother, David, was an advocate well known in Jewish circles in Cape Town and in high government service in Swaziland.[66] When on holiday, I was forced to write home in Hebrew to father (corrected by Mr Cohen), in Yiddish to mother, and in English to the rest. Travelling through that lovely little pass to Tulbagh at night by mule cart, was an exhilarating experience. Stones would rain down on us, flung by baboons from the surrounding mountain tops.

I had just turned 15 when I scraped through Matric. My name went up on the school board for having got the maximum mark for Latin (a few marks were taken off for bad and indecipherable writing, or so I was told). Thereby hangs a tale. The night before the exam, Sam, by intuition — or because he made me lay *tefillin* that day — put me through some unseen Latin translations. He must have had a vision, because that was what confronted me on the morrow. Yes, even the questions in grammar, etc., I knew the lot in detail. My third-class pass was a great disappointment to the family. Anyway, the following Schrires made up for my shortcomings with a vengeance. I was already showing signs of being a light-brown sheep of the family, which became darker during my later varsity days.

I spent most of 1911 and 1912 at the South African College, which was at the top end of the Gardens, taking my first year B.Sc. equivalent to a first-year Medicine. I squeezed through in the company of Ben Cheifitz, who became my best pal. There were Ginger Gillis, who in later life held a high position in government service in charge of mental asylums, his pal Kotze, with a hunchback, both from Oudtshoorn, Rabkin, the *yeshiva bocher* eccentric child specialist, Ariel Goldberg, who specialised as an M.D.F.R.C.S. as a gynaecologist, remained a bachelor, for spite, and a few others whose names I have forgotten.

Prof Hahn and Dr Tietz, both typical square-heads, taught us chemistry. Hahn, overriding and quick-tempered, would bully poor Tietz, mostly in German. He claimed that all South African minerals contained radium. His favourite experiment yearly, to first-year students, was to set a diamond chip in gypsum, concentrate three Bunsen burner flames at full force on it until the stone burst into a blue flame, to show that it was pure carbon. Beattie in physics, Pearson (I think) in botany, and a Scotsman, Gilchrist, in zoology. The first Anatomy Laboratory was started (in 1912?) under Drennan, and the demonstrator was young Lennox-Gordon, newly brought out from Scotland.[67]

The Great Saccharine Venture

I must now relate THE GREAT SACCHARINE VENTURE. A fellow named Matheson (?) arrived from Russia with a wonderful scheme.[68] He induced [seduced] our family into a get-rich-quick undertaking to manufacture saccharine in powder form, 550 strength. Sam, a brand-new lawyer, was most enthusiastic, and became the business manager. Our house, having a dozen rooms, was the ideal location.

They bought mixers, utensils, heaters, zinc sheets, etc., and installed them in a couple of rooms upstairs. Meanwhile raw materials were ordered from Switzerland, consisting of "AMIDE", potassium permanganate, and I don't remember what else. When these huge wooden cases arrived, Matheson insisted on one very important condition. The final mixing must be done only by him, with no other witness present, behind locked doors. The secret was too valuable. (This is easily obtainable now.) The cases remained on the *stoep* for a while and we kids had a great time collecting some of the leaked "pot permang". This was mixed with water and we had a lovely staining material. We were cursed by many neighbours.

Square tins, to hold a pound, were ordered locally, and an additional room was stacked to the ceiling. The secret mixture, spread on trestles and covered with zinc sheets with heater below, took some time to dry out. A beautiful fine snow of white powdered flour emerged, which after being weighed, was packed into the tins, then sealed. The rest was up to Sam and Co. The stuff was sold, at a good profit, to mineral water factories and others, who found the quality as good as imported saccharine but at a much lower price. I think the retail price for small amounts was one pound, at wholesale 14 shillings, the cost being around eight shillings.

Things were booming and new premises were acquired. All I can remember is that the great chemist must have had a rush of blood to the head, and like our pals the Arabs, demanded more and more, and used the big stick. He suddenly disappeared and returned to Europe or Australia for all I know. Peeping through the keyhole, consulting the library, etc., did not help. THAT WAS THAT.

Death of my Father

My father died on 11 October 1912. He had just slaughtered a fowl in the back yard and returned to his study. He was wiping his *chalef* and placing it in its box when he dropped dead. I heard the thud and rushed in. No warning of illness till then — it was sudden and merciful.[69] Before the body was removed, a peculiar thing occurred. A well-known cripple, with twisted neck, body and hands, insisted on touching the body before it was placed in the coffin. He maintained that according to ancient lore, if a cripple touched a dead saint he would surely be cured. I don't think it worked. There was a long string of horse-drawn carriages as the funeral conveyances stopped first at Roeland Street Synagogue, where the coffin was placed on the *bimah,* and the *hesped* proceeded. The same was repeated at the Constitution Street *Beth Ha-midrash*, and again at the Ponevitzer *Beth Ha-midrash*. The Jewish shops en route closed as the cortege wended its way to No 7 Woltemade cemetery, where a large crowd had assembled from all over the Peninsula.[70]

Max and his family were in London. I was told that Max woke up in the middle of the night and felt that something had happened to Father. He cabled South Africa in the morning and was told the sad news. Here was a case of mental telepathy or what-have-you. I followed up Spiritualism from about 1915 to 1921, but dropped it later, because I was not entirely convinced of life after death. Nor am I now, but it does make you think.

I had a personal experience while in Edinburgh during the First World War. A friend of mine, Syd Horwitz, from Bloemfontein, was serving in France and would look me up whenever he came on leave. On his last leave he jokingly remarked that if he got killed, he would visit me that night and tug at my toe. Well — it happened. I later heard that it was the same night. A dream? Coincidence?

Social Life

How many of you remember the old wooden jetty, before the concrete pier was built in 1913? This was a slatted pier jutting into the sea, at the bottom of Adderley Street, and we fished with string and bent pins, through the slats (Fig. 22). We would hire a boat on Sundays and row around the ships. There was swimming as well. When I got back in 1920, the military or naval bands, also

Fig. 22: Old Pier, Cape Town, c.1911.

an orchestra, would perform on summer evenings, attended by everybody and his sweetheart. The same bands would play on the bandstand opposite the Gardens Synagogue. Where are they today?

Or the see-saw, open-sided, single decker trams that travelled up Kloof Nek Road over the pass, on to Camps Bay? The train went from Monument Station, between the trees, to Sea Point. What a thrill!

Or the Opera House, which was replaced by the General Post Office, which imported some of the best companies from overseas? The Tivoli Variety Theatre, under the grand family of Stodel, engaged many world-famous artistes.[71] They were popular and charitable families.[72] The Gradners were another outstanding Jewish family. Mr Gradner was a book-keeper and was a great help to the small Jewish and other foreign dealers in keeping their affairs in order. Mrs Gradner arrived with a Yiddish company as an attractive young actress, and was very popular.[73] What a name she made for herself in later years, devoting herself completely to charity. She will be remembered for a long time for her unstinting labours for the Old Age Home, the Orphanage, hospital visiting, the poor, and what-have-you. Mr Gradner and his son both became mayors of Cape Town.[74]

The strictly kosher Transvaal Hotel and restaurant in Caledon Street absorbed many an immigrant and was a great meeting place for upcountry *Yidden.*[75] The Zionist Hall, lower down on Hope Street, a very small place, was supervised by Mr Gitlin. He ran a small *cheder* (Solly Zuckerman was a pupil). He seemed to me to have only one eye. One of the founders of Zionism in South Africa, he acted as librarian and general factotum, learned and respected.[76] Sarah Goldblatt was the daughter of David Goldblatt the printer.[77] He edited a Yiddish paper in opposition to *Der Advokat*[78] produced by N. D. Hoffmann[79] the printer and my father. Goldblatt was a brilliant outspoken socialist yiddishist, with little pretence of orthodoxy.[80] There was not much love lost between the editors of the two papers. He left his family to go off to America, where he published a Jewish encyclopaedia, and later returned to South Africa and hawked it all over.[81] Sam's wife Sarah remembered him staying at their home in Beaconsfield, Kimberley.

The police in those days were a very friendly lot. They were mostly Scots or Irish and a fine, tolerant set. Drunks, if not in a fighting mood, were escorted to their homes and quietly handed to their wives and put to bed. The policemen were given *matzah* and kosher wine on *Pesach* and other festivals.

There was a Polish Jewess in Wells Square, next to Beinkinstadt, who was known by the name "Kapote". She would order *matzah* for *Pesach*, kosher meat for *Yom Tov*, and most likely fasted on *Yom Kippur*. After many appearances at court charged with running a brothel, she was heavily fined for the umpteenth time. This time the magistrate threatened her with imprisonment if she did not disclose:

"Who is your receiver?"
"You, your worship," was the reply.
Consternation!
"Most of the money my girls earn you take away from me in fines."

Rogge Bay, at the foot of Adderley Street, since filled in, was the place where folk used to buy fresh fish as the boats were pulled ashore. Sixpence to a shilling for a bunch of three or four silver hottentot and other varieties, just the right selection for *gefilte* fish, mostly for Friday night. Snoek, at ninepence each, were taboo for many Jews, as it was not established that it was kosher. It was then the staple food of the coloured people. Most of the fish were sold in the streets from horse-drawn carts. The moment the fish horn was sounded, all the housewives would rush out and haggling began. The best day was Friday morning, as the coloured fishermen knew who their best customers were (Fig. 23).

Fig. 23: Fish market, Cape Town, (n.d.). (S. Schrire coll.)

The farmers from the Cape Flats and the surrounding countryside would do the same, coming round loaded with peaches, apricots, grapes, etc., selling by the handful or basketful. No weighing. There were no factories, no export.[82] Grapes a penny a bunch, watermelons a tickey (three pence) or sixpence, one penny for a handful of peaches, plums, guavas, etc. There was an open market for larger lots, and Indian and Greek shops as well. I don't remember oranges by the bag before World War I. The troops passing through during World War I had a grand time lugging bags of oranges to their boats, costing them one shilling and sixpence or two shillings. Everything in the way of food was very cheap, even taking low wages into account. Luxuries like cars, radios, and other modern necessities were non-existent. Bioscopes (movies) which were only just in their infancy were a novelty. I can remember one small bioscope in Caledon Street, and Fishers and later Wolframs in Adderley Street.

Our Neighbours

From Caledon, Hanover, Harrington, Constitution and Primrose Streets, as they prospered, Jews moved up to Maynard and Mill Streets, upwards to Oranjezicht, and later to Sea Point and Rondebosch. A lot of the oldsters settled in Muizenberg — from all over South Africa. As soon as a substantial *kehilah* community came into being, a synagogue was built with the other accompaniments.

We lived at the corner of 38 Harrington Street[83] and 56 Boom Street (later called Commercial Street) which had about a dozen rooms, and was used as a boarding house. I can recall the people who were our neighbours in Harrington Street. There was Motte Bloch with his stalwart sons, who conducted a wholesale soft goods warehouse on Harrington Street, employing very few outside helpers. Each son would unpack, knock nails into wooden packing cases, do the bookwork, sweep up, etc. What a family of busy bees. They certainly deserved the great success they achieved later on St. George's Street and Johannesburg. The youngest son, Joe, who was at school with me, was in charge of the buying. He married a friend of the Mauerbergers in London, named Tiny Freudenheim. I visited them in a lovely house in London, about 1915 or '16.

Next to M. Bloch was a wholesale grocer, Yekele Hoffman (later Rabkin and Hoffman), a jovial happy-go-lucky businessman. His son, Barney, that natty popular traveller, was one of our gang. Not far from the above was Smith's Jewish bookshop. One of the sons, Jack, was at Edinburgh University with me, became a GP, and remained a bachelor. On the opposite corner was the dairy belonging to old Vilk. His two sons did well in Cape Town and Worcester in stationery and general stores. Next, one came to Gild the harness maker, Hopkins' foundry,

Winer's barber shop (his son Sam, a dentist, was my friend) and the post office, the postmaster being a tiny *Yiddishe* chap, Hurwitz. This man was a godsend to the *greeners* who only spoke Yiddish, enabling them to send money to relatives in Russia. Next came Wortreich the chemist (I think his father previously had a shoe shop not far away).

Across the road, still on Harrington Street, were the grocers Walt and Gorfinkel, then Halperin's Bakery which later became a dairy. His bakery was useful to those of us who sent *cholent* to him on Friday afternoon, to be cooked and kept piping hot overnight for Saturday lunch. Orthodox homes did not cook on the Sabbath. Now came the Clains. What a remarkable woman this widow was. Besides running a boarding house very cheaply and efficiently for young Jews, most of them in poor circumstances, she managed to feed and educate five sons and two daughters. I remember Bunch, Ginger, Harry, all good soccer players and good chaps. She later moved to Buitengracht Street and many an immigrant must have looked back most nostalgically at Mother Clain's cooking and consideration for their needs.

Opposite our house on the corner was Sandler's bottle store. The other corner belonged to the grocer Levinson. They later became wholesalers. The third corner was also a grocery shop run by the Friedmans. The previous owners, from Boer War times, were the Knoxes. Annie Friedman's older sister married Melamed, the Hansa wine man. Their neighbour was Mrs Jackson with a couple of sons, one who had a hotel in Upington and the other in later years was with Ackermans.[84]

Then one came to the Washkansky family.[85] Even after their sons were enrolled into our gang, they were always known as the "*Gruners*".[86] Next was Berman, the horse dealer, with two sons Harry and Jack, and a daughter. Harry took his own life, for reasons unknown, and Jack did well in furniture. Their house was on the corner of Butler Square, opposite the church. Idel Schwartz, the fanatical Zionist, lived in this square. He had the gift and fervour of a Hyde Park Corner speaker.[87] His daughter was Bertha Solomon, MP, one of the first women advocates in South Africa.[88]

On the other side of the street the block was ours. The Winers occupied one of the houses next to the church. In between the houses was a tiny room on the pavement, occupied by a shoemaker, and then another house and a shop. When I was a tiny nipper, before the church was built, the ground was used by the gang as a playground. A piece of old zinc roofing with sacking acted as a first aid dressing station to patch up wounds after clashes with *skollies*[89] or hapless workmen on their way to their jobs. This was just after the Boer War — and fighting fever was still unquenched.

Old bearded Greenblo (Greenblo & Stone) at the lower end of Boom Street, was a bag and bottle dealer. A batch of sons helped to make a success and build a foundation for future prosperity. They were a *balebatishe* family. Old *Bobbe* Gordon lived in Canterbury Street. She was a midwife in Neustadt, and helped to bring my brothers Max and Sam into the world, as well as hundreds of others.

On the corner of Buitenkant Street and Mill Street, was Levenstein, Schloschon the jeweller, Shapiro at the corner shop and above Mill Street, the Zuckermans who were keen Zionists,[90] as was my father.[91] At the bottom of Buitengracht Street was Shagom the watchmaker whose eldest daughter married Greenstein of Stellenbosch, dear friends of mine. There was also Weinberg Bros, makers of cardboard boxes and later printing, who later were absorbed into Herzberg Mullne, which still later became one of the main components of the Nampak Group.

In upper Harrington Street lived the Stones, Peppers, Grusd, Goldberg, Max Schrire, Israel Mauerberger[92] and the Ochbergs. Isaac Ochberg made his pile by buying a shipwrecked vessel and selling it at a nice fat profit. He deserved it because, at his own expense, he brought out a crowd of hopelessly lost and destitute war orphans after the 1914–1918 war. He was instrumental in helping to build an Orphanage in Cape Town.[93] Prisman, on the corner of Caledon Street, had a bottle store. One son became a doctor, the other a lawyer. Arcus, first in Caledon Street then next to our butchery in Canterbury Street, dealt in bicycles. Across the road was Urdang, a leather merchant. Wells Square contained that famous landmark Beinkinstadt, the shop for Jewish requirements in books, *siddurim, talaisim, tefillin, esrog, lulav, matzahs* from Manischewitz, etc.[94] He claimed that he was a "True Schrire".

Also in Caledon Street was Papert, a big man physically, selling tobacco and cigarettes,[95] and Rubin, another dealer in Jewish needs, Lehr's soda fountain and cigarettes, whose son was known as Capt. Isaac, lawyer and town councillor. I can't remember all, but can only recall a few as they come to mind. Mr Hayes, the ultra-anglicised orthodox upholsterer from England, lived next to the Gardens Synagogue. Mrs Hayes was a charming old lady, and her eldest daughter Rayna, who married Sam Kirsch, was the perfect English lady — orthodox and aristocratic. They were the *Unterfuhrers* at my wedding.

Getz, a dairyman with big feet, married a Miss Rubin, daughter of another dairy owner in Caledon Street. Her brother Marcus, a friend of mine, had a handsome Roman look. Swerling had a draper shop in Caledon Street — his sons (or nephews?) became very big wholesale fish dealers. I also remember Zion Getz — I associate the name "Zion" with eggs — and that he married Rav Mirvish's sister. Pevsner from Rhodesia took over from Herman and Canard at the top of Plein Street and also prospered. Policansky brothers, the cigarette manufacturers in Caledon Street, Star Cigarettes, rolled by hand were tops and the family prospered.[96] Every packet contained a card, and after collecting a certain amount or sequence (by swopping and begging) I managed to collect a small library of red-bound books of English literature. Besides these Lithuanians, who were in the majority, there was an influx of Kurlanders, mostly from Riga and Libau. These *Riganiks*, who came from a big European city, were inclined to put on a superior air towards the *Litvaks* and South Africans. This attitude was, and is, not forgotten. They are now leaders in commerce, and are still very fond of the good things in life. It seems they are fond of flowers. Many of them are named Blum, Bloom, Blumenau, Bloomberg, Blumenthal, etc.

Afterwards

Many of the second generation of the above, including those of many others from Cape Town, made great names for themselves, both in South Africa and overseas. Sam married Sarah Senderowitz of Beaconsfield on 8 [sic 28] Dec 1913 and moved to Kimberley. The previous week Annie[97] married Schus, both at Roeland Street *Shul*. She died in the 1918 flu epidemic. I was 17 years old when my father died, and I left District Six soon after to study medicine in Edinburgh. But that is another story.

FOOTNOTES

1 Harry Nathan Schrire (1895-1980) was the youngest son of Yehuda Leib Schrire and his wife Gela, and the only one of their children born in Cape Town. These reminiscences were later used by Gwynne Schrire in a series of articles, namely "Adapting to a New Land: The Greener in Cape Town 1900", *Jewish Affairs*, 1990, 45:5, pp. 42-46; "Mostly *Smouse*? — South African Jews and their Jobs a Century Ago", *Jewish Affairs*, 2000, 55:1, pp. 9-15; " 'Stranger in a Strange Land': Immigration Problems and Community Assistance in South Africa a Century Ago", *Jewish Affairs*, 2002, 57:4, pp. 30-34; "Avraham Meir Solomon, Abba Eban and Early Cape Zionism", *Jewish Affairs*, 2003, 58:1, pp. 27-52; "Jewish Life in District Six before World War 1: A Memoir", *Jewish Affairs*, 2008, 63:2, pp. 22-28. The present version has been partly redrafted and more extensively annotated in order to integrate it more effectively into the Diary and *Tolada* by Yehuda Leib Schrire, this volume.

2 Italics denote a foreign language, and underlining denotes a biblical or religious expression. Inserts for ease of comprehension are bracketed, as are illegible or unusual words.

3 For more extensive analyses, see Carmel Schrire and Gwynne Schrire, Context, this volume; Carmel Schrire, Discourse, this volume.

4 Sarah Senderowitz Schrire was married to his older brother Samuel (1889-1949).

5 It was actually 1892 (Schrire, *Tolada*, this volume, p. 107, stanza 28).

6 He studied at Zufran, Vilna, Volozhin, Volchenik and Alsan in Lithuania (Schrire, *Tolada*, this volume, p. 102, stanza 8).

7 Many of Reb Yehuda Leib Schrire's compositions were printed in Nechemiah Dov Hoffmann's various newspapers, including *Haor*, *Herald*, *Telegraph*, *Volkszeitung*, *Afrikaner*, *Haohev* and *Kinneret* (see Schrire and Schrire, Context, this volume, footnote 10). He also wrote a Hebrew novel Yehuda Leib Schrire, *Shoshanah Novelet* (Warsaw: Warsaw Typography Alexander Ginz, 1879), see Appendix II.6, this volume.

8 "I brought happiness ... with my singing ... I delighted them at *Shabbat* and at festivals" (Schrire, *Tolada*, this volume, p. 103, stanza 13).

9 See Schrire *Tolada*, this volume, footnote 50.

10 Toddy was Theodore Schrire (1906-1990), eldest son of Harry's brother Moshe Mordechai (Max) (1881-1953).

11 See footnote 7, this chapter, p. 179

12 This is unlikely because Sammy Marks left Neustadt in 1868 when Harry's father would have been only 17 years old (Richard Mendelsohn, *Sammy Marks. 'The Uncrowned King of the Transvaal'* [Athens: Ohio University Press, 1991] pp. 5, 206). It is surprising that the acculturated Anglo-German Jews of the Park Synagogue imported a traditionalist like Yehuda Leib Schrire. What we might be seeing here instead is an effort by the founders to ingratiate themselves with the wealthy Sammy Marks by importing a traditionalist from his home town at the behest of Globus.

13 Richard Mendelsohn in *Sammy Marks*, p. 206, says that he gave close to £1,000 to rebuild the synagogue.

14 Yehuda Leib Schrire lists his "wonderful and magnificent talents" as a teacher, *shochet*, *bodek*, cantor, violinist, baker, poet, cobbler and artist (Schrire, *Tolada*, this volume, p. 102, stanza 9).

15 Moshe Mordechai (Max) (1881-1953), Samuel (1889-1949), Annie (1891-1918), Harry (1895-1980). A sepia photograph of Yehuda Leib and his family, inscribed "1883", shows him holding a small boy, presumably Max. His wife is holding a younger child, who was presumably one of the sons that died.

16 This is a mistake, as the Wolmarans Street Synagogue was not yet in existence — Harry Schrire probably meant the Park Synagogue that opened in 1892. Richard Mendelsohn reports much friction in the community in "Oom Paul's Publicist: Emanuel Mendelssohn, founder of the first congregation," in Mendel Kaplan and Marian Robertson (eds.), *Founders and Followers. Johannesburg Jewry 1887-1915* (Cape Town: Vlaeberg Publishers, 1991), pp. 72-91.

17 Theodore (Toddy) Schrire's erudition is evident in *Hebrew Amulets: Their Decipherment and Interpretation* (London: Routledge & Kegan Paul, 1966). For a list of Yehuda Leib's writings see Appendix II, this volume. His Babylonian *Talmud* is now in the possession of his great granddaughter (CS).

18 A town in the Little Karoo in the Western Cape Province, situated about 480 km (298 miles) from Cape Town, that was the epicentre of the ostrich feather boom in the late 19th and early 20th centuries.

19 Ark of the Covenant that houses the *Torah* scrolls. This would have been the St. John's Street's *Griene Shul* built in 1892 by a breakaway, more Orthodox group of Jews from Kelme who tried to reproduce a Lithuanian *heimland* synagogue decorated with original Lithuanian-style Jewish handicraft and an ark like that in their *shul* in Kelme. The Jews from Šiauliai went to the other synagogue built on Queen Street in 1888, called *Der Englishe Shul*. See "The Jewish Community of Oudtshoorn", www.seligman.org.il/oudtshoorn_jews.html; see also Carmel Schrire, *Digging through Darkness: Chronicles of an Archaeologist* (Charlottesville and London: University Press of Virginia, 1995), pp. 12-20; Schrire and Schrire, Context, this volume, footnote 13).

Although Harry describes his father making an ark, there is some confusion here. The large Oudtshoorn ark currently housed in the C. P. Nel Museum in Oudtshoorn, is credited to having been brought to South Africa by Mr Samuel Lazarus of Oudtshoorn and placed in the *shul* in 1892 before Yehuda Leib settled in Cape Town. Correspondence asking for an ark carved by Yehuda Leib to be displayed in a cupboard in the former Jewish Museum, situated in the Old Gardens synagogue, suggests that Yehuda Leib carved a small ark whose whereabouts are unknown (T. Schrire to Jewish Museum, Cape Town, *in litt.*).

20 A number of his woodcuts, carvings and a painting were passed on to his grandson, Toddy Schrire. A characteristic carved plaque is also present in the C. P. Nel Museum in Oudtshoorn, Cape (see Appendix III, this volume, Figs III.4, III.5).

21 *Gaon* of Pumbedita, Babylon, c 906–1006 CE. See M. H., "Sherira ben Hanina Gaon", *Encyclopedia Judaica 14*, pp. 1381–1382.

22 This is hardly surprising given that the Lithuanian census of Oshmanya of 14 May 1858 registered 79 Shriras including six Shmuel Shriras and three Leib Shriras — names common to this day. Yehuda Leib's grandfather was Samuel and his son, Samuel, was the grandfather of Gwynne's brother, Samuel (see Appendix I, this volume).

23 See Schrire, Diary, this volume, p. 42.

24 Chaim Weizmann wrote that he met a wealthy Jew from Baku, an "oil man", called Shrirow, who agreed to support him on a short-term basis to do some research. *Trial and Error: The Autobiography of Chaim Weizmann* (New York: Schocken, 1966), pp. 65, 96, 100.

25 Toddy was Theodore Schrire (1906–1991) and Dave (David, 1908–1991), and Isch (Isidore, 1910–1975) were his brothers. Gwynne Schrire's brother, Samuel, met his daughters who owned correspondence between their father and Weizmann that the eponymous Institute was eager to own.

26 Rami Shrira from Kibbutz Cabri, came to visit the family in Cape Town in 1997 and was a walking history of Israel.

27 See Schrire, *Tolada*, this volume, pp. 120ff, stanzas 80ff.

28 Glass negatives of some of his photographs of the South African War are housed in the Western Cape Archives and Records Service, Schrire Collection, SH1-27.

29 Mendel Kaplan assisted by Marian Robertson, *Jewish Roots in the South African Economy* (Cape Town: C. Struik Publishers, 1986), pp. 308–324.

30 Schrire, *Tolada*, this volume, p. 129, stanza 117.

31 Letter from Theodore Herzl to Rebecca Mauerberger, June 13, 1901, The Nahum Goldman Museum of the Jewish Diaspora, Tel Aviv, Neg. no. EXH. 42.3c.29.11; see also Elie Kedourie (ed.), *The Jewish World: Revelation, Prophecy and History* (London: Thames and Hudson, 1979), p. 298 , pl. 40.

32 Morris Mauerberger (1890–1984) was born in Lazdey, Lithuania (Kaplan, *Jewish Roots*, p. 308).

33 Ackerman's Lithuanian-born father died in 1902, when he was eight. He started work as a traveller for Sacks Futeran, opening the Wynberg shop in April 1916. His son Raymond revolutionised chain stores when he established Pick n Pay. Social and environmental responsibility play a large role in the values and principles of Pick n Pay, and the Ackerman Pick n Pay Foundation supports education and literacy, health care, HIV/Aids, electricity and water accessibility, road safety, the fight against crime, feeding schemes, sport development, the disabled and housing (Kaplan, *Jewish Roots*, pp. 311–324).

34 Sam Kirsch took over Stanhope Drapery in October 1916 (see Kaplan, *Jewish Roots*, p. 312).

35 Born in Bielsk, Poland, Leon Segal (1897-1954) lost his mother when he was one year old and his father when he was 10. He came to South Africa alone, aged 11. He became the founder and joint managing director, Ackermans Ltd; vice president, Board of Directors, Greatermans; former president, Junior Zionist Society; vice-president, South Africa Jewish War Appeal; president, United Communal Fund; vice-president, Rosecourt Jewish Youth Centre; chairman and honorary life member, Jewish Board of Guardians (1942-1946); treasurer, Oranjia Cape Jewish Orphanage; director, Community Chest, and chairman and later vice president, Cape Jewish Board of Deputies (see Kaplan, *Jewish Roots*, pp. 313–318).

36 Harry Schrire managed this store in 1921 when Leon Segal went on a buying trip to England and later was appointed the manager of the Port Elizabeth branch of Ackermans (see Kaplan, *Jewish Roots*, pp. 314, 317).

37 Gus Ackerman, Sam Kirsch and Leon Segal were the founding managers of Ackermans, South Africa's first chain store group established by Morris Mauerberger in 1921 (see Kaplan, *Jewish Roots*, p. 317).

38 Although he himself did not complete high (senior) school, Mauerberger believed in the importance of education and endowed chairs in ophthalmology, neurosurgery and cardiology at the University of Cape Town. He also donated generously to the University of the Western Cape and subsidised a free clinic for poor people in Ottery, Cape. The Mauerberger Foundation has played a key role in community development in South Africa, providing bursaries to students and funding in the fields of education, women's rights, the plight of the poor and homeless, and the importance of sustainable environments.

39 *Potash and Perlmutter*, a popular 1913 comedy by Montague Glass and Charles Klein about the troubles of two partners in the garment trade — later made into a successful silent film.

40 Solomon Harris founded the South African Woollen Mills in 1925, and opened a clothing factory thereafter (see Kaplan, *Jewish Roots*, p. 319).

41 Mauerberger lost an eye in Russia when a child threw a stone at him. His nephew, Arnold, Lord Goodman, presents a scathing character sketch of the "horrible" man he called "Uncle" (Arnold Goodman, *Tell Them I'm On My Way* [London: Chapmans, 1993], pp. 73–77) .

42 Schrire, *Tolada*, this volume, p. 121, stanza 87.

43 Ibid., p. 128, stanza 115.

44 Rebecca Zuckerman's husband, Moses, was the founder of the *Bnoth Zion* Association. She was its third president, and later its honorary life president until her death in 1958. She was the mother of Solly, Lord Zuckerman (1904–1993).

45 Later the University of Cape Town.

46 Municipal districts of Cape Town. District Five lay south of District Six as drawn in a 1909 map in Vivian Bickford-Smith, *Ethnic Pride and Racial Prejudice in Victorian Cape Town* (Johannesburg: Wits University Press, 1995), pp. xxii–xxiii.

47 Rabbi M. Ch. Mirvish (1872–1947) was born in Baisogola, Lithuania, and educated at *yeshivot* in Tels and Slobodka. He came to Cape Town in 1908 as the rabbi to the *Beth Ha-midrash Hachadash* on Constitution Street. He was the first rabbi in the Cape Colony to have full *smichah* and was a founder of the Cape *Beth Din* and the Cape Board of *Shechita*. He was chairman of the United Hebrew Schools, a founder of the Jewish Aged Home, and a member of Cape Executive of the Jewish Board of Deputies from its inception. Mirvish was active in aid to Eastern European Jewish war and pogrom victims (Sidney Mirvish, *The Harris Family: From Poland to South Africa and Beyond* [Omaha, NE: Copycat, 2008], p. 29).

48 Morris Alexander (1877–1946) was born in Czinn, East Prussia, and won a scholarship to study law at Cambridge. A keen Zionist, he was president of the Roeland Street *Shul* and delivered the sermons. He was secretary of the Cape Town Jewish Philanthropic Society, and he established the Cape Jewish Board of Deputies in 1904 and chaired it until 1937. He was a member of the Town Council in 1908 and a member of Parliament from 1910 until his death, serving for many years as representative of the Castle District, which included District Six.

49 Solomon Schechter (1847-1915) was born in Focşani, Rumania, and was appointed lecturer in Talmudics and Reader in Rabbinics at Cambridge University. He recognised the old manuscripts from the Cairo *Geniza* for what they were, and brought them to Cambridge. In 1902 he was appointed second president of the Jewish Theological Seminary in New York, and founded the United Synagogue of America, later called the United Synagogue of Conservative Judaism.

50 Hoffmann refers to this function in his *Sefer Ha-zichronot*: "A few years later Prof Schechter paid a visit to his children in Cape Town. He was given a tremendous welcome at a banquet in the old synagogue ..." (Nechemiah Dov Hoffmann, *Book of Memoirs: Reminiscences of South African Jewry*, trans. from the Yiddish by Lilian Dubb and Sheila Barkusky [Cape Town: Jewish Publications-South Africa, Isaac and Jessie Kaplan Centre for Jewish Studies and Research, University of Cape Town, 1996], p. 34).

51 This was in 1909 when the Roeland Street Synagogue gave a reception to honour Schechter; see Louis Herrman, "A History of Capetown Jewry", in Morris de Saxe (ed.), *The South African Jewish Year Book. Directory of Jewish Organisations and Who's Who in South African Jewry 1929, 5689-90* (Johannesburg: South African Jewish Historical Society, 1929), p. 69.

52 The divorce of Ruth and Morris Alexander fuelled endless gossip and speculation in Cape Town, and was still remembered with horror in the home of Rebecca Schrire in the 1950s (Baruch Hirson, *The Cape Town Intellectuals: Ruth Schechter and her Circle, 1907-1934* (Johannesburg: Wits University Press, 2001).

53 They established their own *Chevrah Gemara*, where he read the *blat*. Originally held weekly, it grew, according to Hoffmann, to about 50 members who would meet every evening to study the *Gemara*. Harry recorded the *Siyyum Ha-Torah* held around *Rosh Hashanah* amid a joyous celebration (Hoffmann, *Book of Memoirs*, p. 29).

54 Rubin had a Jewish bookshop.

55 Leonard Schach (1918-1996) earned post-graduate degrees in history and law before becoming a theatrical producer and director, directing more than 300 plays. When he decided that he could no longer live in a country in which apartheid segregated his audiences, he immigrated to Israel. His final production was *Dear Anne*, based on the diary of Anne Frank, and was staged in Cape Town.

56 Solly, Lord Zuckerman (1904-1993) was a scientist and advisor to the Allies in World War II, a champion of nuclear non-proliferation and an expert on global economic issues.

57 Solomon Harris (1853-1918) came to South Africa in 1880 from Lodz, Poland. In 1911 the Harris family acquired an interest in the Waverley Wool Manufacturing Company run by his son Woolf and his son-in-law Jack Gesundheit. The Harris family built the first major textile factory in South Africa on Beach Road, Woodstock, which later became the South African Woollen Mills (SAWM) that began operating there in 1914, just before World War I. This was the real start of the blanket industry in South Africa (Neville Gottlieb, quoted in "Jewish Pioneers of the Textile Industry", in Kaplan, *Jewish Roots*, p. 286; Mirvish, *Harris Family*, p. 29).

58 Solomon Harris's children were Miriam (b. 1870) who married her uncle Harry; Woolf (b. 1873); Henry (b. 1879); Morris (b. 1881); and Bella Gesundheit (b. 1881). Harry and Miriam's daughter Hilda married Rabbi Mirvish's son Louis, one of the first two doctors to qualify in South Africa and the first gastroenterologist there. Woolf Harris was chairman, Gardens Synagogue, Oranjia Cape Jewish Orphanage, Cape Jewish Board of Deputies (1937-1942), and the Cape Chamber of Industries (Mirvish, *Harris Family*, pp. 18, 20, 31, 59).

59 Given that Jack Gesundheit joined the factory in 1913 and Solomon Harris died in 1918, the *shnoddering* (donating money for honours in the synagogue) must have occurred sometime in that interval; since Harry Schrire left Cape Town in 1912, this information must be based on hearsay.

60 Wealthier Jews like the Harrises gravitated out of District Six to more elegant properties on the mountain slopes. Around 1895 Solly Harris bought Myrtle Lodge in Schoonder Street, Gardens, at the corner of Vriende Street, where the Harris family lived in a compound.

61 For Mr Geffen, see *The Jews of District 6: Another Time, Another Place*, Exhibition catalogue, South African Jewish Museum, Cape Town, South Africa (Cape Town: Jewish Publications, Isaac and Jessie Kaplan Centre for Jewish Studies and Research, University of Cape Town, in association with the South African Jewish Museum, 2012), p. 61. Morrison was appointed beadle in 1902. See also Herrman, "Capetown Jewry", in De Saxe, *South African Jewish Yearbook*, p. 69.

62 Dr Deborah Sagorsky was the chairman, *Bnoth Zion* Association, the first woman to chair the Western Province Zionist Council (1963-1966), and honorary life president, Women's Zionist Council of South Africa.

63 The *Jewish Chronicle*, 9 January 1903, reported that "Rev. Glushak RAM [sic] left Southampton by the *Saxon* to take up his duties as reader to the New Hebrew Congregation, Roeland Street".

64 Appointed *chazan* in 1906 (Herrman, "Capetown Jewry", in De Saxe, *South African Jewish Year Book*, p. 69).

65 An 18th century house bought by the Dutch Reformed Church in 1878 that served as a teachers' training college; the Cape Town High School occupied the property from 1925 to 1957. It is now part of the Iziko Museum system.

[66] David Cohen was Chairman, Students Jewish Association; chairman, South African Legion of the British Ex-servicemen's League, the Discharged Soldiers' Rehabilitation Committee, and the Governor General's War Fund. He practised as a solicitor in Kimberley, but since racial discrimination was offensive to his sense of justice, he moved to Swaziland where he became Solicitor-General and legal adviser to King Sobhuza II. He later became a judge of the High Court. Subsequently he served as chairman, United Communal Fund; member, Western Province Zionist Council; chairman, Israel Maritime League; chairman, Jewish Board of Deputies (Cape Council) 1953–1957; and national vice-president, South African Jewish Board of Deputies.

[67] For these teachers, see Jan H. Louw, *In the Shadow of Table Mountain: A History of Cape Town Medical School and its Associated Teaching Hospitals up to 1950, with Glimpses into the Future* (Cape Town: Struik, 1969).

[68] He might have been related to M. Matuson who was a partner with Schrire and Hoffmann in *Die Judishe Folkszeitung* in 1905. See Joseph Abraham Poliva, A *Short History of the Jewish Press and Literature of South Africa From its Earliest Days Until the Present Time* (Johannesburg: Prompt Printing, n.d.), p. 17.

[69] There must have been some warning of illness because Gela Schrire's declaration in the Insolvency Court two years earlier, on 4 April 1909, describes her husband as a "chronic invalid, not able to do anything for himself" (Cape Archives, 19-9, MOIB 2/3251/991). The date given here of Yehuda Leib's death is wrong: the death certificate (Western Cape Archives and Records Service, 1912 MOOC vol. 6/9/701 ref. 2880) records the day as 9 October. His actual gravestone is also apparently wrong in that it reads 1 *Cheshvan* 5673, which implies that he died on 12 October (Gail Flesch, London, 2013, *in litt.*). In addition, inasmuch as he died at home, the certificate apparently misstates his place of death as 180 Commercial Street, Cape Town, when in fact he lived at number 80 (see Schrire, *Tolada*, this volume, footnote 171).

[70] Yehuda Leib's friend and partner in the newspaper *Die Judishe Folkszeitung*, N. D. Hoffmann, published *The Jews in South Africa: Of all Matters Concerning Jews and Judaism in South Africa* in 1916. It was the first Yiddish book printed in South Africa. In it he included a photograph and obituary of his friend (see Hoffmann, *Book of Memoirs*, pp. 39–40) as well as a lament for him by Mr B. Turtledove (ibid., p. 39). See also, Naomi Dison Kaplan, "A lament on the death of Yehuda Leib Schrire", *Jewish Affairs*, 2009, 64:2, pp. 28–29.

[71] Harry Stodel bought the Tivoli Music Hall on Darling Street in 1910, which supplied Cape Town with a continuous string of overseas musical and variety artists. In 1908 he established a film-distribution agency and in 1912 he bought the Alhambra Theatre, St. George's Street, Cape Town. Later he became the Cape Town director for I. W. Schlesinger's African Theatres.

72 Harry Stodel, born in London in 1869, became a town councillor for the Gardens Constituency; a director of Africa Theatres Trust Ltd, the African Film Co; chairman of the Peninsula Licensed Victuallers' Association; choirmaster, Gardens Synagogue; member, *Chevrah kadisha*; a great contributor to the Russian-Jewish Relief Fund; active in various philanthropic organisations (Hoffmann, *Book of Memoirs*, p. 31).

73 Her daughter, Vera Gradner Blumberg, was equally popular and charitable as was her granddaughter, Adele Searll (1939–1998), who campaigned for the treatment of drug abuse.

74 Louis Gradner was mayor from 7 September 1933 to 5 November 1935. Walter Gradner was mayor from 3 September 1965 to 7 September 1967.

75 The minute book of the Cape Town Jewish Philanthropic Society (1897–1903) gives the Transvaal Restaurant, Caledon Street, as the address of six of its applicants for assistance.

76 Jacob Gitlin was the honorary secretary, *Dorshei Zion* Asssociation for over 40 years and became the first chairman of the Western Province Zionist Council, 1943-1952 and later its life president. Today, the Jacob Gitlin Library in Cape Town bears his name.

77 Goldblatt's daughter, Sarah, was also the literary executor of the Afrikaans poet, C. J. Langenhoven.

78 Harry Schrire is mistaken. It was David Goldblatt who published *Der Yiddisher Advocat* from 1904 to 1914. His father and Hoffmann launched *Die Judishe Folkszeitung*, which was published from 11 September 1905 to October 1905 (Poliva, *Short History*, p. 28). Hoffmann wrote that "a friend of my youth Reb Y L Schrire (of sacred memory) became my partner with the co-operation of a Warsaw Jew, Mr M Mathuson. However, owing to financial circumstances this partnership only lasted 6 months" (Hoffmann, *Book of Memoirs*, p. 55).

79 The pioneer of Yiddish journalism in South Africa, Nechemiah Dov Hoffmann (1860–1928), was born in Gavre, Lithuania, and came to South Africa in 1890 bringing with him Hebrew-Yiddish type-sets, hoping to establish himself as a journalist and publisher in South Africa. He was an ambitious, if unsuccessful, journalist who wrote for the European Yiddish papers, including the Warsaw daily *Hatzefirah* and *Hamelitz*. In South Africa he was involved in at least seven attempts to publish Yiddish newspapers, none of which lasted very long — his bad temper did not help. His book, *Sefer Ha-zichronot* (1916), which contains an obituary of his friend, Reb Schrire, was the first book in Yiddish to be published in South Africa.

80 Born in Radom, Poland, David Goldblatt (with Morris Alexander) arranged a successful deputation to visit the attorney-general to change a clause in the Immigration Act preventing Yiddish-speakers from entering the Cape Colony. Goldblatt published a brochure, *Yiddish — is it a European Language?* (*Jewish Advocate*, Cape Town, 1905). The two men established the Cape Jewish Board of Deputies. Goldblatt published a number of Yiddish newspapers here, including *Der Kriegstraphet*, *Der Yiddisher Advocate* and *Afrikaner Telegraph*. In 1914 he moved to New York.

81 *Die Algemeine Illustrierte Enziklopedia*, 1905.

82 It was not quite as simple as this; the wool, wine and veld product (feathers, skins) industries began long before the main thrust of Jewish immigration and certainly long before he was born.

83 The 1899 Juta's *Cape Town and Suburban Directory* lists Scheire L, Butcher, 38 Harrington Street and Scheira, Mrs, Boarding House, Leicester House, 56 Boom Street. The 1904 Cape Town directory lists Louis Schira as living at 62 Harrington Street.

84 Born in Cork, Ireland, Abraham Jackson (1884-1967) came to South Africa in 1900 and was chairman, Furniture Traders' Committee; president and life trustee of the Green and Sea Point Hebrew Congregation; president of both the Cape Town Hebrew Congregation and of the Jewish Orphanage; chairman of the Cape Jewish Board of Deputies (1946-1948); former chairman, United Council of Orthodox Hebrew Congregations; chairman, Revisionist Movement; member, Provincial Council representing Sea Point; life member, Cape Peninsula Council, United Party, and chairman of its Sea Point Division; member, Cape Peninsula Cemeteries Board of Trustees; member, SANTA; director, Community Chest; chairman, Sea Point Public Library; chairman, Sea Point Boy's School committee; treasurer, United Relief, Reconstruction and Orphan's Fund. He was known as the "fighting Irishman" and was militant in his opposition to those matters with which he could not agree.

85 In 1967 Louis Washkansky became the first human recipient of a heart transplant. The Professor of Cardiology and a leader of the transplant team transplant was Harry's nephew, Velva (Va) Schrire, Sam's son, who enjoyed an international reputation. He graduated from the University of Cape Town medical school with 10 gold medals and four scholarships and went on to establish the Cardiac Clinic at Groote Schuur Hospital. He authored many books and papers and received many fellowships and honours. See Lawrence William Piller, *The Cardiac Clinic: Groote Schuur Hospital 1951-1972: The Schrire Years* (Cape Town: Groote Schuur Hospital Cardiac Clinic, 2000).

86 Probably meaning *grienes*, newcomers.

87 One of the founders of the *Dorshei Zion* Society

88 A leading suffragette and proponent for women's rights. As a Member of Parliament, Solomon was responsible for the passing of the Married Women's Property Act — previously the husband had controlled his wife's assets. In 1938 she established a soup kitchen for the poor in Jeppestown, Johannesburg, which she operated for 20 years and which developed into the Bertha Solomon Recreation Centre.

89 *Skollie* (Afrikaans) is a ruffian, street gangster.

90 Moses Zuckerman, a keen member of the mens' *Dorshei Zion* Association, founded the *Bnoth Zion* Association for women. His wife, Rebecca Zuckerman, became its third president, lived to witness the birth of the State of Israel, and remained involved as honorary life president until her death in 1958.

91 Reb Yehuda Leib Schrire established the short-lived *Bnei Zion* Society in 1897.

92 Born in 1879, Israel Mauerberger was one of the founders, Cape Board of Hebrew Education.

93 Isaac Ochberg (1879-1937) was born in Uman, Ukraine, Russia, and came to Cape Town in 1895. He became a successful businessman and property developer. Life president of the *Dorshei Zion* Society, he represented South Africa at a World Zionist Congress in Switzerland and made generous bequests to purchase land in Israel and to the Hebrew University of Jerusalem. He named one of his buildings on Adderley Street, Cape Town, "Balfour House" and a street in his Edinburgh estate in Claremont "Balfour Avenue", in honour of the Balfour Declaration of 1917 that mandated the establishment of the State of Israel. Member of Cape Executive of the Jewish Board of Deputies, vice president of the Roeland Street Hebrew Congregation, and active in the Hebrew Order of David, he identified strongly with the community's welfare concerns and worked for the Helping Hand Society, the Old Aged Home and the Jewish Orphanage. His daughter, Bertha Epstein, wrote that he did not confine himself solely to the alleviation of distress among Jewry but was always ready to proffer help whenever and wherever it was needed, irrespective of race, colour or creed. As president of the Jewish Orphanage, he was responsible for bringing out 200 Jewish war orphans from the Ukraine in 1921 with permission from General Smuts. He had travelled to the Ukraine after the civil war with much difficulty and danger and spent three months visiting orphanages all over the war-ravaged countryside to rescue these children and bring them back with him to South Africa.

94 Beinkinstadt, like Yehuda Leib Schrire, came from Oshmanya, and founded a Jewish bookshop in District Six that became a meeting place for immigrants and the main source of Jewish books and ceremonial objects until it closed in 2008. Hoffmann said it became the largest bookshop in South Africa within 10 years (Hoffmann, *Book of Memoirs*, p. 46; Mendelsohn and Schein, p. 76-77). In the early years he imported Manischewitz *matzoth* from Cincinnati. His daughter, Bertha, published an anthology of poem translations from the Hebrew and Yiddish in 1930 (Bertha Beinkinstadt, *An Anthology of Poem Translations* [Cape Town: City Printing Works, 1930]).

95 Born in 1851 in Wilkomir, Israel Mordecai Papert was active in educating the youth and frequently got into trouble for promulgating his ideas about the Enlightenment. He moved to London where he started a tobacco business and then re-located to Cape Town where he did the same. He was a poet, scholar and essayist, devoted his time to Zionist causes, became president of the *Bikkur Cholim* and served on the educational committee of the *Talmud Torah* school (Hoffmann, *Book of Memoirs*, pp. 41-45).

96 The Policansky brothers were born in Russia and learned their trade through contacts with Turkish soldiers who rolled cigarettes. They opened a cigarette factory on Plein Street that employed 80 to 160 workers.

97 Annie Schrire (1891-1918) was Yehuda Leib's only daughter.

5. A DISCOURSE ON THE AUTHORS OF THE SCHRIRE MANUSCRIPTS

Carmel Schrire

None of the three manuscripts in this book has been published before nor subjected to critical analysis. This essay is an attempt to scrutinise them in order to try to gain some deeper insight into the authors and their world.

Our earliest manuscript is the diary of Yehuda Leib Schrire. It was written in or around 1893 and describes events between April 1892 and November 1893.[1]

Although we call it a "diary", it is not a daily log and the uniformity of script, pen and ink, and narrative flow suggest that it was transcribed from earlier versions and notes. This is patent in the inclusion of non-narrative elements such as the section on "Israel and its Baggage" or "The Sins of my People and his Goods", that was apparently first written in Yiddish and later translated into Hebrew for inclusion here. Likewise, discourses on gold mining and indigenous people were also added later. In addition, odd pages carry apparent reminders or prompts, such as a page with a Yiddish poem, and another with a run of calculations of Hebrew dates ending in the Gregorian year 1893. Most touching is the name and address of Nechemiah Dov Hoffmann, journalist, publisher, writer and scholar, and, above all, a man who counted Yehuda Leib Schrire as one of his "dearest friends",[2] which reads "Hoffmann bros, Hottentos [sic] Kloof Ceres".[3] It is clear that he expected this diary to be read because he refers on occasion to a "reader" or "dear reader". More specifically, he notes that it was written for himself and his sons, in order that they might benefit from his observations and learn geography.

The timeline of the narrative runs for about 18 months from April 1892 to November 1893. On 21 April 1892 Yehuda Leib began his preparations to leave Europe for Africa. He travelled from Neustadt to his birthplace at Oshmanya near Vilna, in order to further his practical religious studies prior to leaving for Africa, and at the same time to say goodbye to his beloved parents. Six weeks later he returned home, packed his books and food (having sent his clothes on ahead) and travelled by steam train through Germany via Berlin and Hamburg to his port of departure in Vlissingen (Flushing), Holland. Boarding the steam ship *Dunbar Castle*, he reached Las Palmas on 14 July 1892 and then sailed for the Cape. After a brief stopover, he set off for Johannesburg by train and wagon and arrived there on 8 August 1892. His sojourn was briefer than he had expected and he returned to the Cape on 1 November 1893.

The overall tone of the Diary differs radically from the mordant *gravitas* of his later epic poem, or *Tolada,* possibly because the diarist was almost 20 years younger than he was when he penned the poem and could still rhapsodise about the sweetness of his life.[4] This doesn't mean his diary was always optimistic. Threads of conflicting emotions are braided through the narrative; there is his wrenching decision to leave his family and travel to Africa, a decision whose implications roar in on him repeatedly. He weeps with his parents, with his wife, his eldest son and, later, alone as his journey proceeds. Tears pour down his face on leaving his family and he "melted like wax ... with tears" at the prospect of leaving them.[5] Anxiety overwhelms him at times; he worries about money constantly and his original excitement about "the good hope shining on me from Africa"[6] wavers when he meets the rabbi in Cape Town. Even before he reaches Johannesburg "my heart told me that in Africa I was not going to do well".[7] Once there, the "good hope" withers and dies in the face of the irreligious community he had come to serve. He falls out with them within a few weeks. He tries unsuccessfully to support himself in other ways before deciding to return to Lithuania. In anger he sends off a bitterly critical Yiddish article entitled "Israel and its Baggage" or "The Sins of my People and his Goods", later copying it into the diary in Hebrew. In this article he attacks the entire Johannesburg Jewish community, including its synagogues, rabbis, organisations and various functionaries. He calms himself with nicotine, being "addicted to this wretched desire ... this bad habit", and he smokes twice as much when he is angry, even though he knows that this pleasure "would eat half of my flesh".[8]

A striking aspect of the diary is its attention to detail. The author's intellectual fervour is revealed by the fact that before leaving home he sent his chest of clothes ahead and carried his treasured science and religious books with him. Passing through strange lands he is inspired by new things and is compelled to try and understand and record the world around him. Although like many Jews at that time, he had never studied science, his meticulous attention to detail goes beyond geography, evoking the intensity of a nineteenth-century naturalist or "natural philosopher" as he happens upon something new.

Take for example his description of a life jacket, that even includes the way it would help to retrieve a drowned body:

> *... it was made out of square pieces of cork trees sewn together on a strong piece of material like a woman's apron with six strings of linen attached to it, two to tie around one's neck, two on one's body and two under one's knee, so that all one's body from the face and neck until the knee would be covered with a thick dress from a cork tree the width of three fingers, and if one*

> *were to lie in the water with one's face down, one would not sink into the depths of the sea.*[9]

More poetic is his rendition of the wharf at Vlissingen:

> *The walls of the mountain on the other side were built of strong stones from the foundation to the top like the wall of a fortification. ... The noise of the waves sounded loudly and forcefully with foam on the top of the water like a foaming pot. The force of the water hit the mountain wall and the waves washed very strongly backwards and then forwards again ... I did not feel any wind. The air was tranquil and quiet and when I turned to the sea I saw the waves shining like gold and sparkling with precious stones from the sun's rays before she collected up her light and a cold wind blew on me.*[10]

More mundane is his clinical description of a seasick passenger:

> *... his friend was also lying down like a beaten corpse, his mouth vomiting whatever he had eaten with great pain. A little bit of green water [bile] was washing down from his mouth and nose.*[11]

His blunt account of his brothers sounds like the old countdown "Ten Green Bottles", in that two died young, two went to America and were swallowed up, and the fifth was dispatched by a wife who was not only an adulteress but also a murderess.[12] He has no qualms about describing how sewage is handled on board ship ("clean hollow pipes pass with water to wash away all vomit and faeces.")[13] nor in telling how he was nearly swept overboard when he went to pee over the side.[14]

The dominant characteristic of Yehuda Leib Schrire, however, is not his lucid observations of people and places, nor his temper, his contentiousness and his restless soul, but his faith. He has many roles — as a ritual slaughterer, a cantor and a teacher — and on occasion, he seems more than anything like a wandering man looking for a place to settle. But whatever he may seem to be, he knows who he is: an Orthodox Jew, devoted to the teachings and precepts of his forebears and primed at all times to recognise his ancient enemies.

Consider his wary defensiveness in Vlissingen:

> *The owner of the hotel too was not Jewish and mocked the Jewish guests and watched our movements. I ate a small piece of cake that I had taken with me secretly to use for a* Kiddush. *I had hidden it from their eyes because I did not want them to say the people of Israel were always hungry.*[15]

In contrast to this is his instinct for his own kind. On *Shabbat*:

> *I noticed a man go out holding hands with his wife. Their faces were Jewish faces, only [he had] a pipe in his mouth and a thing for the protection from rain [umbrella] in his hand. From afar they also looked at me. I said to the boy who stood next to me: "Please go and follow him and look where they are going because their faces are the faces of Jews but their doings are the doings of* goyim.*" Fifteen minutes later the boy came back and said: "You saw well. Let's go to the synagogue because they went there too."*[16]

His orthodoxy never flags. It is unthinkable that he should ride on *Shabbat*, and dragging his crippled leg he walks the long distance to the ship at Vlissingen:

> *I found three honest people who came with me and we walked according to my ability. Drops of sweat poured from me, and my hands were wet with water but in my heart I was happy because I was honouring* Hashem *and the Sabbath when I went walking about two Russian* versts *on my pathetic legs.*[17]

Adherence to his faith is not congruent with gentleness or acceptance nor does it mean that he is forgiving and tolerant in his dealings with Jews who do not meet his standards of orthodoxy. He excoriates the rabbi of Neustadt as a smooth-tongued snake, and his *rebbitzin* as "born to her parents, scum of the earth and nameless".[18] He shortens his old-fashioned coat before reaching Johannesburg, in anticipation of the distaste that would come his way for his sartorial orthodoxy, yet when the English Jews there insist that he shave his side locks and further tailor his clothes, his outrage turns to scorn. He defies them by refusing to socialise with President Kruger at the inauguration of the Park Synagogue, and deliberately uses Yiddish or Hebrew on this occasion, ostensibly to reach the Russian Jews, but implicitly to challenge his English audience. He dismisses a rabbi from Grodno as "frivolous"[19] and likewise the English Rev. Ornstein of Cape Town as lacking in the spirit of the *Torah*.[20] I had always imagined that ignorance, like uniqueness, was unqualifiable. Yehuda Leib employs three levels to denigrate his colleagues: one *chazan* is "... not a very small ignoramus", Rev. Harris is a "simple ignoramus", and Rev. Wolfers a "real ignoramus".[21] He occasionally tempers his contempt with irony, as in his prediction that the dead might not be able to rise if their coffins were secured with iron pegs or when mocking an ostentatious gold watch worn by the president of the *Chevrah kadisha*.

On a broader level, his diary presents Yehuda Leib on the verge of a major transition. For all the comfort and strength of conviction that he draws from his orthodoxy, the *Reb* is about to be catapulted from membership in an oppressed European minority to the upper reaches of the social pyramid, as part of the ruling white minority in the British colonial world. His *shtetl* life is over, and with it the constraints and controls that governed that small universe are in the process of being reconfigured in a transplanted immigrant community at the far reaches of the world.

He realises this more fully in his second manuscript, the epic poem that we call *Tolada.* Its narrative overlaps to some extent with that of the Diary, but continues for 17 years thereafter, ending in 1910. Its uniformity of script and ink suggests that it might have been transcribed in one go at this time.[22] It is a story whose basic outline resembles that of many other immigrant autobiographies, with their struggles, hopes and joys. What makes this one so different — and certainly it is without peer in South African immigrant Jewish literature — is its particular format as a lyrical poem which incorporates the formal language of biblical and religious tracts ("songs and epigrams", says its title) into a late nineteenth- early twentieth-century narrative. Its first translation was commissioned by Carmel Schrire without annotations.[23] However, these are such an integral part of the text that the present translator agreed to cross-reference them in order to emphasise the breadth of scholarship and erudition of the author. Given the unlikelihood that Yehuda Leib ever spoke this way — a perfectly colloquial voice emerges in his Diary — he might deliberately have chosen this mock-heroic voice for the *Tolada*, so as to confer *gravitas* upon his narrative and thus to transform a typical immigrant saga into something more weighty and important.

Yehuda Leib was familiar with the world of learning, having penned a number of texts himself; but this *Tolada* was a private thing. It was never intended for publication. Instead, like the Diary, its purpose was to serve as a "souvenir ... forever and ever" which would educate his descendants about the facts, joys and sorrows of his life and encourage them to work hard, keep their faith and make honest and moral decisions at all times.[24]

The first third of *Tolada* reiterates some of the events related in the Diary. It covers his birth in 1851 in Oshmanya, Vilnius (now Belarus), and goes on to describe how he travelled first to a *yeshiva* and later on to Kovno and Lodz where he picked up numerous skills, both religious (cantor and ritual slaughterer) and mundane (violinist, baker and cobbler).[25] In 1879 he married Gela Globus and moved to Warsaw where he encountered the new Emancipation movement. He went on to spend the next eight years in Neustadt Sugind as a ritual slaughterer and cantor. Around this time he was invited to go and minister to the English Jews on the burgeoning goldfields of Johannesburg, and the prospect of a new life and a stable income pleased him.[26] He landed at the Cape in 1892 and went on from there to Johannesburg. As things turned out it was a bad fit all round: Schrire despised his congregation of English Jews with their ostentation and lack of piety, and in return, he smarted at their contempt for his traditional ways.[27] He left 15 months later, fully intending to return to Lithuania, but on his arrival in Cape Town he was offered a job and he decided to settle there.

The *Tolada* now continues where the Diary leaves off. Yehuda Leib set up a home for his family in Cape Town. He and his wife made their living by working in a butcher's shop, while he diversified (as we now say) working as a cantor, slaughterer, teacher and leader of his flock. The economic boom engendered by the South African War (1899–1902) engulfed the Schrires and they prospered to such an extent that by the time the war was over they owned 11 rental properties as well as a boarding house.[28] Unfortunately, at this point, a cascade of misfortunes began: in 1901 bubonic plague hit the Cape and Gela apparently succumbed. Fearing for her life, Yehuda Leib shipped the family abroad and settled in Frankfurt where he met up with his elderly parents. No sooner had he relaxed in a city he called the "eternal miracle"[29] than they were threatened with ruin: after the war, refugees from the Witwatersrand went home, and this, together with the post-war depression (1903–1909) left rental properties without paying tenants. The Schrires had no choice; their gold had turned to dross. Leaving one son behind they returned to the Cape where, in the face of imminent bankruptcy, they resumed working in the meat trade.

Unlike the engaging tone of the Diary with its ebullient embrace of new sights and vile people, the *Tolada* presents life as a relentless and often bitter struggle. Yehuda Leib portrays himself as a victim of circumstance, a decent man, buffeted by fate and circumstances. Happiness is transient and nothing good lasts long. His achievements dissolve like sea foam, success vanishes like a "spider's web" or "melting snow", or is "washed away by the chimneys of the sky".[30] By the time he is 50 years old he feels as though he has been a slave for most of his life.[31] Turning inward, he blames himself for his tribulations: in spite of all his youthful skills and education, he seems always to have lacked "sense [and] purpose", lurching from joy to despair as he "escaped from one danger and fell into another".[32] When he made the biggest decision of his life, to go to the "tumultuous city" of Johannesburg, the frivolity, ignorance and acculturated nature of the community sent him scuttling back to the orthodoxy of his European home. He was deflected by an offer in Cape Town, only to see its promise evaporate almost immediately. No sooner did things look up in Cape Town than his wife was struck by the plague. Running, as it were, for their lives, they set sail for Europe only to see their youngest child crash down to the deck of the ship. They recovered in "jolly Frankfurt" only to have their daughter fall deathly ill. No sooner does she recover than the economy at the Cape collapses taking their new-found assets along with it. In a sad coda, they return to the Cape, where the humiliation of insolvency slams the lid on their hopes of prosperity.[33]

He is not imagining this nor is it simply a matter of the way he looks at the world. Misfortunes do seem to strike continuously and he records them with relish so that his children will know how it was and how it felt so that they might, on occasion, they might cut him a break when they realise why the old man often seemed preoccupied and anxious.

The final manuscript presented here was written by Yehuda Leib's youngest son Harry Nathan (1895–1980). Like his father, Harry compiled his memoir for his children, remarking with a dry humour that is singularly lacking in his father's work: "Before I become decrepit, and while my memory still functions, with gentle urgings from my family and friends, I willingly submit these efforts."[34] It is easy to understand their encouragement. The memoir reveals a prodigious memory for names and events in the 17 years between 1895 and 1912. He describes his childhood growing up in and around District Six, his family and his friends. He goes door by door in an extended riff on "Jewish Geography", itemising who lived where, what they did, and what became of them. The pranks of his friends, who were known as the "Harrington Street Loafers", are related[35] as are tales of the synagogue and community. Interwoven with all these details is a picture of his father Yehuda Leib up to his death in 1912.

Unlike his father's Diary, and completely unlike the *Tolada*, this account is written by an outwardly self-deprecating man, whose own achievements are often dwarfed by those of others. It begins in the Old Country, expanding here on the early life of his father and continues thereafter in a more autobiographical framework. South Africa in the early twentieth century is bursting with social and economic promise for its new, immigrant populations. Gone are the many constraints and regulations that bound the Jews of East Europe into their communities, excluded by religion and culture from the upper reaches of society.

Here, in their new diasporic world, the emigrants have become part of a European, white society in a British colony, with ties to a new Motherland of Great Britain. Jewish children are trilingual. Their horizons stretch beyond the confines of *cheder* and religious schools. Some become professionals and businessmen, and the most successful hone their skills in London and Edinburgh. In due course many achieve international fame in science, commerce and philanthropy, endowing institutions with reputations undreamed of when they and their parents first stumbled ashore at the wharf at Cape Town.

Harry's Memoir bridges the confines of Jewish Eastern Europe and the expanses of South Africa. No one personifies this link better than the *pater familias*, Yehuda Leib Schrire. By the time the Memoir really gets going, he is no longer the itinerant immigrant of his Diary and the early *Tolada*, but a Cape Town resident, settled there with his wife and children. His fortunes are admittedly unpredictable, buffeted as they are by economic booms and busts, but he has survived and flourished by virtue of his ability to re-invent himself. He juggles a judicious mixture of *chazones*, religious study, violin playing, woodwork, journalism, butchery and ritual slaughtering, while his wife Gela runs a boarding house and butchery. The same strong sense of identity that propelled him out of the unorthodox ministry in Johannesburg holds fast. He knows who he is and he thinks he knows what his children will become: they are raised to read and write in three languages, and to observe the strict rituals of Orthodox Judaism. Yehuda Leib remains adamant about what he believes in and what is his due, and he is not intimidated by local personalities like the guest cantor at the *shul* whose father purloined his composition, nor indeed by visiting dignitaries like Professor Solomon Schechter who failed to meet his high standards of religious observance.[36]

Detailed analysis of his parents is not to be found here. Harry presents them as active, bustling members of a new world, and never probes their health or moods[37] nor does he mention his father's thwarted desire to be somewhere else. Being the youngest, he was only 17 years old when Yehuda Leib died suddenly in 1912. His death, when it comes, is somehow shocking. His passing saddened many people who looked to this small, bright-eyed man as an anchor to the past and a guide to the future.

Before concluding, let's try and dig a little deeper into the patriarch himself. In *Heshel's Kingdom*, elegiac memoir of his grandfather, Dan Jacobson has only one photograph and a spectacle case to add to the memories of his grandfather and is forced to draw on their shared genetic legacy to illuminate his own past and

Fig. 24: Yehuda Leib Schrire with his wife Gela and two sons, Vilna, 1883. (G. Schrire coll.)

Fig. 25: The Schrire family, Cape Town, May 1895. (C. Schrire coll.)

Fig. 26: The Schrire family, Cape Town, c.1897. L. to R. Harry, Gela, Annie, Max, Yehuda Leib and Sam. (C. Schrire coll.)

future.[38] Unlike Jacobson, we have a rich archive of writings as well as images and art with which to explore Yehuda Leib. Our photographic collection spans more than three decades (1883-1914) and includes formal studio portraits as well as casual family snapshots. He appears as a small, pale-eyed, neat-featured man, fully bearded in accord with the Orthodox tradition. The earliest studio portrait was taken in Lithuania in 1883, and shows him and his wife, each holding a child, the larger of whom appears to be his oldest son, Max, and the younger one, a son who must have died in infancy (Fig. 24).[39] A later studio portrait of the family taken in 1895 when he was 44 years old (Fig. 25) shows him in his top hat and long black coat, carrying a long cane, and this sartorial formality is repeated in three further views taken in 1897, including two portraits (see Schrire, Diary, this volume, Figs. 18, 19) as well as a full family scene (Fig. 26). In contrast we also have two rare informal snapshots. In the first, he sits with his wife and three youngest children at the dining table wearing his everyday clothes, sporting small, wire-rimmed glasses and a gold watch chain (Fig. 27). In another, apparently taken on the same day, he poses in his ritual regalia while his daughter, Annie, stands proudly next to him, clutching the back of a chair (Fig. 28). These casual images belie the implied prosperity of the studio portraits by showing clearly that these are not rich people. The faded wallpaper, mismatched table legs and scuffed bentwood chairs all speak of a frugal existence. Bulging bags stacked up against the wall suggest that a journey might be in the offing and this, together with the absence in both shots of his eldest son, suggests that these pictures were probably snapped by Max, an aspiring photographer intent on capturing these images before the family left him behind to sail to Europe in 1901 (see Fig. 9, this volume).[40]

A view of the couple in Cape Town, that might date around 1905-9, conveys a certain propriety in the placement of his right hand on the back of her neck (Fig. 29). A later, formal portrait taken for public display, reveals the strain of his advanced years and his fine features; his beard is white now and his face is lined (Fig. 30). Our final image of Yehuda Leib brings everyone together as if for a grand finale. It shows three generations decked out in their finest with white starched collars for the men and lace for the women. The patriarch sports a full white beard and is dressed in his long coat and cap. The baby on his lap is his youngest Cape Town grandson, Isidore (Isch), who was born in December 1910, suggesting that the picture must date to the following year, 1911. The author of the Memoir, Harry, aged 16, stands behind his father. Although the shabby walls and handdrawn dartboard suggest that they are posing in the back yard of their home, the photograph was apparently taken by a professional photographer, J. Kagan of Cape Town. Yehuda Leib Schrire looks every inch the *pater familias*, surrounded by the family that he has reconstituted out of his East European past. He seems to be rich in love and happily settled in the sunshine of a burgeoning new land (Fig. 31).

His grandson, Toddy Schrire, who was a small child when Yehuda Leib died in 1912, recalled that his grandfather was a man who made people laugh, adding that he was nicknamed the "cap maker of Cape Town" for his ability to top a story with the

Fig. 27: The Schrire family at dinner in Cape Town, c. 1901. From left, Harry (6), Gela (45), Sam (12), Annie (10) and Reb Yehuda Leib (50). (C. Schrire coll.)

Fig. 28: Yehuda Leib Schrire and his daughter, Annie, at home in Cape Town, c. 1901. (C. Schrire coll.)

Fig. 29: Yehuda Leib and Gela Schrire, in the fullness of their years in Cape Town, c. 1905-09. (C. Schrire coll.)

perfect aphorism, much as a hatter fits his client with the absolutely correct hat. I think he said "*kapelush makher*", which I am told might denote a complicated etymological usage.[41] On the other hand, his great-grandson, Jonathan Schrire, who never knew the Old Man, sees the *Tolada* as a "hymn of unhappiness and even bitterness" that gives, what he calls:

> *... a deeply unimpressive picture of a man who can't keep a job or earn a living, who is filled with self-pity, who withdraws into the contentious world of communal Jewish life, leaving his wife to go out into the real world (albeit as a slum landlord), to grow their assets, and deal with the legalities until their whole enterprise collapses into insolvency.*[42]

Fig. 30: Yehuda Leib Schrire, official portrait c. 1911-12, retrieved from display in unspecified context in Cape Town (C. Schrire coll.).

"Deeply unimpressive" may be going too far. Gela was certainly no victim. A portrait taken in her late forties shows a handsome, confident woman, her wig conferring stature while her gold rings, chain and fob watch imply prosperity (Fig.32). Then as now it was common for Jewish women to work and Gela worked alongside Yehuda Leib for many years, until 1909 when she herself testified that her husband was too ill to work.[43] True, the episode when Yehuda Leib breaks the quarantine restrictions in both Cape Town and London and exposes innocent people to what he imagines to be bubonic plague reveals a high degree of social irresponsiblity.[44] Yehuda Leib does not deny his faults, and spends a lot of time recording his mistakes as a man like any other, being smart and stupid, moral and venal, elated and depressed, open-minded and dogmatic, all at one and the same time. Despite often feeling that the waters are closing over his head he nevertheless finds time to contribute meaningfully to his new, diasporic life — founding the first Zionist society in Cape Town,[45] establishing the first *Talmud Torah*, running study groups, while all the time writing and teaching in pre-Ben Yehuda Hebrew in order to promote Zionism by resurrecting Hebrew as a modern language.[46]

Nevertheless, Jonathan has unwittingly hit on the dark undercurrents in the *Tolada*. Throughout its narrative the author seems unable to understand why, as a decent, honest man, bad things keep happening to him. It is hard to gauge the depth of his frequent bouts of depression, despair and self-reproach and given the

Fig. 31: The Schrire family, Cape Town, 1911. Standing L. to R. Sam, Annie, Harry, Max. Seated L. to R. Gela with David, Yehuda Leib with Isidore (Isch), Rebecca with Theodore (Toddy). (C. Schrire coll.)

happy family photograph that was shot in the very same year that the epic poem was penned, one might be tempted to view them as exaggerations. But the ups and downs in his woeful chronicle are nothing compared to a revelation found in the very last stanzas of the poem, where he confesses that his whole life has been a failure! Neither he nor his wife have achieved their greatest aim, namely, to make *aliyah*, and return to the nest by settling in Palestine and Jerusalem. This, he insists, was their only wish throughout their time in Africa, and one that to his despair, they have not fulfilled.[47]

This grim admission seems to come out of nowhere. Although his Zionism is patent in his teachings and his scholarly language, Palestine itself is largely if not altogether absent in the memoirs of this Jewish father, reverend, butcher, scholar, artist and landlord. So the question now is, given that his South African family had taken root in this new land, how genuine was his self-castigating regret that he had not settled in the Holy Land? Perhaps he never actually had the means to go, but he mentions two opportunities: first after he left the goldfields in 1893 bound for Oshmanya, he might have joined a larger pilgrimage to Palestine;[48]

and second in 1901, when he left the Cape and chose to go not to Palestine but to Frankfurt, "a good town in Israel".[49] As things turned out he regretted both moves quite quickly, falling as he so often did a victim to a series of economic disasters over which he had no control. Yet the fact remains that on neither occasion did he actually make tracks for the Holy Land. Instead, he settled in Cape Town and lived his life as a Zionist in the Jewish diaspora.

Fig. 32: Gela Schrire in her prime, Frankfurt-am-Main, c.1901-03. (C. Schrire coll.)

It seems that this residency did not bring him the peace and contentment he craved, and nowhere is this anguish more patent than in his art, where his carvings and paintings may be read as an evocative expression of his predicament. Those pieces that survive and are catalogued in Appendix III were probably all fashioned in Cape Town, yet despite the fact that he was living at the foot of the most powerful iconographic symbol in Africa, he carves the place name only once and never ever depicts the mountain backdrop that cradles the town.[50] Instead, his work resonates with his longing for Palestine in its reiteration of the icons of Zionist nostalgia — the tombs of the Patriarchs, Rachel's Tomb, the Western Wall, the Cedars of Lebanon, the Star of David, and the founder of the movement, Theodore Herzl. The art reflects long hours spent in his workshop, tinkering, smoothing and engraving away with obsessive care, to create things of beauty and memory that might decorate his actual home so far away from where he wanted it to be. It confirms both his deepest desire — to make *aliyah* — and his deepest regret — that he never settled in Palestine. This thwarted purpose explains why Yehuda Leib left his estate to his children on condition that they settle in Palestine — thus imposing upon his heirs the responsibility that he had failed to achieve. The children contested the will and stayed right where they were.[51]

When their father died the older boys were getting established and Harry was only 17 years old. He was born at the Cape and educated in the orthodox tradition, but never actually lived in the insular world of the *shtetl*. In the years that followed, he diverged from his father's precepts and rules. His childhood naughtiness and pranks morphed into something more serious, outwardly pursuing medical studies at Edinburgh University while doing any number of things that he was not prepared to divulge in his memoir. When his brother visited him in Edinburgh and learned that he was no longer studying medicine, the family cut off his allowance and ordered him to return home at once. His father would have been outraged at the deception, though he might have been comforted to know that on his return to South Africa, Harry was folded into the larger family enterprise and settled down with apparently good nature, to work and raise a family.

The Schrire manuscripts reach far beyond their intended purpose as souvenirs of times past written purely for family consumption. They present accounts of one of the great demographic movements that reconfigured the world and its Jewish people a century ago. The Diary describes the massive transition from Eastern Europe to Africa, and the poem straddles the turn of the twentieth century when South Africa moved from its full-scale dependency as a British colony towards the establishment of a Union that would eventually become a fully independent nation state. Harry Schrire's Memoir provides a detailed first-generation catalogue of his peers that epitomises the Jewish explosion from the repressive darkness of Europe into the invigorating sunshine of the Cape. Together, these two Schrires end up presenting their experiences of the the Jewish diaspora, as well as a textured picture of community formation in South Africa in the early twentieth century.

FOOTNOTES

1 Yehuda Leib Schrire, Diary, this volume.

2 Nechemiah Dov Hoffmann, *Book of Memoirs: Reminiscences of South African Jewry*, trans. from the Yiddish by Lilian Dubb and Sheila Barkusky (Cape Town: Jewish Publications-South Africa, Isaac and Jessie Kaplan Centre for Jewish Studies and Research, University of Cape Town, 1996), p. 39.

3 See *Jewish Life in the South African Country Communities*, vol. 2 (Johannesburg: South African Friends of Beth Hatefutsoth, 2002), pp. 70–71.

4 Schrire, Diary, this volume, p. 57.

5 Ibid., p. 46.

6 Ibid., p. 42.

7 Ibid., p. 68.

8 Ibid., p. 41.

9 Ibid., p. 58.

10 Ibid., p. 50.

11 Ibid., p. 57.

12 Ibid., p. 42.

13 Ibid., p. 54.

14 Ibid., p. 61.

15 Ibid., p. 51.

16 Ibid., p. 51.

17 Ibid., p. 52.

18 Ibid., p. 39.

19 Ibid., p. 64.

20 Ibid., p. 64

21 Ibid., pp. 81, 82, 85.

22 Yehuda Leib Schrire, *Tolada,* this volume, pp. 99-100.

23 Carmel Schrire, *Digging through Darkness: Chronicles of an Archaeologist* (Charlottesville and London: University Press of Virginia, 1995), pp. 255-56.

24 Schrire, *Tolada*, this volume, pp. 100-101, stanzas 2-5.

25 Ibid., p. 102, stanza 9.

26 Ibid., p. 105, stanza 23

27 Ibid., p. 108, stanzas 33–35.

28 Ibid., p. 118, stanza 74. Harry Schrire, Memoir, this volume, p. 147, footnote 171.

29 Schrire, *Tolada*, this volume, p. 124, stanza 98.

30 Ibid., p. 106, stanza 25; p. 135, stanza 141.

31 Ibid., p. 120, stanza 80.

32 Ibid., p. 102, stanza 10; p. 104, stanza 18.

33 Ibid., pp. 133-135, stanzas 134–140.

34 Schrire, Memoir, this volume, p. 157.

35 Ibid, p. 170.

36 Ibid., p. 165.

37 Yehuda Leib was described as a "chronic invalid" in his wife's court testimony in 1909 (see Carmel Schrire and Gwynne Schrire, Context, this volume, p. 20).

38 Dan Jacobson, *Heshel's Kingdom* (London: Penguin Books, 1999), p. 5.

39 Schrire, Memoir, this volume, p. 180, footnote 15.

40 For preparations for the European journey, see Schrire, *Tolada*, this volume, pp. 120-121, stanzas 80–84. These snaps are similar to one taken of Max Schrire while he was photographing his Boer War images (Western Cape Archives and Records Service, Schrire Collection, SH1-27). We are grateful to Dr Janet Monge, Department of Anthropology, University of Pennsylvania, who dated these images using her knowledge of forensics and human development.

41 According to Professor Dovid Katz of the University of Lithuania, there is a Yiddish expression "*Oys kapelush-makher*" — literally, "no longer a hat-maker", but used when someone has abruptly lost a position, been fired/demoted, sidelined. This surviving expression implies an older meaning of "*kapelush makher*" in the sense of someone of authority and status in the community and beyond, and the like (Katz, *in litt.*, 30 November 2012).

42 Jonathan Schrire, *in litt.*, 1 April 2012.

43 Schrire, Memoir, this volume, p. 186, footnote 69.

44 Schrire, *Tolada*, this volume, pp. 120-122, stanzas 83–91.

45 Marcia Gitlin, *The Vision Amazing: The Story of South African Zionism* (Johannesburg: Menorah Book Club, 1950), p. 43; Israel Abrahams, *The Birth of a Community: A History of Western Province Jewry from Earliest Times to the End of the South African War, 1902* (Cape Town: Cape Town Hebrew Congregation, 1955), p. 104; Gustav Saron and Louis Hotz, *The Jews in South Africa: A History* (Cape Town: Oxford University Press, 1955), p. 37.

46 I am grateful to Gwynne Schrire for this insight.

47 Schrire, *Tolada*, this volume, p. 137, stanzas 149–150. It may be of interest here that the ethical will of Meyer Dovid Hersch written in Yiddish in 1922 expresses the same wish in almost the same words: "In my lifetime it was not possible for me to attain my greatest ambition — which was to visit the Land of our Fathers — Eretz Israel... I appeal to you to make good this ambition." Meyer Dovid Hersch, "The Ethical Will of Meyer Dovid Hersch", in Levy (ed.), p. 193.

48 Schrire, Diary, this volume, p. 90.

49 Schrire, *Tolada*, this volume, p. 120, stanza 80.

50 See Appendix III, Fig. III.2, this volume.

51 His daughter-in-law, Rebecca, remained a strong Zionist all her life. His son Samuel moved to Palestine in 1935 and started a poultry farm, with the hope of moving his family there once it succeeded. It failed and he had to return home; Samuel's son Louis (Yehuda Leib) was made an honorary member of the Cape Town *Bnoth Zion* Association, his wife was its longest serving executive member, and their son, Samuel, made *aliyah* in 1975. Toddy Schrire briefly entertained the idea of *aliyah* when the State of Israel was declared in 1948. The will and contestation are housed in the Western Cape Archives and Records Service, 1912 MOOC vol 6/9/701 ref 2880 (Paul Cheifitz, pers. comm.).

APPENDIX I

GENEALOGY of SCHRIRE FAMILY

Compiled by Paul Cheifitz, Tel Aviv, 2015

1 Itsko (Yitzchak) ben Shmuel SCHRIRE b: 1821 d: 1911

..+Basia Malka (Batya) KINOLOVSKY b: 1828 m: Unknown d: Unknown

.......2 Yehuda Leib (Louis/Morduch Leyb) SCHRIRE b: 1851 in Ashmyany, Belarus d: 10 Oct 1912 in Cape Town, South Africa

...........+Gertrude (Gerte/Gele) GLOBUS b: 1855 in Dieveniskes, Lithuania m: 14 Oct 1879 d: 30 Mar 1934 in Cape Town, South Africa

................3 Max (Mordechai) SCHRIRE b: 1881 in Ashmyany, Belarus d: 11 Feb 1953 in Cape Town, South Africa

....................+Rebecca MAUERBERGER b: 14 Mar 1882 in Lazdai, Lithuania m: 17 Aug 1905 in Whitechapel, Middlesex, England d: 06 Jun 1963 in Cape Town, South Africa

.........................4 Theodore (Toddy) SCHRIRE b: 06 Nov 1906 in Cape Town, South Africa d: 06 May 1991 in Cape Town, South Africa

.............................+Sylvia SOHN b: 05 Nov 1913 in Cape Town, South Africa m: 22 Feb 1938 in Cape Town, South Africa d: 12 Apr 1999 in Cape Town, South Africa

..................................5 Tamar SCHRIRE b: 18 May 1939 in Cape Town, South Africa d: 28 Apr 1997 in Cape Town, South Africa

......................................+Myer Mervyn SMITH b: 20 Jul 1937 in Vereeniging, South Africa m: 10 Jul 1960 in Cape Town, South Africa d: 15 Nov 2014 in Cape Town, South Africa

....6 Debora (Debbie) SMITH b: 12 Aug 1962 in Cape Town, South Africa

....+Neil David GINSBERG b: 26 Feb 1956 in Cape Town, South Africa m: 16 Feb 1986 in Cape Town, South Africa

....7 Michael Ryan GINSBERG b: 28 Sep 1990 in Cape Town, South Africa

....7 Robyn Amy GINSBERG b: 28 Sep 1990 in Cape Town, South Africa

....7 Matthew Jonathan (Matt) GINSBERG b: 13 Jul 1999 in Cape Town, South Africa

....6 Paul Pesach (SMITH) AMIT b: 21 Jan 1965 in Cape Town, South Africa

....+Beverly Jo COHEN b: 03 Dec 1967 in Glasgow, Scotland m: 1994 in Tel Aviv, Israel

....7 Taya Neve AMIT b: 19 Jan 2000 in Kfar Saba, Israel

....7 Tomer Oliver AMIT b: 31 Aug 2001 in Israel

....7 Ellie Rose AMIT b: 19 Mar 2004 in Brighton, England

....6 Rinah SMITH b: 29 Mar 1970 in Cape Town, South Africa d: 19 Apr 1979 in Cape Town, South Africa

....6 Raphael Schrire SMITH b: 29 Nov 1973 in Cape Town, South Africa

....6 Abigail Rinah SMITH b: 18 Mar 1982 in Cape Town, South Africa

....+Ryan David EPSTEIN b: 24 Apr 1981 in Cape Town, South Africa m: 22 Mar 2010 in Stellenbosch, South Africa

....7 Malachi Smith EPSTEIN b: 28 Jan 2014 in Cape Town, South Africa

.................................5 Carmel SCHRIRE b: 15 May 1941 in Cape Town, South Africa

.....................................+John Peter WHITE b: 1939 in Christchurch, New Zealand m: 1963 in Cape Town, South Africa

.................................*2nd Husband of Carmel SCHRIRE:

.....................................+William STEIGER b: 17 Nov 1939 in Cedarhurst, New York, USA m: 02 Feb 1971 in Montreal, Canada

....6 Reuben Schrire STEIGER b: 17 Mar 1971 in Montreal, Canada

....+Hilary CONNORS b: 20 Mar 1972 in San Francisco, California, USA m: 21 Sep 2003 in San Francisco, California, USA

....7 Theodore Handlin STEIGER b: 16 Jul 2004 in San Francisco, California, USA

....7 Phoebe STEIGER b: 01 Mar 2006 in Mill Valley, California, USA

....6 Nina Micol STEIGER b: 01 Jul 1975 in Princeton, New Jersey, USA

....+Andrew Olav MUIR b: 25 Nov 1968 in Poole, Dorset, England m: 04 Sep 2010 in London, England

....7 Zachary Arlo MUIR b: 03 May 2012 in London, England

.................................5 Sharon SCHRIRE b: 09 Jun 1943 in Cape Town, South Africa

.....................................+David Nigel GODFREY b: 16 Nov 1943 in Harrogate, England m: 16 Aug 1970 in Cape Town, South Africa

....6 Mark Benjamin GODFREY b: 12 Jul 1973 in London, England

....+Rachel Elena LEWIS b: 14 Jun 1973 in London, England m: 21 Jul 2002 in Cobham, England

....7 Noah Joseph GODFREY b: 03 Mar 2005 in London, England

....7 Hannah Evie GODFREY b: 23 Aug 2007 in London, England

....6 Sarah Lisa GODFREY b: 09 Feb 1977 in London, England

....+Joel Bryan GAMSU b: 25 Jun 1979 in Durban, South Africa m: 19 Jan 2012 in Cape Town, South Africa

....7 Ruby Gabriella GAMSU b: 11 Jun 2013 in Cape Town, South Africa

....7 Marni Eden GAMSU b: 11 Dec 2014 in Cape Town, South Africa

....................................5 Gail SCHRIRE b: 20 Apr 1945 in Cape Town, South Africa

....+Michael Charles FLESCH b: 11 Mar 1940 in London, England m: 02 Aug 1972 in London, England

....6 Dina Jane FLESCH b: 06 Dec 1973 in London, England

....+Stephen Bryan LUCAS b: 14 Dec 1968 in London, England m: 04 Aug 2002 in London, England

....7 Jack Solomon LUCAS b: 20 Dec 2003 in London, England

....7 Adam Harry LUCAS b: 18 Nov 2005 in London, England

....7 Sam Reggie LUCAS b: 23 Feb 2008 in London, England

....6 Daniel Joe FLESCH b: 29 Oct 1976 in London, England

....+Melinda Gillian FRASER b: 13 Jan 1976 in Cape Town, South Africa m: 07 Dec 2008 in London, England

....7 Dylan Joshua FLESCH b: 20 Oct 2009 in London, England

....7 Mia Levia FLESCH b: 22 Mar 2012 in London, England

...........................4 David SCHRIRE b: 13 Oct 1908 in Cape Town, South Africa d: 15 May 1991 in Cape Town, South Africa

...............................+Esther Lynette ROBINSON b: 03 Feb 1912 in Harare, Zimbabwe m: 1940 in Cape Town, South Africa d: 22 Dec 1976 in London, England

....................................5 Jonathan Paul SCHRIRE b: 08 Dec 1945 in Cape Town, South Africa

....+Gail Marilyn MILLER b: 28 Jan 1953 in Port Elizabeth, South Africa m: 10 Jan 1977 in Westminster, London, England

....6 Katherine Anne (Kate) SCHRIRE b: 01 Dec 1983 in Westminster, London, England

....+Kyle COLLAIR b: 22 Jun 1983 in Cape Town, South Africa m: 02 Jan 2010 in Franschhoek, South Africa

....6 Nicola Lucy (Nicky) SCHRIRE b: 22 Aug 1986 in Westminster, London, England

....6 Matthew Sam SCHRIRE b: 04 Apr 1990 in Westminster, London, England

.................................5 Amanda Jane SCHRIRE b: 27 May 1948 in Cape Town, South Africa d: 23 Oct 2009 in London, England

.....................................+Simon A RENTON b: 11 Dec 1948 in England m: 1977 in Westminster, London, England

....6 Julia Esther RENTON b: 09 Sep 1979 in Hammersmith, London, England

....+Toby COLEGATE-STONE b: 03 Sep 1979 in England m: 01 Mar 2008 in Sandwich, Kent, England

....7 Imogen Irene COLEGATE-STONE b: 01 Oct 2009 in London, England

....7 Mabel Amanda COLEGATE-STONE b: 30 Oct 2011 in London, England

....6 Claudia Jessamine RENTON b: 19 Aug 1981 in Hammersmith, London, England

.................................*2nd Husband of Amanda Jane SCHRIRE:

.....................................+Derek CONTENT b: 29 Jun 1945 m: 16 Apr 1992 in London, England

........................4 Isidore (Isch) SCHRIRE b: 21 Dec 1910 in Cape Town, South Africa d: 28 Jul 1975 in London, England

............................+Ruth Joyce BLUMBERG b: 14 Feb 1917 m: 1938 in Kensington, London, England d: Mar 2001 in East Sussex, England

........................*2nd Wife of Isidore (Isch) SCHRIRE:

............................+Alma Evelyn A GLAUM b: 04 Oct 1916 in Forest Gate, London, England m: 09 Jul 1955 in Kensington, London, England d: 10 Feb 2004 in Bath, Somerset, England

...............3 Samuel SCHRIRE b: 21 Mar 1889 in Neustadt Sugint, Lithuania d: 02 Sep 1949 in Cape Town, South Africa

...................+Sara Neche (Sarah) SENDEROWITZ b: 11 Nov 1891 in Kimberley, South Africa m: 28 Dec 1913 in Kimberley, South Africa d: 29 Jun 1981 in Cape Town, South Africa

........................4 Louis SCHRIRE b: 29 Sep 1914 in Kimberley, South Africa d: 12 Sep 1986 in Cape Town, South Africa

............................+Mary KATZ b: 06 Jan 1918 in Johannesburg, South Africa m: 02 Nov 1941 in Johannesburg, South Africa d: 09 Dec 2008 in Cape Town, South Africa

.................................5 Gwynne Yvonne SCHRIRE b: 22 May 1943 in Johannesburg, South Africa

......................................+Ashley ROBINS b: 24 Sep 1940 in Harare, Zimbabwe m: 31 Mar 1968

....6 Evan Malcolm ROBINS b: 17 Feb 1969 in Cape Town, South Africa

....+Karen KALLMANN b: 26 Apr 1971 in Johannesburg, South Africa m: 27 Jun 1999 in Johannesburg, South Africa

....7 Yael Lerato ROBINS b: 14 Sep 2004 in Cape Town, South Africa

....7 Eitan Inkosinathi ROBINS b: 11 Aug 2006 in Cape Town, South Africa

....7 Aryeh Andile ROBINS b: 06 Feb 2008 in Cape Town, South Africa

....7 Ma'ayan Nandi ROBINS b: 18 Apr 2010 in Cape Town, South Africa

....7 Ayelet Thabiza ROBINS b: 24 Aug 2012 in Cape Town, South Africa

....6 Estelle ROBINS b: 01 Apr 1971 in Cape Town, South Africa

....+Daniel PFEFFER b: 13 Mar 1964 m: 22 Apr 2001 in Jerusalem, Israel

....7 Ariella PFEFFER b: 22 Nov 2002 in Jerusalem, Israel

....7 Gabriella PFEFFER b: 15 Dec 2004 in Ra'anana, Israel

....6 Roy Joshua ROBINS b: 29 Apr 1979 in Cape Town, South Africa

..................................5 Martyn Roy SCHRIRE b: 21 Apr 1945 in Cape Town, South Africa d: 26 Mar 1977 in Johannesburg, South Africa

..................................5 Samuel Rodes SCHRIRE b: 11 Feb 1950 in Kimberley, South Africa

......................................+Sarah MOISE b: 11 Jan 1951 in Alexandria, Egypt m: 17 Dec 1972 in Cape Town, South Africa

....6 Dani SCHRIRE b: 24 Nov 1974 in Cape Town, South Africa

....+Yamit RACHMAN b: 05 Oct 1977 in Jerusalem, Israel m: 01 Aug 2004 in Jerusalem, Israel

....7 Yannai SCHRIRE b: 11 Jan 2006 in Jerusalem, Israel

....7 Hillel Avner SCHRIRE b: 18 May 2011 in Berlin, Germany

....6 Arnon SCHRIRE b: 29 Jan 1978 in Jerusalem, Israel

....+Odelia LEVY b: 28 Feb 1980 in Tsfat, Israel m: 21 Aug 2005 in Hadera, Israel

....7 Lia SCHRIRE b: 11 Mar 2007 in Haifa, Israel

....7 Nevo SCHRIRE b: 19 Aug 2009 in Haifa, Israel

....7 Lavie SCHRIRE b: 24 Aug 2013 in Haifa, Israel

....6 Ray Yehuda SCHRIRE b: 06 Apr 1986 in Jerusalem, Israel

........................4 Wolfe (Velva/Va) SCHRIRE b: 24 Oct 1916 in Kimberley, South Africa d: 16 Feb 1972

............................+Ruth Miriam GOLDBERG b: 09 Jun 1923 in Kimberley, South Africa m: Unknown d: 03 Jun 1979 in Cape Town, South Africa

.................................5 Robert Arthur SCHRIRE b: 20 Dec 1944

.....................................+Christine June AKERSON b: 06 Jun 1950 in Los Angeles, California, USA m: 23 Jun 1970 in Santa Barbara, California d: 04 May 2010

....6 Margot L SCHRIRE b: 27 Feb 1972

....+James R BOWYER b: Unknown m: Jan 1994 in Harrow, England

....*2nd Husband of Margot L SCHRIRE:

....+Tore LERAAND b: 26 Dec 1961 in Oslo, Norway m: Unknown

....7 Torbjorn Tyler Schrire LERAAND b: 08 Feb 2008

....7 Sofie Marie Schrire LERAAND b: 21 Oct 2009

....6 Carmel Lauren SCHRIRE b: 27 Mar 1974

....+Nicolaus Alexander VON GYMNICH b: 18 May 1974 m: Unknown

....7 Spencer Thomas VON GYMNICH b: 03 Aug 2011

....7 Mackenzie Elizabeth VON GYMNICH b: 05 Jul 2013

.................................*2nd Wife of Robert Arthur SCHRIRE:

.....................................+Veronique ? b: Unknown m: Unknown

.................................5 Stephen David SCHRIRE b: 02 Jun 1951

.................................5 Jeremy Richard SCHRIRE b: 21 Aug 1957

.....................................+Beverley ROSE b: 07 Aug 1957 m: 02 Jul 1983 in Ealing, Middlesex, England

....6 Timothy Daniel SCHRIRE b: 31 May 1990 in Camden, London, England

....6 Harriet Rose SCHRIRE b: 11 Feb 1993 in Camden, London, England

.................................5 Barbara Jill SCHRIRE b: 18 Oct 1947 in Cape Town, South Africa

.....................................+Brian ARENSON b: 17 Mar 1945 in East London, South Africa m: 02 Feb 1969 in Cape Town, South Africa

....6 Jenny Lynne ARENSON b: 03 Aug 1971 in Grahamstown, South Africa

....7 Melissa Dorothy ARENSON b: 02 May 2012 in Perth, Australia

....7 Phoebe Edna ARENSON b: 02 May 2012 in Perth, Australia

....6 Ricky Val ARENSON b: 24 Jul 1973 in Cape Town, South Africa

....+Katherine Jane BRODRICK b: Unknown m: 09 Jan 2001 in Cape Town, South Africa

....7 Daniel ARENSON b: 07 Dec 2003 in Perth, Australia

....7 Adam Joshua ARENSON b: 28 Dec 2005 in Perth, Australia

....7 Joshua Eli ARENSON b: 27 Aug 2009 in Perth, Australia

....7 Abby Dinah ARENSON b: 15 Sep 2011 in Perth, Australia

....6 David Graham ARENSON b: 14 Apr 1976 in Cape Town, South Africa

.........................4 Annie (Anita Ruby) SCHRIRE b: 23 Feb 1920 in Kimberley, South Africa d: 21 Feb 2015 in London, England

.............................+Bertram (Bertie) LENTIN b: 1916 m: 23 May 1943 in Muizenberg, South Africa

...................................5 Annette LENTIN b: 09 Jun 1944

....+Sonny MEYERSON b: Unknown m: Unknown

....6 Velva MEYERSON b: Dec 2013 in Perth, Australia

...................................*2nd Husband of Annette LENTIN:

....+? PIZZI b: Unknown m: Unknown

....6 Nicky PIZZI b: Unknown

...................................5 Kenneth Michael LENTIN b: 31 Jan 1947

....+? ? b: Unknown m: Unknown

...................................5 Ronald LENTIN b: 24 Feb 1951

....+? ? b: Unknown m: Unknown

.........................*2nd Husband of Annie (Anita Ruby) SCHRIRE:

.............................+Isaac KAHN b: Unknown m: Unknown

.........................4 Edna Bessie SCHRIRE b: 24 Aug 1922 in Kimberley, South Africa d: 23 May 2011 in Port Elizabeth, South Africa

.............................+Leo SCHACHTER b: 19 Mar 1914 in Leipzig, Germany m: 08 May 1947 in Cape Town, South Africa d: 11 Mar 1995 in Port Elizabeth, South Africa

...................................5 Shoshana Lee SCHACHTER b: 29 May 1949 in Port Elizabeth, South Africa

......................................+Ronald SHAPIRO b: 22 Oct 1943 m: 13 May 1990

..................................5 Elisabeth Selima SCHACHTER b: 13 Nov 1951 in Port Elizabeth, South Africa

......................................+Vernon Michael NEPPE b: 16 Apr 1951 in Johannesburg, South Africa m: 29 May 1977

....6 Jonathan Samuel NEPPE b: 12 Jan 1980 in Johannesburg, South Africa

....6 Shari Elanna NEPPE b: 22 Jun 1982 in Johannesburg, South Africa

....+Jonathan David SCHWARTZ b: 24 May 1975 in New York, New York, USA m: 06 Aug 2006

....7 Liam Stanley SCHWARTZ b: 22 Dec 2010 in Seattle, Washington, USA

....7 Eliana Miriam SCHWARTZ b: 01 Jun 2012 in Seattle, Washington, USA

....7 Gabriella Lillian SCHWARTZ b: 15 Jan 2015 in Seattle, Washington, USA

.........................4 Cynthia Frances SCHRIRE b: 17 Jul 1924 in Kimberley, South Africa d: 11 Apr 2014 in Sydney, Australia

.............................+Aubrey Morris GREEN b: 28 Jun 1915 in Oudtshoorn, South Africa m: 06 Apr 1948 in Muizenberg, South Africa d: 27 Aug 1982 in Oudtshoorn, South Africa

..................................5 Isabel Sandra GREEN b: 02 Mar 1950 in Oudtshoorn, South Africa

......................................+Barry Alec GOTTHEINER b: 21 Jul 1950 in Cape Town, South Africa m: 01 Oct 1972 in Cape Town, South Africa

....6 Neil Cyril GOTTHEINER b: 08 Mar 1973 in Cape Town, South Africa

....+Cigalle HAMMERMAN b: 24 Mar 1974 in Afula, Israel m: 25 Jan 2001 in Sydney, Australia

....7 Avital GOTTHEINER b: 14 Mar 2004 in Sydney, Australia

....7 Ella Mina GOTTHEINER b: 15 Oct 2005 in Sydney, Australia

....7 Eitan Jack GOTTHEINER b: 04 Jul 2008 in Sydney, Australia

....6 Lianne Verity GOTTHEINER b: 18 Aug 1976 in Oudtshoorn, South Africa

....+Joshua (Josh) WERMUT b: 19 Jan 1977 in Sydney, Australia

....7 Meisha Coda WERMUT b: 09 Aug 2011 in Sydney, Australia

....7 Tala WERMUT b: 09 Jan 2015 in Sydney, Australia

..................................5 Jeremy Robert GREEN b: 17 Aug 1955 in Cape Town, South Africa

......................................+Beverley Moira SHER b: 04 Oct 1955 m: 15 Feb 1981

....6 Daniel Saul GREEN b: 16 Feb 1982

....+Keren ORBACH b: 26 Jul 1979 m: 03 Apr 2011

....7 Joshua GREEN b: 31 Jul 2012

....6 Michelle Ami GREEN b: 11 Jan 1986

....+Luke BIRKETT b: 08 Jul 1981 m: 23 Oct 2011

..................................5 Cheryl GREEN b: 21 Dec 1960 in Cape Town, South Africa

......................................+Alan MARGOLIN b: 16 Dec 1955 in Cape Town, South Africa m: 07 Feb 1988

....6 Emanuel MARGOLIN b: 18 May 1989 in Cape Town, South Africa

....6 Gadiel MARGOLIN b: 25 Jun 1995 in Cape Town, South Africa

................3 Annie SCHRIRE b: 1891 in Neustadt Sugint, Lithuania d: 14 Oct 1918 in Cape Town, South Africa

....................+Hersch (Harry) SCHUS b: 1882 in Byel, Russia m: 21 Dec 1913 in Cape Town, South Africa d: 12 Jun 1959 in Cape Town, South Africa

................3 Harry Nathan SCHRIRE b: 15 Sep 1895 in Cape Town, South Africa d: 28 Apr 1980 in Cape Town, South Africa

....................+Leah (Lily) FINBERG b: 28 Jan 1898 in Spitalfields, Middlesex, England m: 12 Mar 1922 in Cape Town, South Africa d: 03 Dec 1992 in Cape Town, South Africa

.........................4 Leonard (Lennie) SCHRIRE b: 20 Feb 1923 in Stellenbosch, South Africa d: 23 Oct 1999 in Johannesburg, South Africa

.............................+Bertille BUTLER b: 01 Feb 1928 in Youghall, Ireland m: 30 Aug 1952 in Johannesburg, South Africa d: 29 Apr 2003 in South Molton, England

..................................5 Brian SCHRIRE b: 20 Oct 1953 in Johannesburg, South Africa

......................................+Susyn ANDREWS b: 02 Mar 1953 in Howth, Ireland m: 19 Oct 1988 in Durban, South Africa

.........................4 Arthur SCHRIRE b: 06 Dec 1926 d: 03 Dec 2014 in Cape Town, South Africa

.............................+Sylvia Gertrude BENSON b: 31 Jul 1934 m: Unknown

..................................5 David Ian SCHRIRE b: 16 Sep 1958

......................................+Monica ? b: Unknown m: Unknown

....6 Daniel SCHRIRE b: 1990

..................................5 Tania SCHRIRE b: 17 Feb 1960

....6 Tammy SCHRIRE b: 2000

..................................5 Joel Adam SCHRIRE b: 14 Apr 1963

......................................+Sally MILTON b: Unknown m: Oct 2000 in Ealing, London, England

..................................5 Michael A SCHRIRE b: 1967

......................................+Judy L MENCZEL b: Unknown m: Jul 1994 in Westminster, London, England

....6 Zoe SCHRIRE b: 1995

..................................*2nd Wife of Michael A SCHRIRE:

......................................+Ana G VIDAL POLANIA b: Unknown m: Nov 2003 in Camden, London, England

....6 Lily SCHRIRE b: 2007

.........................4 Vivienne Myra SCHRIRE b: 15 Aug 1928

.............................+Philip Maurice (Pip) FREEDMAN b: 14 Jul 1925 in Swellendam, South Africa m: 06 Oct 1949 in Cape Town, South Africa d: 19 May 2003 in Cape Town, South Africa

..................................5 Gail FREEDMAN b: 18 May 1951 in Cape Town, South Africa

......................................+Edsel Keith HELFET b: Jul 1946 in Cape Town, South Africa m: 23 Aug 1981 in Warwickshire, England

....6 Charlotte Amy HELFET b: 19 Mar 1984 in Warwickshire, England

....6 Nicola Claire HELFET b: 29 Apr 1988 in Warwichskire, England

..................................5 Jeremy Louis FREEDMAN b: 03 May 1955 in Cape Town, South Africa

.........................*2nd Husband of Vivienne Myra SCHRIRE:

.............................+Lionel STEIN b: 26 Oct 1918 in Cape Town, South Africa m: 09 May 1974 in Cape Town, South Africa d: 17 Aug 2008 in Cape Town, South Africa

.......2 Slava SCHRIRE b: 1857 d: Unknown

APPENDIX II

WRITINGS and NOTEBOOKS of YEHUDA LEIB SCHRIRE

Compiled by Carmel Schrire and translated by Andrew Plaks

1. Poem

Tolada: The history and happenings, reasons and adventures, from the day of my birth to the day of my death, with a short criticism in a clear language, in songs, and prose, in remembrance for all time.
Notebook. Handmade. Handwritten in Hebrew. 150 eight-line stanzas printed with vowels. 19 x 14.5cm (7½ x 5¾in), unlined, gold embossed.
Ca. 1910–11.

2. A mirror (*shpiegel*) from my family biography (or a building of nature with practical family life)

The real (not exaggerated) story written here, is not legend and is not mythical history. The writer writes a series of facts, the honest truth. No fine language or embellishment often used by writers. The most interesting and effective for the reader (being) the stories of a Jewish family ...
Notebook. Handwritten. Yiddish. 120 pages. 22.5 x 17.8cm (9 x 7in).

3. Address book

Hebrew, English and Yiddish (?). One sketch. Addresses, accounts and narrative. Missing first few pages. Late in book there is a stamp for Samuel Schrire, Frankfurt a. M., Uhland Str. 53.

Handwritten 15.5 x 10cm (6 x 4in).

(C.C. must be Cape Colony and O.R.C. Orange River Colony).

(Hebrew) *Shmot Haneirim* (Names of ?)

Hopefield CC Singer & Schapire

Sank Brothers, Grortfontein CC (nr Hopefield)

S. Milwitzky Biesjspoort Siding CC (nr Victoria West)

S. Liberman LadyBrand O.R.C. (on Lesotho border)

P.O. Kenhardt C.C. H. Rogow (founded 1868, in N Cape 120 km /74½ miles from Upington)

Rev. (deleted) Rabbi Judah L. Levin (Heb. M'lah? Sherira) Detroit, Mich

Kenadu 140 Division Street.

G. Kramer Roets P/O Boeresdorps Namaqualand

Mr Pickfords, 44 Burg Str.

M. Nobel Swakopmund

H. Globus Johannesburg P.O. Box 5032

Page dated 1891, 1897

395 S. Robey Str. Chicago, ill (street name changed 1927 to
Damen Ave).

Sam Schrire America

J. Smoless Grand Hotel Vryburg (in North West province between Kimberley and Mafikeng)

Stamps with initials (?) HS

R ---- Brena (? Bueno) Vista Hig(h) Level Road, Green Point

Meir[?] Mishulch[?] probably Meschulach (Heb.)
Russia M. Moemkobaui Br noc. Parku Cybourkckou rye.

Page headed: "Cigaress"
S (?Y) Katz Geinzenhausen, Y. B"ayern (or ez ayern) Gerberstr;

H. Schus stud chim in Fribourg (Schweiz);

5 Seime Str. Cnr Buniamo Barrimorvitsch

Stamps: Samuel Schrire Frankfurt a.M. Uhland Str, 53. (semi-detached building standing next to no. 51. pre-War?)

cnr Jul. Gans, - Sem. Schrire, Uhland strasse 53, Frankfurt a m.

Vir E. Beniamowitz Seimel Stra 5

Mr. Max Schrire, Johannesburg P.O. Box 5951

Frankfurt a m. Musikantenweg 66,
S. Marcus
H. Katz

L. Berman Esq. 17 Faure Str. Cape Town

Hot. Ulman Frankfurt?

Eim ???

Jampter just Baaer??

A.S. Ginsburg, 26 Buitenkant Str. (razed: opposite Perseverance Tavern)

Mr J. (?J) Mauerberger 39 Fashan (? Fashion) Street Spitalfields London E. (nr Brick Lane, now Tower Hamlets)

Mr Sam Schrire 141 Sholto Street Chicago ill America

Mr E. Rame (? Rome) 17 Betty Str Cam (? Carr..) Rd London E.

Sam. Schrire 287 W 15th Street Chicago ill.

Yetta Bryer 18 Lion Sq, Union St, Whitechapel E.

Mr in Lirbr... John ... Little Graff

Last page: *Ich habe ihness ein Buch ??? jahn ifnan??*

4. Proverbs. *Dedicated to Tuvia bar Moshe Mordechai (Toddy) and Rivka (Rebecca)*
Copied from Hebrew and Yiddish.
Quotations and commentaries on 342 entries.
Dictionary.
Notebook. Handwritten. 19 x 12.7cm (7½ x 5in).

5. *Mishneh Milon*
Mishneh auxiliary dictionary.
Notebook. Handwritten. 20 x 16.5cm (8 x 6½in).

6. *Shoshanah Novelet*. *Original book by Yehuda Leib Schrire.*
Warsaw Typography. Alexander Ginz. Warsaw. 1879.
Stamp on right:
Beit akad sefarim
A. Zuckerman
Warsaw, Nelerki 15

Published book. 17.8 x 11.4cm (7 x 4½in). Rebound in black.
Stamped L. Schrire Frankfurt a M.
Stamped in red on top of title page: "Please don't ruin the books".

Pocket contains invoice for 9d, from Standard Bank of South Africa, Limited. Debited to S. Senior Sons Ltd.... Dated 20/2/34.

Plaks translations:

i. Facing title page:

Short Message (by Zuckerman)
When I took this story to be printed, I saw and I blushed; numerous mistakes were made in it, in grammar, organisation and sequence. And since I love my nephew who wrote this true story, I took upon myself the burden to edit it and to compile it for the reader who will remember me for better as the one who brought it to print.

ii. Facing first page:

Honour
My pleasant parents dearest to my heart, life of my spirit, Yitzchak and Batya Malka, God be with them, that they will live and the generation of the honest will be blessed.

7. *Yelakot Shila. Shirim v'[?] Micklamin[?]* Yiddish.
Some are copies.
Small square notebook, 12.7 x 12.7cm (5 x 5in). Handwritten (?). Handmade.

8. *Megilat S'tarim*. A fine story found in an old manuscript from the kings of Kusaria Khazar.
Shiny black notebook. 22.9 x 17.8cm (9 x 7in). Handwritten.
Fiction copied from a German ms. by Y. L. S.

9. Talmudic studies, serious discussions.
Shiny black notebook. 22.9 x 17.8cm (9 x 7in). Handwritten.

10. Alexandria: The Queen. A historical tale of Alexander Yannai reign in 3670 (2000 years ago).
Yiddish.
Marbled covered notebook. 22.9 x 17.8cm (9 x 7in). ? Handmade. Handwritten. 286+ pages.

11. *Seleg Bogdim*. Notebook of traditions for young Jewish boys that they should know.
Fiction. Hebrew.
First lines read: *"When I was 18, I published "Shoshana Novelet". Printed in Russia under Uncle Abraham Zuckerman. He corrected the mistakes ...".*
Brown notebook. 22.9 x 17.8cm (9 x 7in). Handwritten. 135 pp +.

12. Sokain the King. Agent of the King.
Warsaw. Ginz 1900.
Title page is stamped L. Schrire Frankfurt a. M. At the bottom is written *"Father's Uncle"* in what might be T. Schrire's hand. The publisher writes: *"The original was in German, the fruit of the imagination of Dr Lehman in Mainz and I have brought it to the field and its mother and the chamber of its progenitress (the holy tongue) because its real sense is in the character of the Jewish people. Why should it be to the people of our nation who understand only ... like a closed book at a time when the contents affect them wherever they may be ...".*

"The amazing reason is the book is as a model to R' Berl Lehman. He is not a fabrication or imagination, but from the world of reality; an author who spoke in a clear language. He also was on the threshold of Yeshiva House which R' Berl had established and called by name those great people who served there...".

Handbound. 17.8 x 11.4cm (7 x 4½in).

13. Diary (n.d.)
Notebook, 18 x 11.4cm (7 x 4½in).
Bound, handmade.
Hebrew, handwritten, faded.
The book has two parts separated by numerous blank pages. It was written first from one cover (Part 1 in our pdf), then turned upside down and written from the other (Parts 2, 3 in our pdfs).

Part 1: Title page: (upside down) "Hoffmann bros, Hottentos Kloof Ceres)."
Over: Calculation of date: 3708+ 1893= 5701. The calculation is wrong but the date of the manuscript might be 1893.
Paginated 1–48.
Unpaginated 6, including sections numbered 1-8, ending with "Finis".
Blank page with mirror image of Finis.
Page with poem in Yiddish.
Content: A biblical history of Joseph, Mary and Jesus.

Part 2: Paginated 1–44.

Part 3: Paginated 45–81.
Unpaginated 6.
Paginated 82.
Unpaginated 6.

14. Miscellaneous musical compositions
One is annotated as being composed by Mr L. Schrire on the occasion of Harry's *bar mitzvah*, 1908.
14 verses.
Notated: "Adagio" and "Sung by Bertha" [?].
Transcribed by Toddy Schrire Nov. 22 1971.

Preliminary translation: Andrew Plaks :

1. About the daughter of my people I will weep
2. I will cry like a jackal, tears of water
3. Her greatness is brought down and her honour is brought low
4. And all her hope under the heaven is hopeless
5. She and only she, why and wherefore
6. Shall she bear and suffer, really made for slaughter
7. All the money is but she has not been treated mercifully
8. Worn out little sheep to the slaughter
9. Every leper and person inflicted with disease, robber and thief
10. Murder and theft in every corner of the land
11. Every unjust person and traitor, and evil doer
12. No mercy or justice, no one to stand in the breach
13. Oy! Oy!
14. He hid his face and didn't vanish

APPENDIX III

ARTWORK of YEHUDA LEIB SCHRIRE

Transcribed, translated and annotated by Devis Iosifzon

III. 1. Memorial tablet carved and painted by Yehuda Leib Schrire, dedicated to the memory of Sarah, wife of Joseph Theodore Mauerberger. The five eggs in the nest represent her five children, one of whom was his daughter-in-law, Rebecca. (C. Schrire coll. Photo C. Schrire)

Letters in bold form Sarah's name combined with her father Aharon — finished in a different colour (font bold and enlarged here).

Translation:

In Memoriam (*Yarzheit* in Yiddish spelling)

There in heaven she chose to be

Merciful the gentle mother

She is still alive she is still standing

In God's shadow the wings of the divine spirit [*Shechina*]

A place which will be lit by God's candle

An arm of light for an honest soul

A temple of mercy high above

An estate she has found our mother Sarah

Daughter of Meir Aharon bless his soul [abbreviated Hebrew version]

Lag Ba'omer 5652 [Gregorian 15 May 1892]

May his/her soul be bound up in the bundle of life [abbreviated Hebrew version]

שם במרום בחרה שבת
רחמניה אם העדינה
היא עוד חיה עוד נצבת
בתוך צל אל כנפי שכינה
מקום אשר יאיר נר אלוה
אור זרוע לנפש ישרה
היכל רחמים מעל גבוה
נחלה מצאה אמנו שרה
בת מאיר אהרן ז״ל
ל״ג בעומר תרנ״ב
תנצב״ה

III.2. Painted relief wood cutout carved by Yehuda Leib Schrire, showing Holy Land sites, framed by vines and grapes, converging on artist's initials "LS" at the base. Central medallion is backed with silver foil, possibly from a cigarette pack. Dedicated to the memory of Theodore Herzl, Cape Town, 1907. (C. Schrire coll., photo C. Schrire)

Translation and Transcription:
The Dearest Herzl Benjamin Ze'ev
Son of Jacob rest in peace [in abbreviation Hebrew version] has passed away [word used for deceased — only for Jews]
July the 3rd 1904 [in Hebrew calendar] rest in peace [Hebrew version]
Rachel's tomb
The cave of *Machpela* [Hebron]
The Western Wall
Cape Town 1907

III.3. Painted relief wood cutout of the Holy Land sites, carved by Yehuda Leib Schrire, showing Jerusalem, Wailing Wall and cedars, with lions of Judah rampant alongside the Tablets of the Law. The blank tablets suggest that this picture is unfinished. (Sharon Godfrey coll. Photo: David Godfrey)

Upper text in centre:
Psalm 113
Transcription: *Mi'mizrach Shemesh ad Mevo'o*
ממזרח שמש עד מבואו
Translation: From the rising of the sun to the place where it sets
In the frame on each side of the lions are the letters of his name, LAMED and SHIN on the left, which are the Hebrew of the letters "L" and "S" on the right side.

Lower text in centre:
Right part of text, three words from the right, refer to the domed building on the right part of the lower register in the inner frame: 1 Samuel 10:2
קבורת רחל אמנו
Transcription: *Kvurat Rachel Imeinu*
Translation: Tomb of Rachel our Mother (in a format which appears in 1 Samuel 10:2)

Two following words in the centre, referring to the illustrated wall, above the centre text:
כותל מערבי
Transcription: *Kotel Ma'aravi*
Translation: Western Wall

Four remaining words on the end part of the line:
קברות מלכי בית דוד
Transcription: *Kivrot Malchei Beit David*
Translation: The tombs of the king from the dynasty of (King) David

III.4. Ark of the Covenant, supposedly carved by Yehuda Leib Schrire

This was commissioned by the St. John's Street's *Griene Shul* built in 1892 by a breakaway, more orthodox group of Jews from Kelme who tried to reproduce a Lithuanian *heimland* synagogue decorated with original Lithuanian-style Jewish handicraft and an ark like that in their *shul* in Kelme. The Jews from Šiauliai went to the other synagogue built on Queen Street in 1888, called *Der Englishe Shul*. *The Jewish Community of Oudtshoorn.* www.seligman.org.il/oudtshoorn_jews.html. (C. P. Nel Museum Oudtshoorn, Western Cape)

III.5. Memorial tablet carved by Yehuda Leib Schrire (C. P. Nel Museum, Oudtshoorn, Western Cape. Photo: C. Schrire, 2005)

Translation:
The day of the death my Father Abraham son of Yehud'
Zikhrono l'vracha[1] who was dying and was *gathered to his kin*[2] 4 Shvat[3]
1887 and my gentle Mother Rachel Leah daughter of Zvi
Last of Pessach 1895/6 in the town of Labischin[4]
County of Posen *May their soul be bound up in the bundle of life*[5]

---

1. "Of blessed memory", in Hebrew, appears here in abbreviation.
2. Genesis 49:29. Abraham saying that about himself.
3. Saturday, 29 January 1887.
4. The closest approximation I found in the county of Posen to the spelling here.
5. Abbreviation in Hebrew letters.

This pile[6] is testimony and this tombstone is a testimony
That I their son Zvi Hirsh Levin who respects[7]
Their memory have donated a donation to *Beth Midrash*[8]
Knesset of Israel[9] in the town of Oudtshoorn
Their names to be inscribed in the book of mentioning
[of] Their pure souls on every *Yahrzeit*
And during *Shalosh Regalim*[10] year after year until
The *end of the days.*[11]

III.6. Oil on board painted by Yehuda Leib Schrire, showing the Tablets of the Law, Zion and Ark of the Covenant wreathed in roses. (C. Schrire coll. Photo C. Schrire)

Top verse split over the two sides of the crown:

שויתי יהוה לנגדי תמיד

Transcription: *Shiviti Hashem (YHVH) l'negdi tamid*

Psalms 16, 8: I have set the LORD always before me; *Shiviti* (or in Ashkenazi pronunciation *Shivisi*).

6. Refers to heap or a pile of stones, as an ancient form of burial.
7. Cherishes.
8. Place of *Torah* study.
9. Meaning the Jewish community.
10. The three pilgrimage festivals: Pesach (Passover), Shavuot (Feast of Weeks) and Sukkot (Festival of Tents or Booths), when the Israelites living in ancient Israel and Judea would make a pilgrimage to Jerusalem.
11. Daniel 12:12 (the year 1887).

In the Ashkenazi tradition these are boards in a synagogue which in some Jewish communities are used as a tool for pronouncing God's name. Normally located on the pillar in front of the pulpit from which the cantor conducts the prayers, or on the *parochet* (also *paroches*), which is the screen or the curtain of *Aron Kodesh* (*Torah* Ark), or on a special illustrated page in the *siddur*. Sometimes the "Shiviti" board is also called the "Mizrach" (East). This tradition is based on the verse from Psalms 16:8. In medieval times, Kabbalists developed special imagery and meditative techniques, which help to concentrate the thought on names of God, trying to lift the spirit and to connect with spiritual worlds. In the eighteenth and nineteenth centuries, this tradition grew into a field of Jewish artistic craft.

On both sides of the boards of the Ten Commandments above the left and right Stars of David, the two words on each side of the boards read:
יהוה אחד
Transcription: *Hashem (YHVH) Echad*
Translation: God is one (as it appears in the *Shema Israel* prayer verse).

In the centre of each of the two Stars of David is the word Zion, in Hebrew: **ציון**

The separate letters in each of the triangular edges of both Stars of David are:
מגן דוד
Transcription: *Magen David*
Translation: Star of David
The two boards in the centre have a shortened version of the Ten Commandments with Hebrew letters in between from the first (*aleph*) to the tenth (*yud*).

In the semi-circle on top of the open arc, in the lower register is the word:
שדי
Transcription: *Shaddai*
Translation: One of the names of God
Under this, appears again "God is one".

In the centre of the illustrated open arc:
ואהבת לרעך כמוך
Transcription: *Ve'ahavta lere'acha kamocha*
Translation: Love your neighbour as yourself; a *mitzvah* based on Leviticus 19:18. Amongst the many commentaries to be found about it, the best-known is by Rabbi Akiva who said it is the great rule of the *Torah*.

Lowest register in form of banner, the three words in the centre:
יהוה שומר ישראל
Transcription: *Hashem (YHVH)* Shomer Yisrael
Translation: God the Guardian of Israel.

Under the bottom Star of David on the right side is the word:
שנת
Transcription: *Shnat*
Translation: the year of

Under the bottom Star of David on the left is the Hebrew year:
התלג
Transcription: He, Tav, Lamed, Gimel
This is a mistake. It would denote 1672-3 which is patently not the date of manufacture.

APPENDIX IV

Certificate presented to Gela Schrire by the Cape Town Jewish Orphanage, the Board of Guardians and the Aged Home, ca. 1931–32

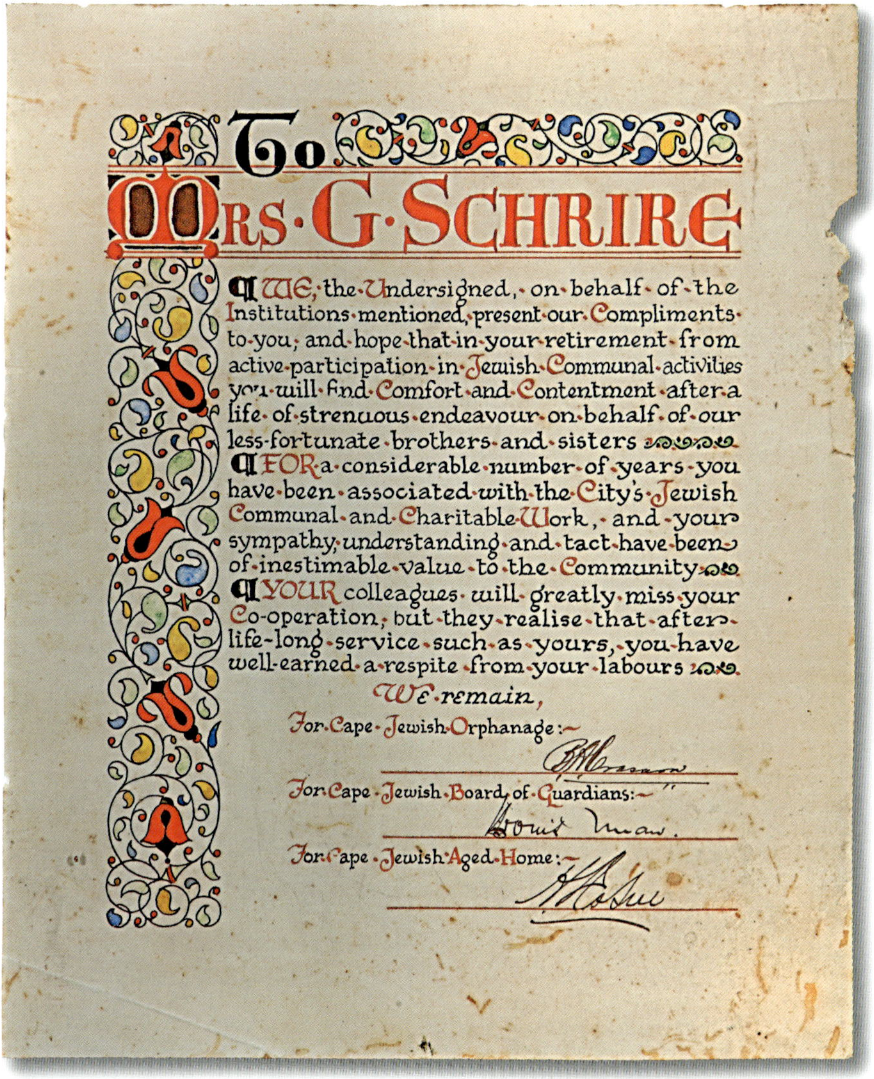

To
Mrs G. Schrire

WE, the Undersigned, on behalf of the Institutions mentioned, present our Compliments to you, and hope that in your retirement from active participation in Jewish Communal activities you will find Comfort and Contentment after a life of strenuous endeavour on behalf of our less-fortunate brothers and sisters

FOR a considerable number of years you have been associated with the City's Jewish Communal and Charitable Work, and your sympathy, understanding and tact have been of inestimable value to the Community

YOUR colleagues will greatly miss your Co-operation, but they realise that after life-long service such as yours, you have well-earned a respite from your labours

We remain,

For Cape Jewish Orphanage:–

For Cape Jewish Board of Guardians:–

For Cape Jewish Aged Home:–

GLOSSARY

(All words are Hebrew unless otherwise indicated)

Agudat Achim — Association of Brothers

Aliyah — honour of being called up to the *Torah* to recite the blessings

Arba kanfoth — four-cornered garment with fringes on the corners worn under the clothes by Jewish men

Ashkenazi — European Jews (from Ashkenaaz, Germany, as opposed to Sephardi Jews from Sepharad, Spain. When used in reference to language in Chapter 2, *Ashkenazi* denotes Yiddish

Ba'al teshuvah — return of secular Jews to traditional Judaism

Balebatishe (Yiddish) — respectable, in good standing in the community

Bedek chometz (Yiddish), *bedikat chametz* (Heb.) — searching for leavened food like breadcrumbs on the night before Passover

Beth din — rabbinical court

Beth ha-knesset — synagogue

Beth ha-olam — cemetery

Beth ha-midrash — a study hall, often located in the synagogue

Be'ezrat Hashem — with the help of G-d

Bimah — platform in the synagogue on which stands the desk from which the *Torah* is read

Blat Gemara/Gemora — a page of the *Gemara*

Bnei Zion — Sons of Zion, branch formed in 1897 in Cape Town

Bnoth Zion — Daughters of Zion, branch formed in 1901 in Cape Town

Bobbe (Yiddish) — grandmother

Bocher (Yiddish) — lad

Bodek — an examiner, a highly qualified officer who inspects the *shochet*'s knives to determine if they are free from nicks and sufficiently sharp and also inspects animals after slaughter

Bundu (Bantu, Xhosa) — outback, back of beyond

Chalef — a special knife used for kosher slaughter

Chalitzah — ceremony by which a childless widow and her husband's brother could avoid the duty to marry after the husband's death

Challah — loaf of bread, usually eaten on the Sabbath and other Jewish festivals

Chanukah — Feast of Lights

Chasid (pl. *Chasidim*, f. *Chasidot*) — a follower of an orthodox, pious, Jewish sect founded in Poland c. 1750

Chazal — acronym, for *Chachameinu Zichronam Livrocho* (Our Sages of Blessed Memory), referring to the rabbinic authorities of the *Talmud*

Chazan (pl. *chazanim*) — cantor

Chazones (Yiddish) — chants of the *chazan*

Cheder — lit. "room", an elementary school teaching Hebrew and Judaism

Cheshvan — month of the Jewish year

Chevra/Chevrah — lit. "friends", also denotes "society"

Chevrah kadisha — organisation that prepares bodies for burial

Chevrah Mishnaot — *Torah* scholars who study the *Mishnah*

Cholent — slow-cooked stew put on the fire on Friday and eaten on the Sabbath

Chup (Yiddish) — a catch, good match

Chupah — wedding canopy

Daven (Yiddish) — pray. Observant Jews pray three times daily in formal worship services

Dayanim — people knowledgeable in Talmudic law.

Dennebal (Afrikaans) — pine cone bearing *dennepitte* (pine nuts)

Dorp (Afrikaans) — village

Dorshei Zion — Seekers of Zion, men's Zionist association formed in 1899 in Cape Town

Draidlech (Yiddish) — four-sided spinning tops played with on *Chanukah*

Drosha (Yiddish) — sermon

Drush (Yiddish) — rabbinic literature, commentaries on the Bible.

Elul — month of the Jewish year

Erev Shabbat — Sabbath eve (Friday night)

Etrog — *Citrus medica,* a yellow citron used during the festival of Sukkot

Frumme (Yiddish) — religious

Gabbai (gabba) — treasurer or president

Gaon — honorific, possibly denoting "genius", originally applied to heads of major Jewish academies at Sura and Pumbedita in Babylon, 589-1040 CE

Gefilte fish (Yiddish) — stuffed fish, a popular *Ashkenazi* dish

Gemara (Gemora) — comprises rabbinical analysis of and commentary on the *Mishnah*

Gemilut Chesed (pl. *Chasadim*) — charitable organisation

Goniff (Yiddish) — thief

Goyim (adj.), *goyishe* (Yiddish) — often used in a derogatory way to mean "non-Jews", non-Jewish"

Griene (*griener/greener*) (Yiddish) — a raw, new immigrant

Hallel — praise prayer

Hashem — lit. "the Name", used as a substitute for "G-d"

Haskalah — Enlightenment movement

Havdalah — religious ceremony marking the end of the Sabbath and the beginning of a new week

Heim (adj. *heimisher)* (Yiddish) — home. *Der heim*, the home, adj. homely

Hesped — funeral oration

Ivris b' Ivris — lit. "Hebrew into Hebrew", a method of teaching Hebrew using only that language

Kaddish — prayer recited by mourners, requiring a quorum of 10 men

Kaparot — atonement, refers to an ancient folk custom that involves whirling a chicken above one's head before *Yom Kippur*, while reciting a prayer in the belief that one's sins will be transferred to the chicken

Kehilah — community, used here to denote a Jewish community

Kiddush — blessing recited over wine or grape juice to sanctify the Sabbath and Jewish holy days

Kinnot — laments

Kvetch (Yiddish) — v. complain, n. someone who complains a great deal.

Latkes (Yiddish) — potato pancakes

Litvaks (Yiddish) — Lithuanians

Lulav — a palm branch bound together with willow and myrtle branches used during the festival of *Sukkot*

Ma'ales — good points

Ma'ariv — evening prayers

Mashgiach — person who inspects and supervises the kosher status of a kosher establishment

Maskilim — enlightened ones, referring to persons of great intellectual achievement

Matzah (pl. *matzot)* — unleavened bread eaten during Passover

Melamed (pl. *melamdim)* — teachers

Meshulach — charity collector

Mezuzah — ritual object affixed to the doorposts of Jewish homes, containing verses from the *Torah*

Mikvah (mikveh) — ritual bath

Minchah — afternoon prayers

Minyan — a quorum of 10 men required for reciting certain communal prayers

Mishnah (pl. *mishnayot*) — the oral tradition of debates on Jewish law between scholars living between the first century BCE and second century CE and the judgments given

Mitzvah (pl. *mitzvoth)* — precepts and commandments from G-d

Mohel — person who performs circumcisions

Moshiach/Mashiach — Messiah

Mussaf — additional prayer service, recited on the Sabbath and holy days

Neilah — concluding service of *Yom Kippur*

Nissan — month of the Jewish year

Parnass — president of the congregation

Parnosse (Yiddish) — way of making a living

Parshat Shalach, parsha — weekly portion of the *Torah* read in the synagogue. The *Shelach Lecha,* starting "Send for yourself" (Numbers 13:1- 5:41), is read nine weeks after the end of Passover

Pashkvil (pl. *pashkvilim*) — broadsheet, poster on public wall

Payot — side locks worn by religious men

Pesach — Passover

Purim — lit. "lots", a holiday commemorating the Jewish deliverance from the threat of annihilation in Persia in the fourth century BCE

Rav (pl. *rabbanim* or *rabbonim*) — rabbi

Reb — title of respect for a man

Rosh Hashanah — New Year

Rebbitzen (Yiddish) — rabbi's wife

Seder — feast and ritual of Passover

Sefer Torah — scroll of the *Torah*

Shabbat — Sabbath

Shacharit — morning service

Shadchan (m.), *shadchente* (f.) (Yiddish) — match-maker

Shalach mones (Yiddish) — custom of sending gifts before *Purim*

Shammes (Yiddish) — beadle or sexton who looks after the synagogue

Shatz — abbreviation of *shaliach tzibbur* ("emissary of the congregation"), designates leader of prayer services

Shavuot — Feast of Weeks

Shechter, see *Shochet*

Shechting/Shechita (Yiddish) — the act of kosher slaughtering

Shlogen shaines (Yiddish) — idiosyncratic expression used by Harry Schrire, combining *shlogen* (beat) and *shaines* (?*hashana rabe*, the seventh day of *Sukkot)*

Shnodder (Yiddish) — donate money in *shul* for honours

Shnorrer (Yiddish) — beggar

Shocher (Yiddish) — black person, from *schachor* (black)

Shochet or *shechter* (pl. *shochtim*) — ritual slaughterer who slaughters and inspects cattle and fowl in the ritually prescribed manner for kosher consumption. In order to train as a *shochet*, a Jew is required to study for a number of years and is examined, in theory and practice, in the laws of *shechita* (ritual slaughtering), animal anatomy and pathology. He serves as an apprentice with an experienced *shochet* before becoming fully qualified. The position of *shochet*, as a G-d-fearing person of integrity, is a respected one in the Jewish community.

Shofar (pl. *shofarim)* — ram's horn that is customarily sounded at the *Rosh Hashanah* and *Yom Kippur* services

Shtetl (Yiddish) — village

Shtiebel (pl. *shtiblach*) (Yiddish) — a small synagogue, usually just a room

Shul (Yiddish) — synagogue

Siddur — prayer book

Simchah — lit. "happiness", used to refer to a joyous celebration like a wedding

Sivan — month of the Jewish year

Siyyum HaTorah — completion of reading of the *Torah*

Slichot — penitentional poems and prayers recited on some on major holy days

Smichah — traditional rabbinic ordination

Smous (Yiddish) — v. *smousing*, peddler

Stoep (Afrikaans) — veranda

Sukkot — Feast of Tabernacles that follows the High Holy Days of *Rosh Hashanah* and *Yom Kippur*

Tallis (Yiddish) — prayer shawl

Talmud — central text of Rabbinic Judaism containing the *Mishnah* and *Gemara*

Talmud Torah — primary school originally intended for boys

Tammuz — month of the Jewish year

Tashlich — ceremony conducted during the 10 days before *Yom Kippur*, in which one's sins are symbolically cast into a body of water

Tefillah — prayer(s)

Tefillin — phylacteries

Tehillim — psalms

Teruah — *shofar* blast

Tisha B'Av — the ninth day of the Jewish month of *Av*, a day of mourning for the destruction of the Temple in Jerusalem

Torah — first five books of the Old Testament

Treif (Yiddish) — not kosher

Tzaddik — a righteous person

Unterführer (German) — the person who gives the bride away

Warnung tzetl (High Dutch) — warning notice

Yasher Koach — lit. "May your strength be firm", a way of congratulating those who do an honourable job

Yeshiva bocher (Yiddish) — religious school student

Yichus (Yiddish) — distinguished lineage

Yidden (Yiddish) — Jews

Yom Kippur — Day of Atonement

Yom Tov — lit. "good day", Jewish festival, Holy Day

Yortzeit (Yiddish) — anniversary of a person's death

INDEX (caption pages are denoted in italics)

CONTRIBUTORS

Devis Iosifzon (1967-2013) held an MA (*cum laude*) in Art History and a Librarianship and Information Specialist Diploma from Tel Aviv University and was a member of the South African Translators' Institute. He was the Director and Head Librarian of the Jacob Gitlin Library, Cape Town. His sudden passing remains a great loss to the community.

Carmel Schrire was educated at the University of Cape Town, Cambridge University and the Australian National University. She is a Distinguished Professor in the Department of Anthropology, at Rutgers, The State University of New Jersey, New Brunswick, NJ, USA. She has directed archaeological excavations in South Africa, Australia and Poland, and has published widely on the impact of colonialism at the Cape.

Gwynne Schrire has BA and B.Soc.Sci degrees from the University of Cape Town and is the Deputy Director of the Cape South African Jewish Board of Deputies. She is an independent researcher who has published on numerous topics relating to the history of Jews in South Africa.

Michal Solomon has a BA in Jewish History and English Literature from the University of Haifa, Israel. She is a former Hebrew teacher and principal of a Hebrew school in Westchester County, USA.

Paul Cheifitz is a professional genealogist, born in Cape Town and now based in Israel, who specialises in South African Jewish genealogical research.